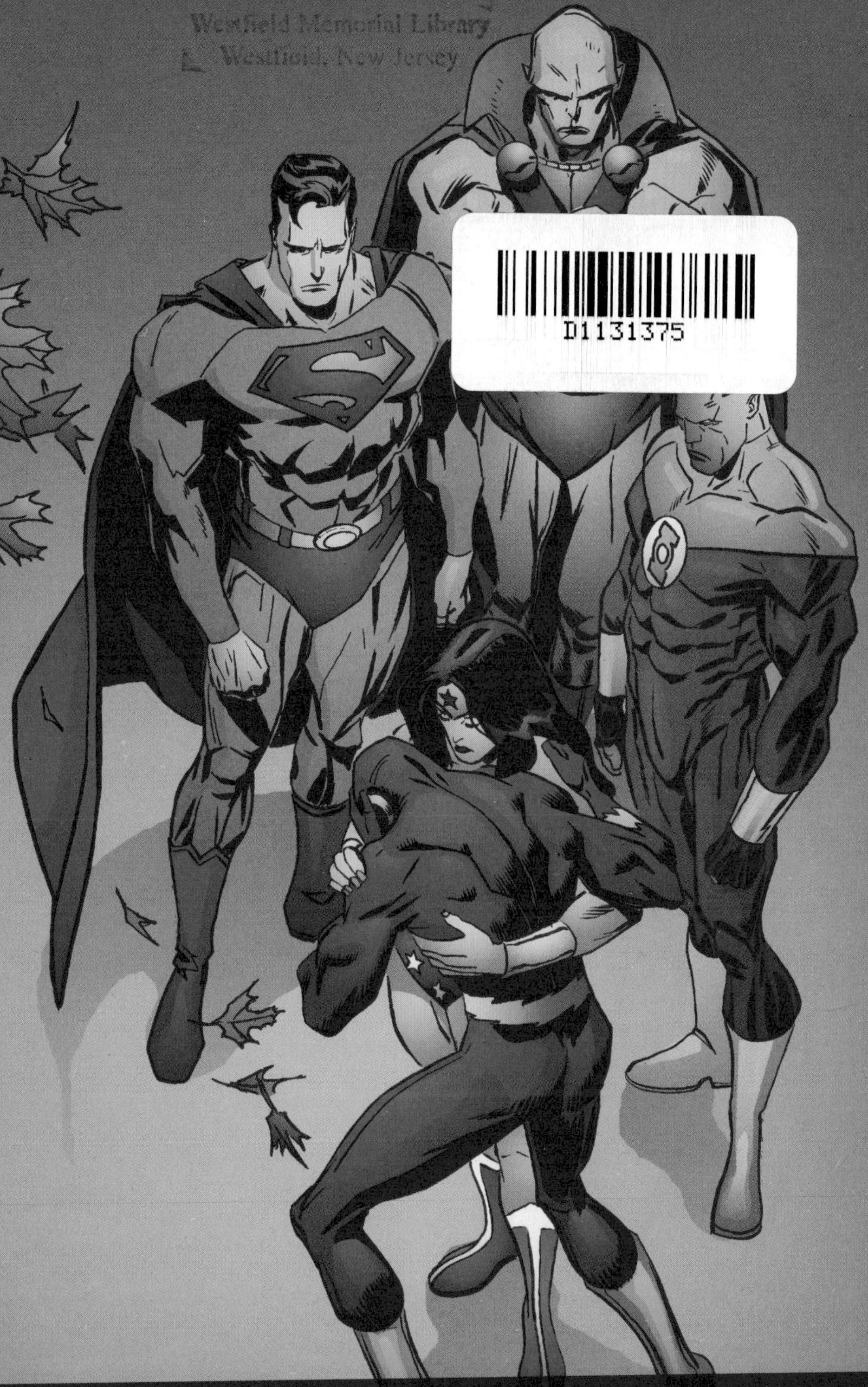

JLA PAIN OF THE GODS

Chuck Austen Writer **Ron Garney** Artist and original series covers **David Baron** Colorist **Ken Lopez** Letterer **Superman** created by **Jerry Siegel** and **Joe Shuster** **Batman** created by **Bob Kane** **Wonder Woman** created by **William Moulton Marston**

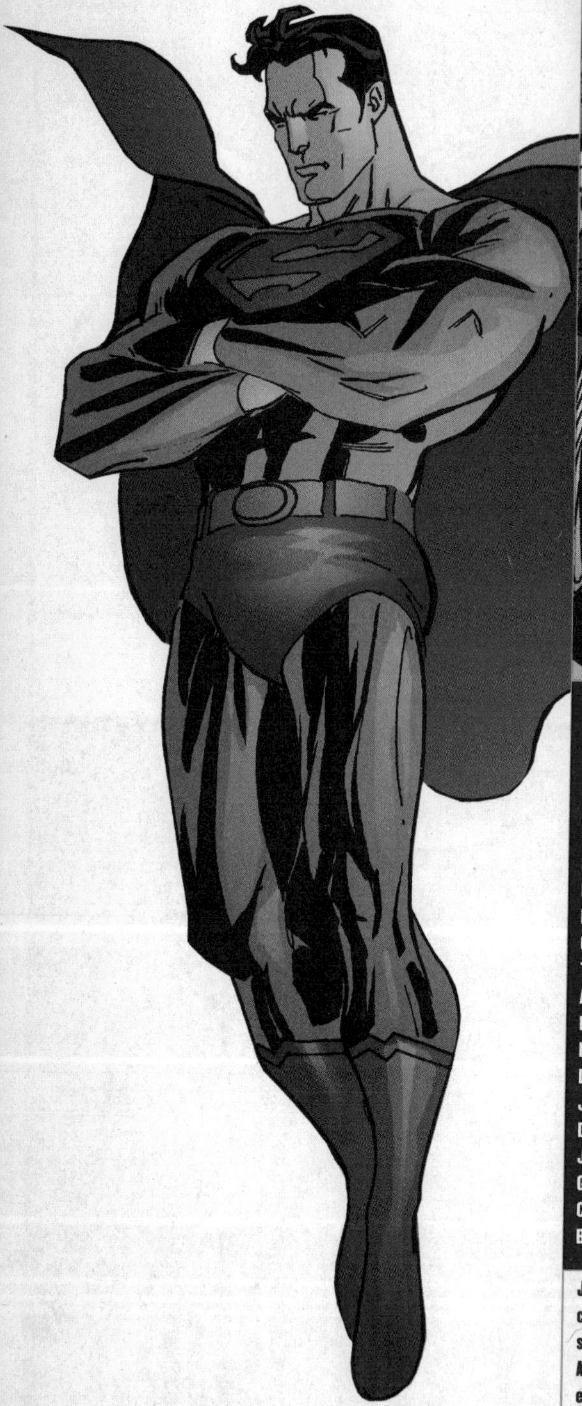

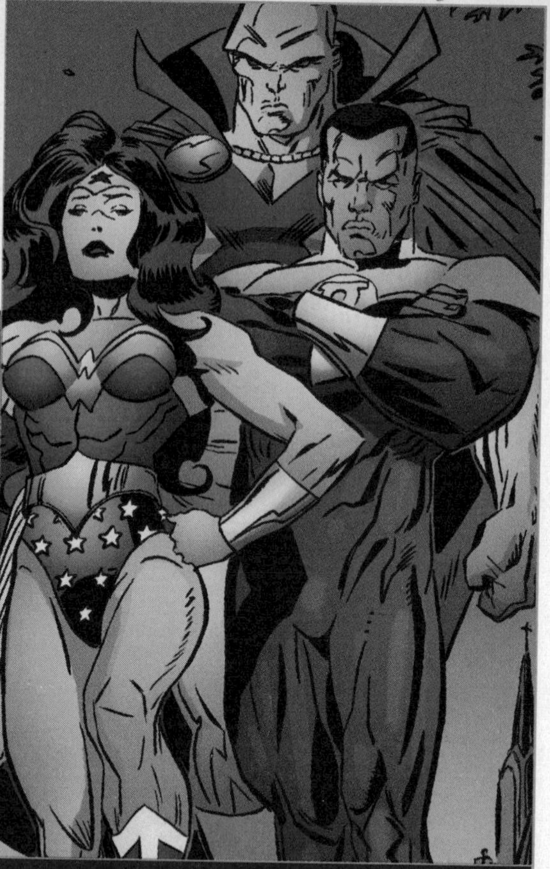

JLA: PAIN OF THE GODS. Published by DC Comics. Cover and compilation copyright © 2005 DC Comics. All Rights Reserved. Originally published in single magazine form as JLA 101-106. Copyright © 2004 DC Comics. All Rights Reserved. All characters, their distinctive likenesses and related elements featured in this publication are trademarks of DC Comics. The stories, characters and incidents featured in this publication are entirely fictional. DC Comics does not read or accept unsolicited submissions of ideas, stories or artwork. DC Comics, 1700 Broadway, New York, NY 10019. A Warner Bros. Entertainment Company. Printed in Canada. First Printing. ISBN: 1-4012-0468-6. Cover illustration by Ron Garney. Cover color by David Baron.

JLA

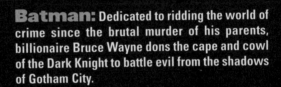

JLA: The Justice League of America is Earth's first and last line of defense, a pantheon of super-powered protectors watching over the Earth from a fortress on the Moon.

Superman: The last son of the doomed planet Krypton, Kal-El uses his incredible powers of flight, super-strength, and invulnerability to fight for truth and justice on his adopted planet, Earth. When not protecting the planet, he is *Daily Planet* reporter Clark Kent, married to fellow journalist Lois Lane.

Batman: Dedicated to ridding the world of crime since the brutal murder of his parents, billionaire Bruce Wayne dons the cape and cowl of the Dark Knight to battle evil from the shadows of Gotham City.

Wonder Woman: Born an Amazonian princess, Diana was chosen to serve as her people's ambassador of peace in the World of Man. Armed with the Lasso of Truth and indestructible bracelets, she directs her gods-given abilities of strength and speed toward the betterment of mankind.

The Flash: A member of the Teen Titans when he was known as Kid Flash, Wally West now takes the place of the fallen Flash, Barry Allen, as the speedster of the Justice League.

Green Lantern: John Stewart has worn the power ring, symbol of the intergalactic Green Lantern Corps, during several tours of duty. Controlled by his will power, the ring makes his imagination manifest, and being an architect, he conceives some pretty cool objects.

Martian Manhunter: J'onn J'onzz has been a member of the JLA for every one of the team's many incarnations. His strength rivals that of Earth's mightiest heroes, and his shape-shifting abilities allow him to pass anonymously among our planet's populace. His awesome mental powers serve to link the entire League in thought.

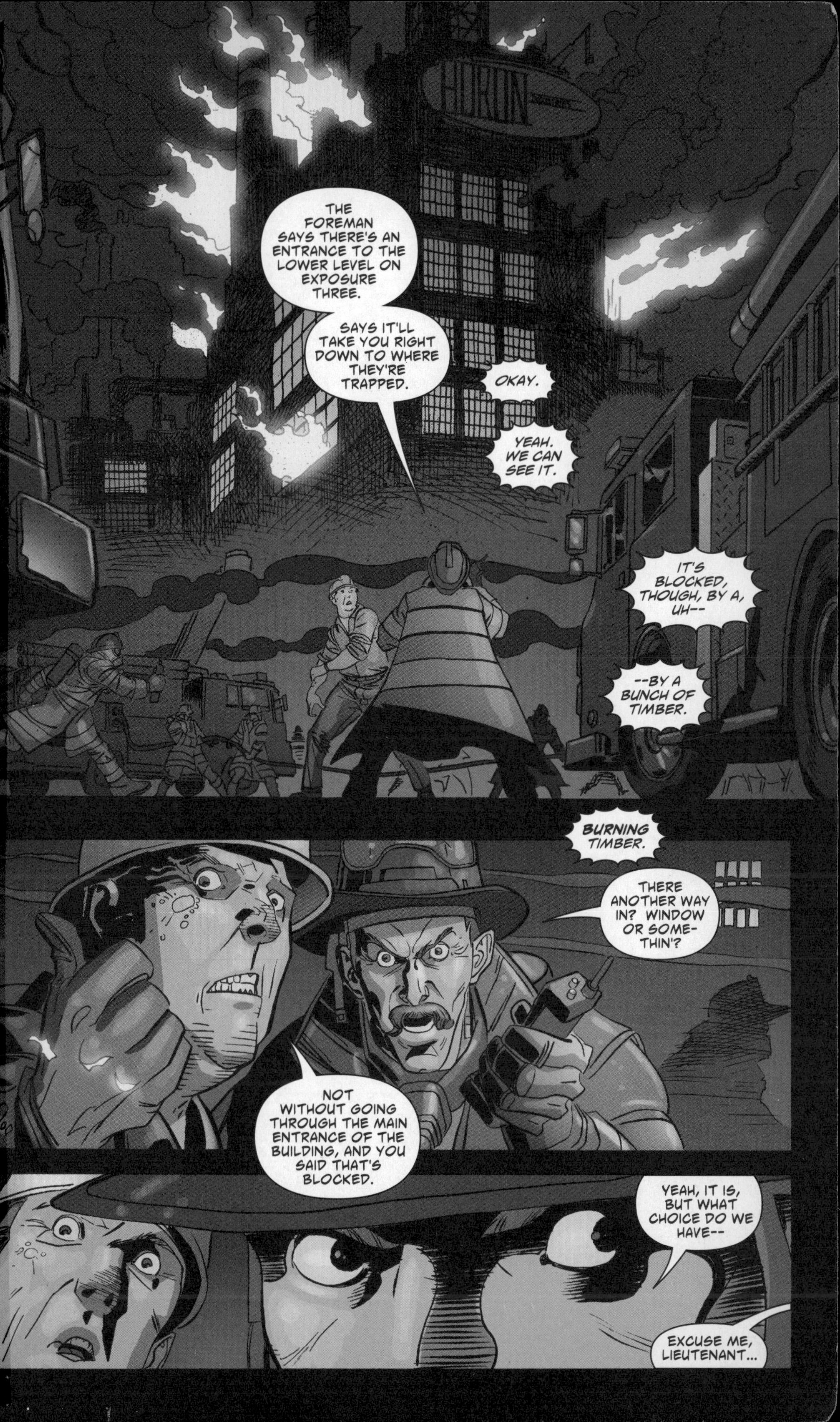
HORUN
THE FOREMAN SAYS THERE'S AN ENTRANCE TO THE LOWER LEVEL ON EXPOSURE THREE.
SAYS IT'LL TAKE YOU RIGHT DOWN TO WHERE THEY'RE TRAPPED.
OKAY.
YEAH. WE CAN SEE IT.
IT'S BLOCKED, THOUGH, BY A, UH--
--BY A BUNCH OF TIMBER.
BURNING TIMBER.
THERE ANOTHER WAY IN? WINDOW OR SOME-THIN'?
NOT WITHOUT GOING THROUGH THE MAIN ENTRANCE OF THE BUILDING, AND YOU SAID THAT'S BLOCKED.
YEAH, IT IS, BUT WHAT CHOICE DO WE HAVE--
EXCUSE ME, LIEUTENANT...

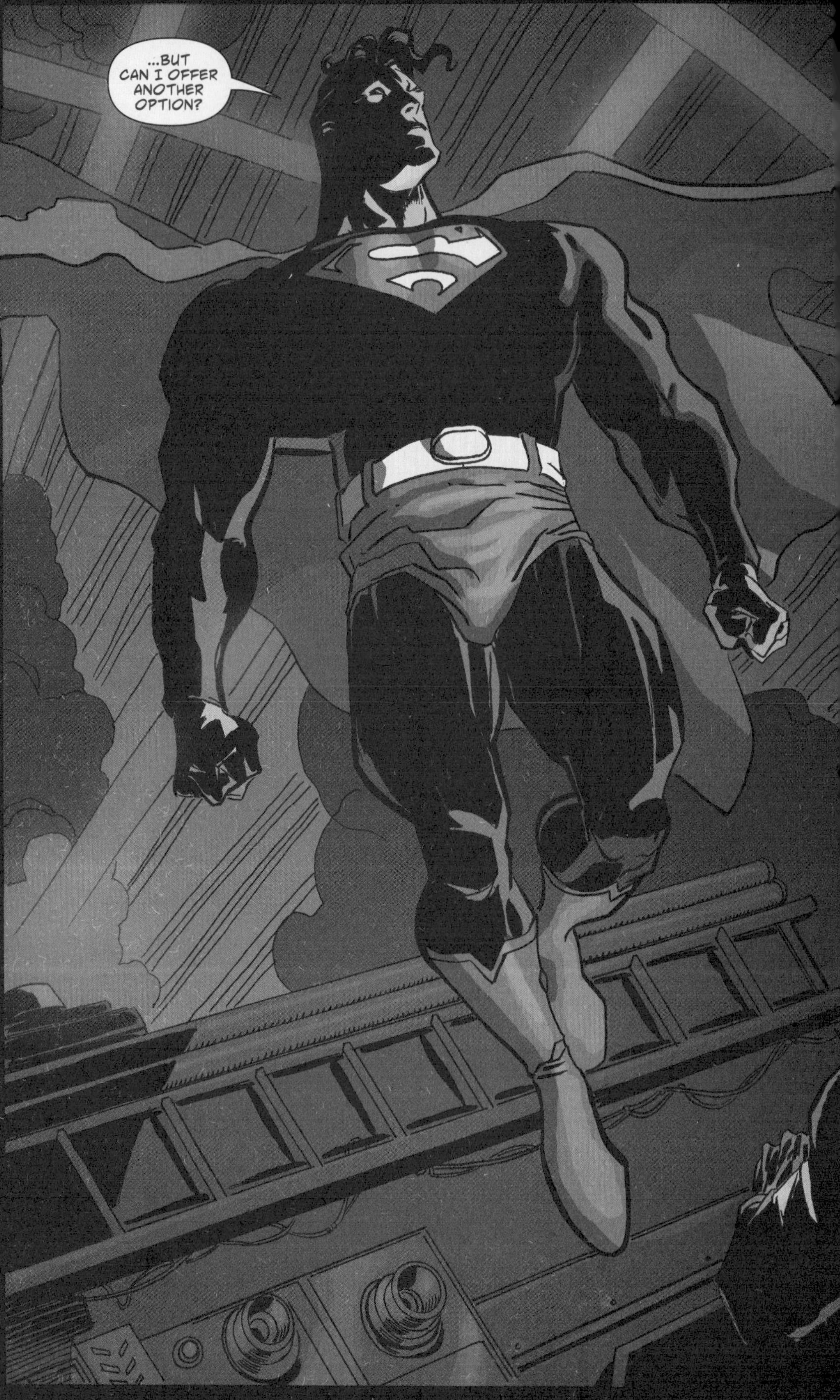
...BUT CAN I OFFER ANOTHER OPTION?

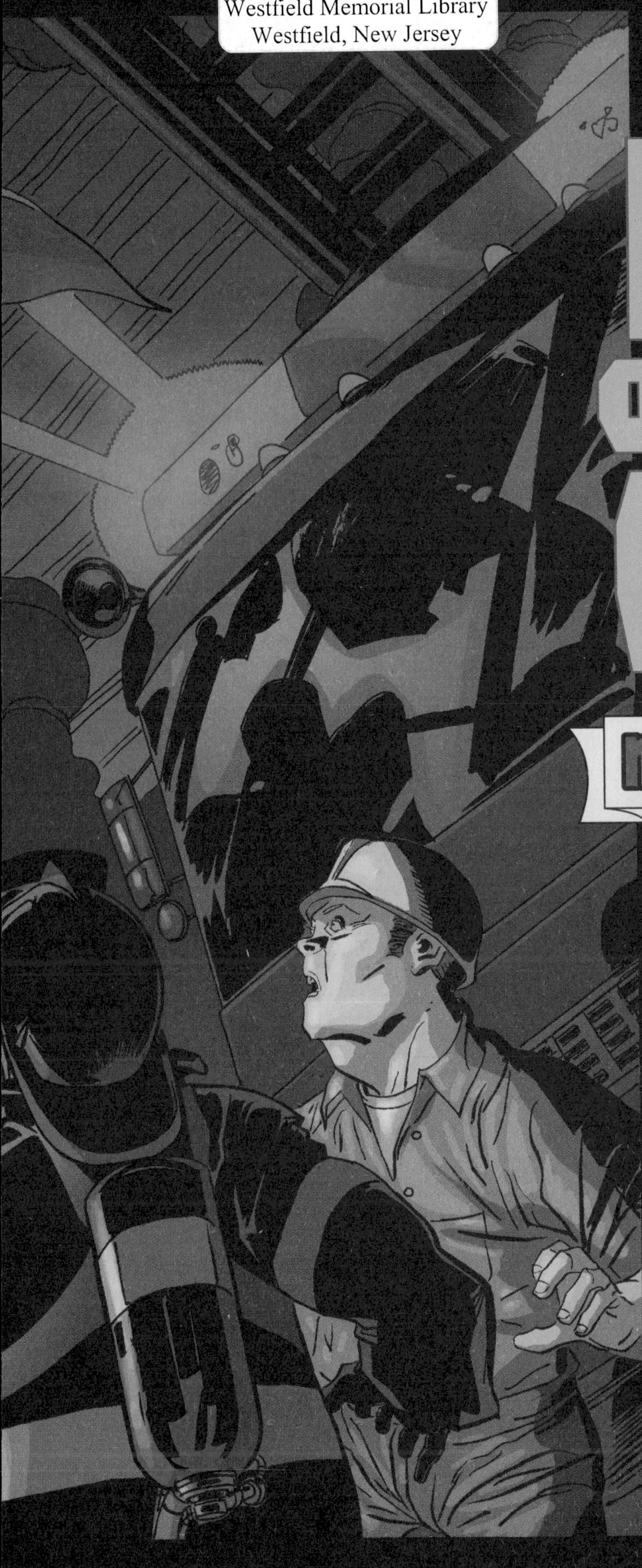

THE PAIN OF THE GODS

MAN OF STEEL

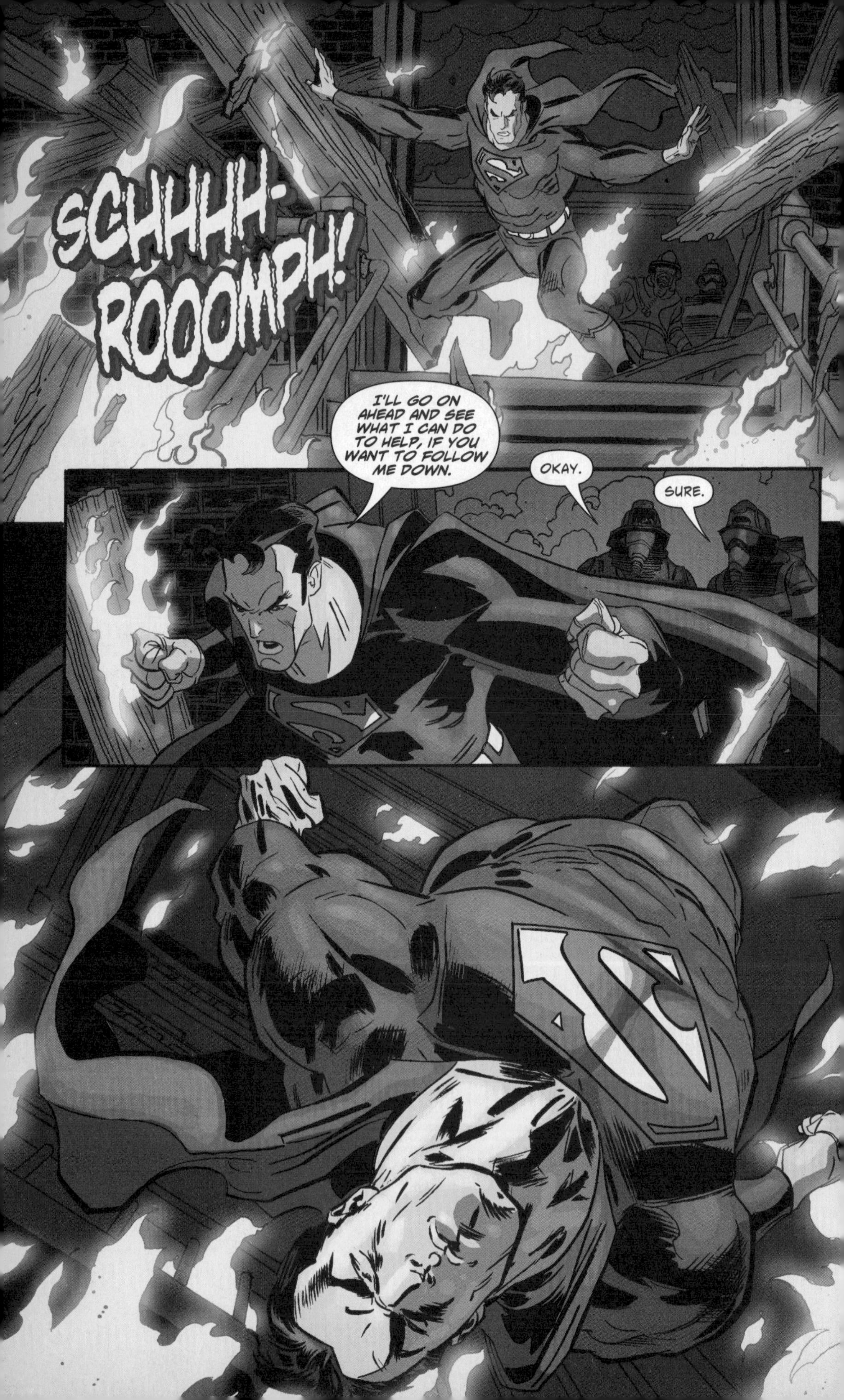
SCHHHH-
ROOOMPH!
I'LL GO ON AHEAD AND SEE WHAT I CAN DO TO HELP, IF YOU WANT TO FOLLOW ME DOWN.
OKAY.
SURE.

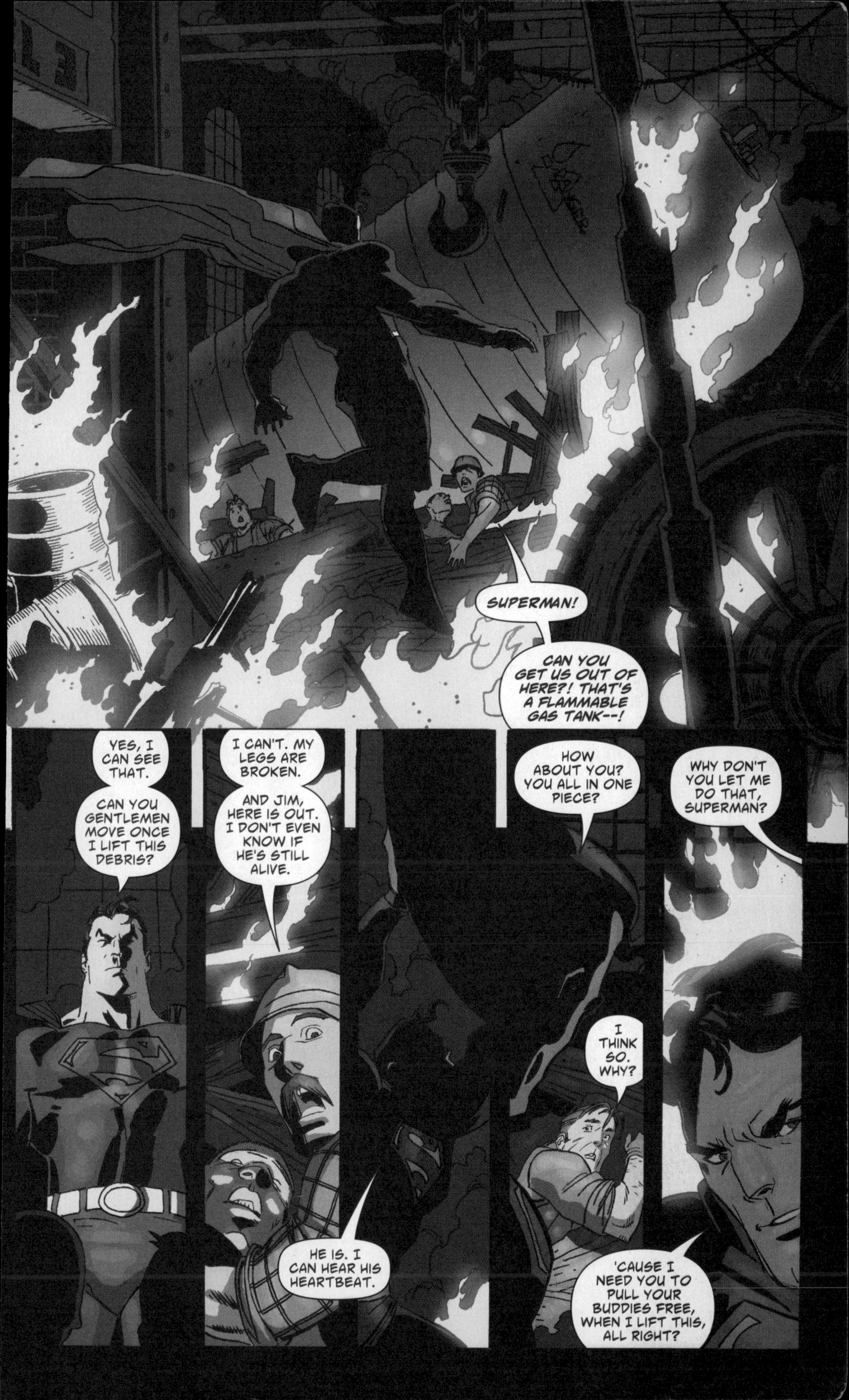
SUPERMAN!
CAN YOU GET US OUT OF HERE?! THAT'S A FLAMMABLE GAS TANK--!
YES, I CAN SEE THAT.
CAN YOU GENTLEMEN MOVE ONCE I LIFT THIS DEBRIS?
I CAN'T. MY LEGS ARE BROKEN.
AND JIM, HERE IS OUT. I DON'T EVEN KNOW IF HE'S STILL ALIVE.
HE IS. I CAN HEAR HIS HEARTBEAT.
HOW ABOUT YOU? YOU ALL IN ONE PIECE?
I THINK SO. WHY?
WHY DON'T YOU LET ME DO THAT, SUPERMAN?
'CAUSE I NEED YOU TO PULL YOUR BUDDIES FREE, WHEN I LIFT THIS, ALL RIGHT?

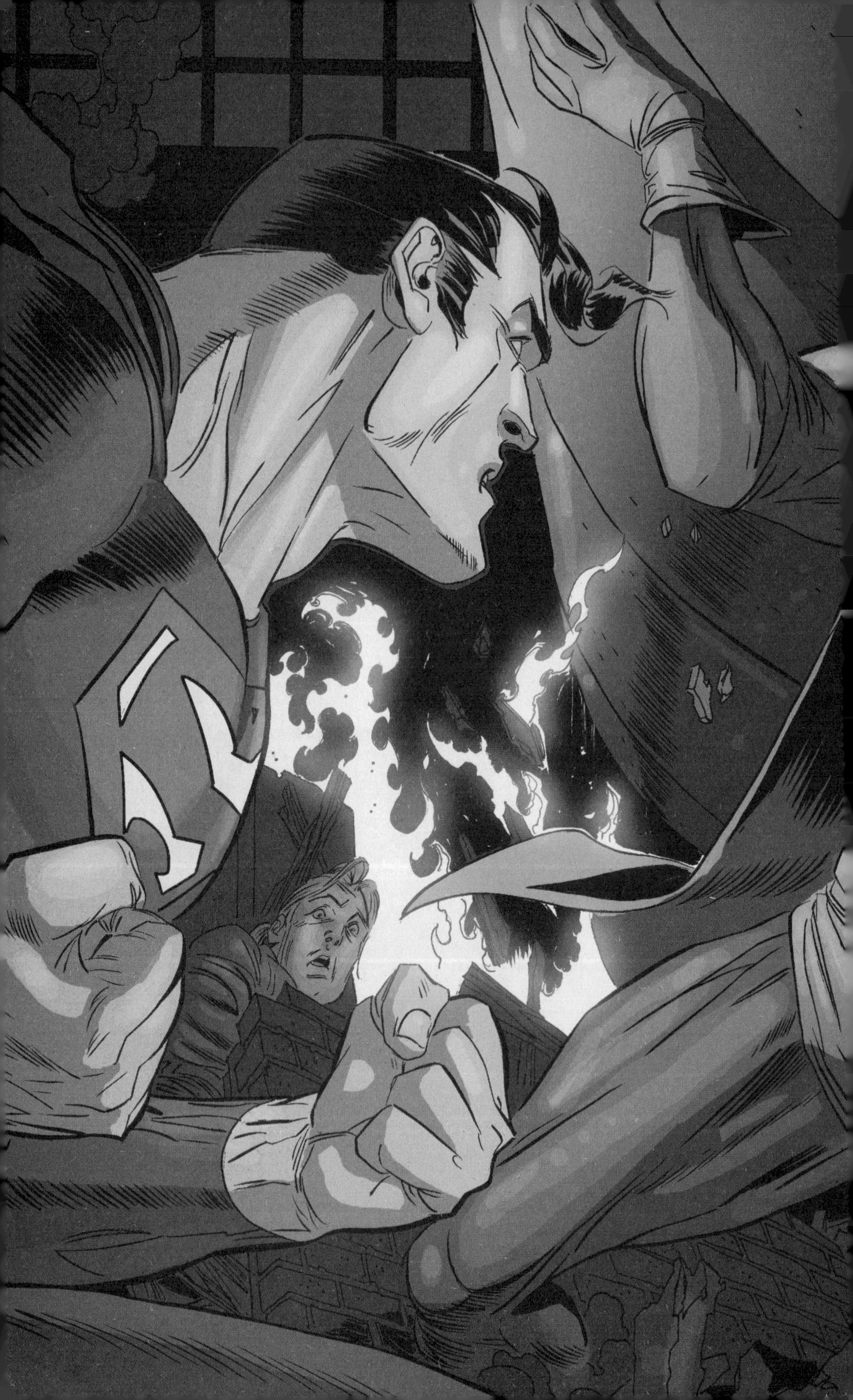

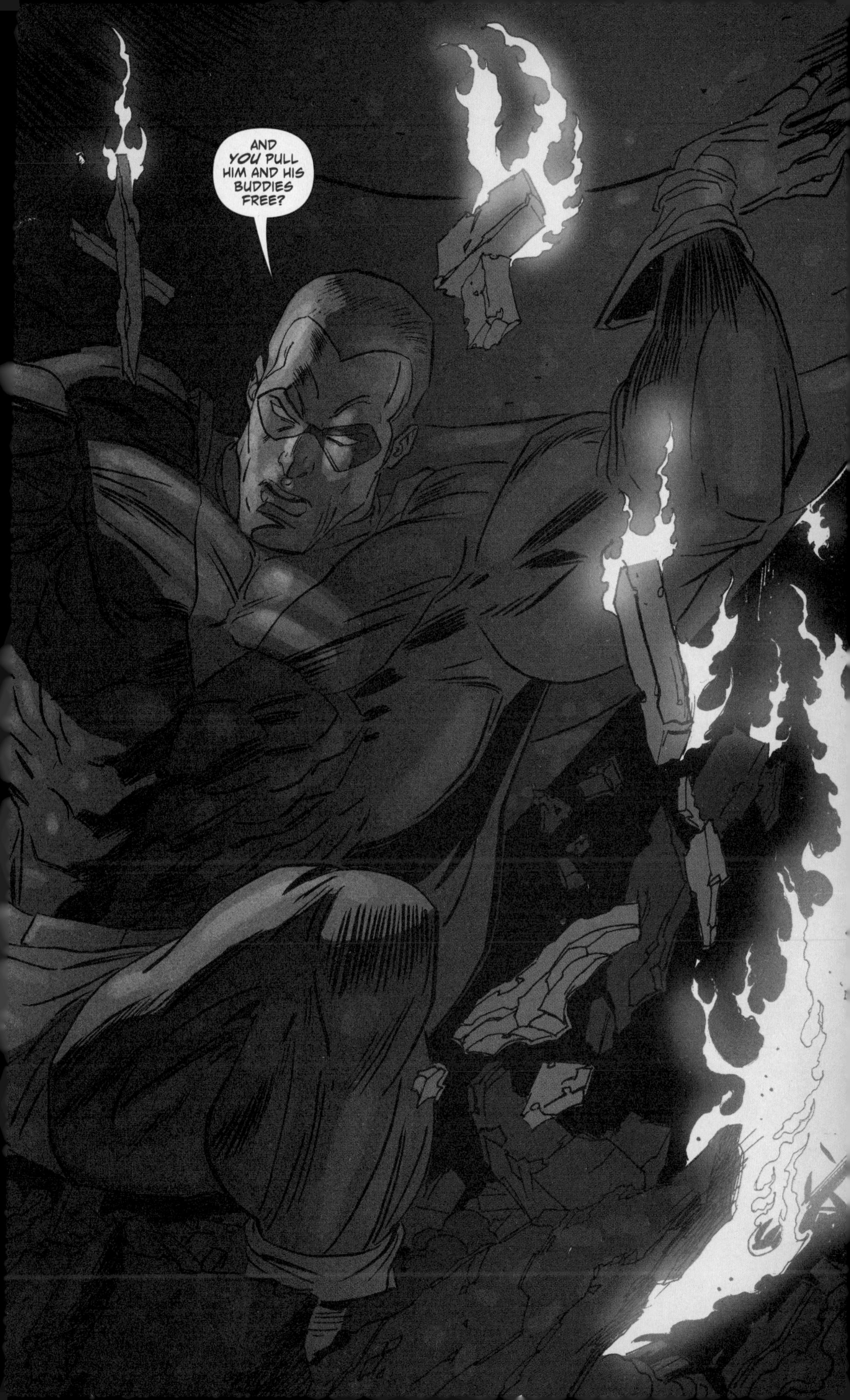
AND YOU PULL HIM AND HIS BUDDIES FREE?

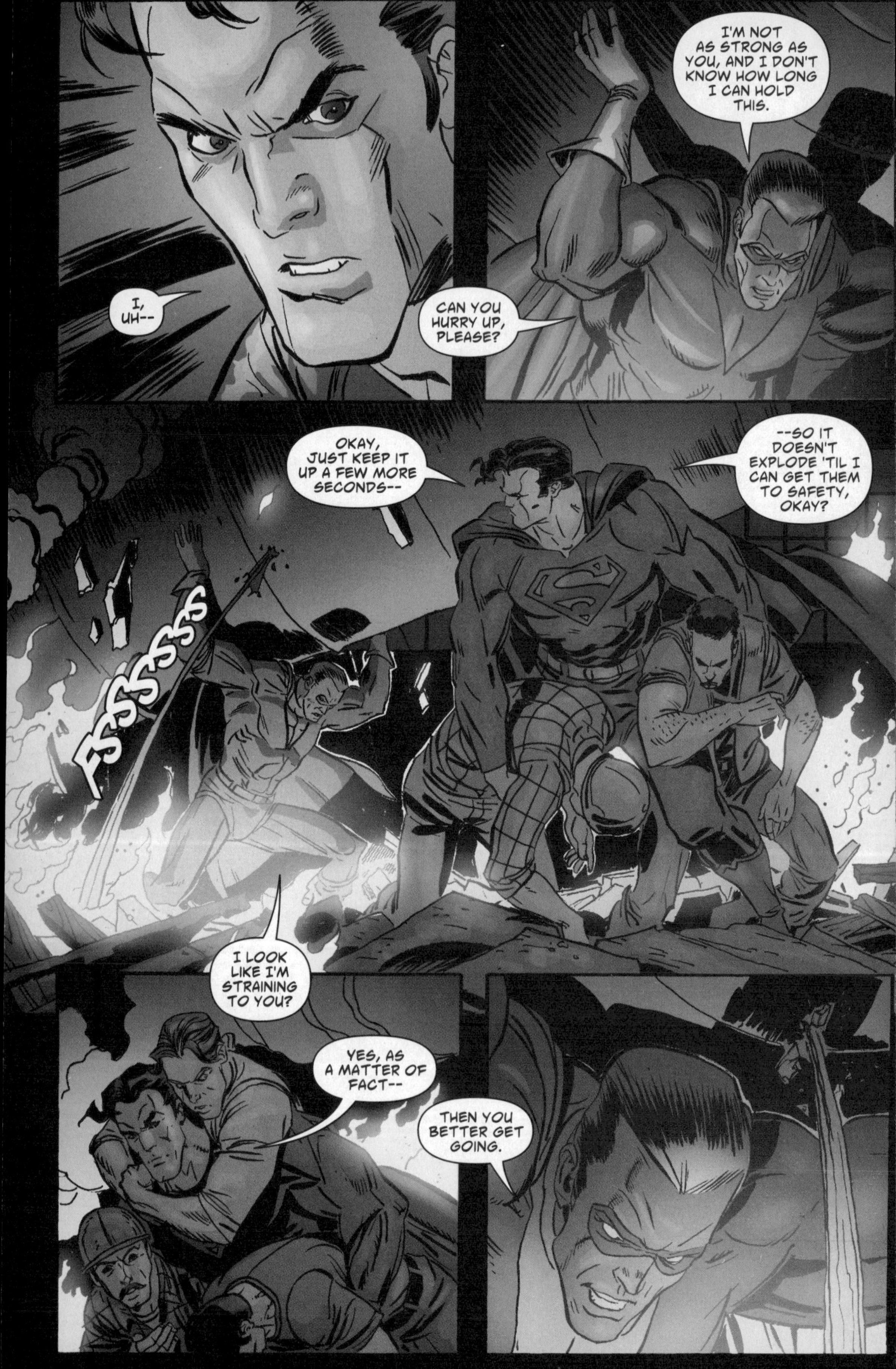
I, UH--
I'M NOT AS STRONG AS YOU, AND I DON'T KNOW HOW LONG I CAN HOLD THIS.
CAN YOU HURRY UP, PLEASE?
OKAY, JUST KEEP IT UP A FEW MORE SECONDS--
--SO IT DOESN'T EXPLODE 'TIL I CAN GET THEM TO SAFETY, OKAY?
FSSSSSSS
I LOOK LIKE I'M STRAINING TO YOU?
YES, AS A MATTER OF FACT--
THEN YOU BETTER GET GOING.

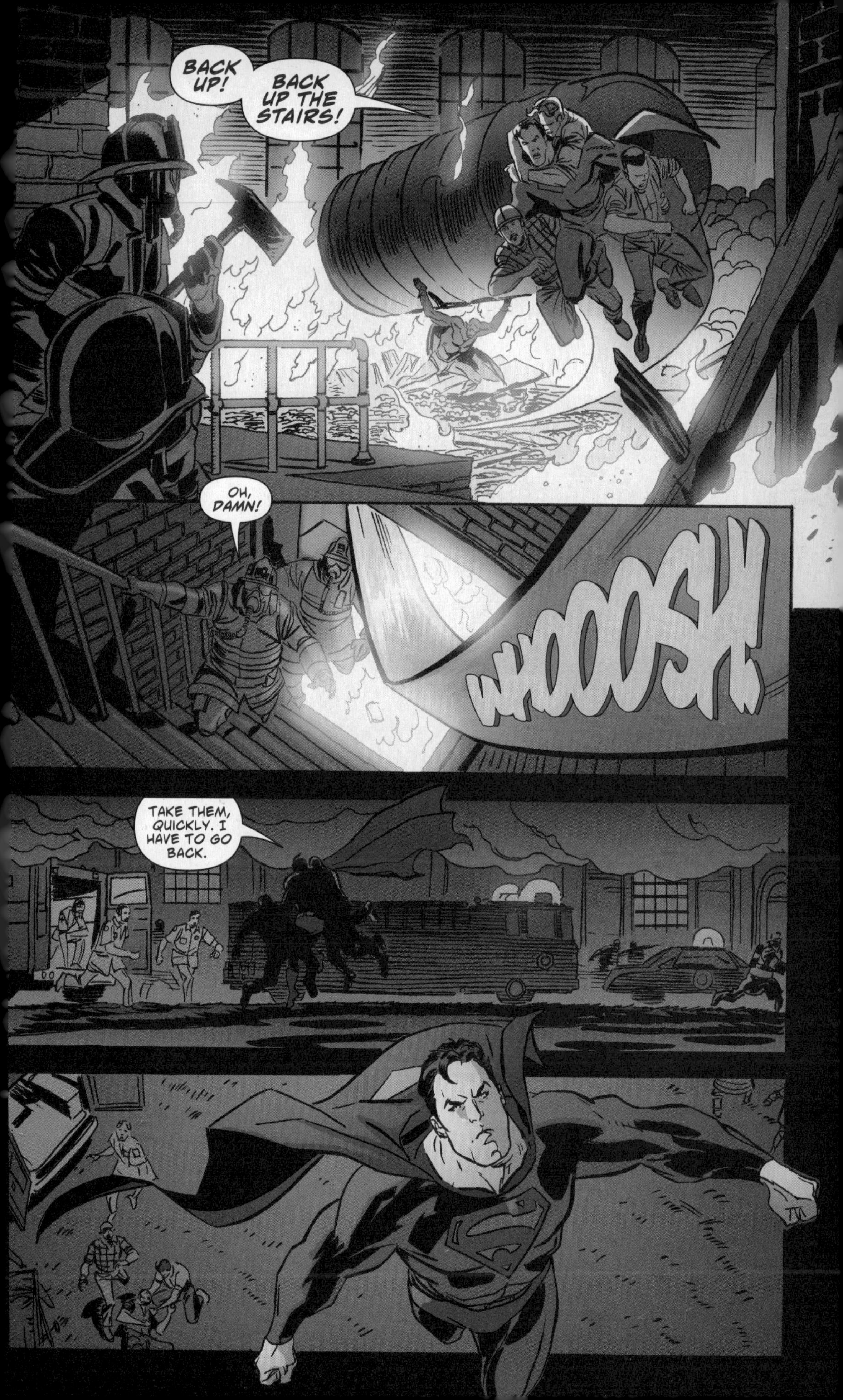
BACK UP!
BACK UP THE STAIRS!
OH, DAMN!
WHOOOSH!
TAKE THEM, QUICKLY. I HAVE TO GO BACK.

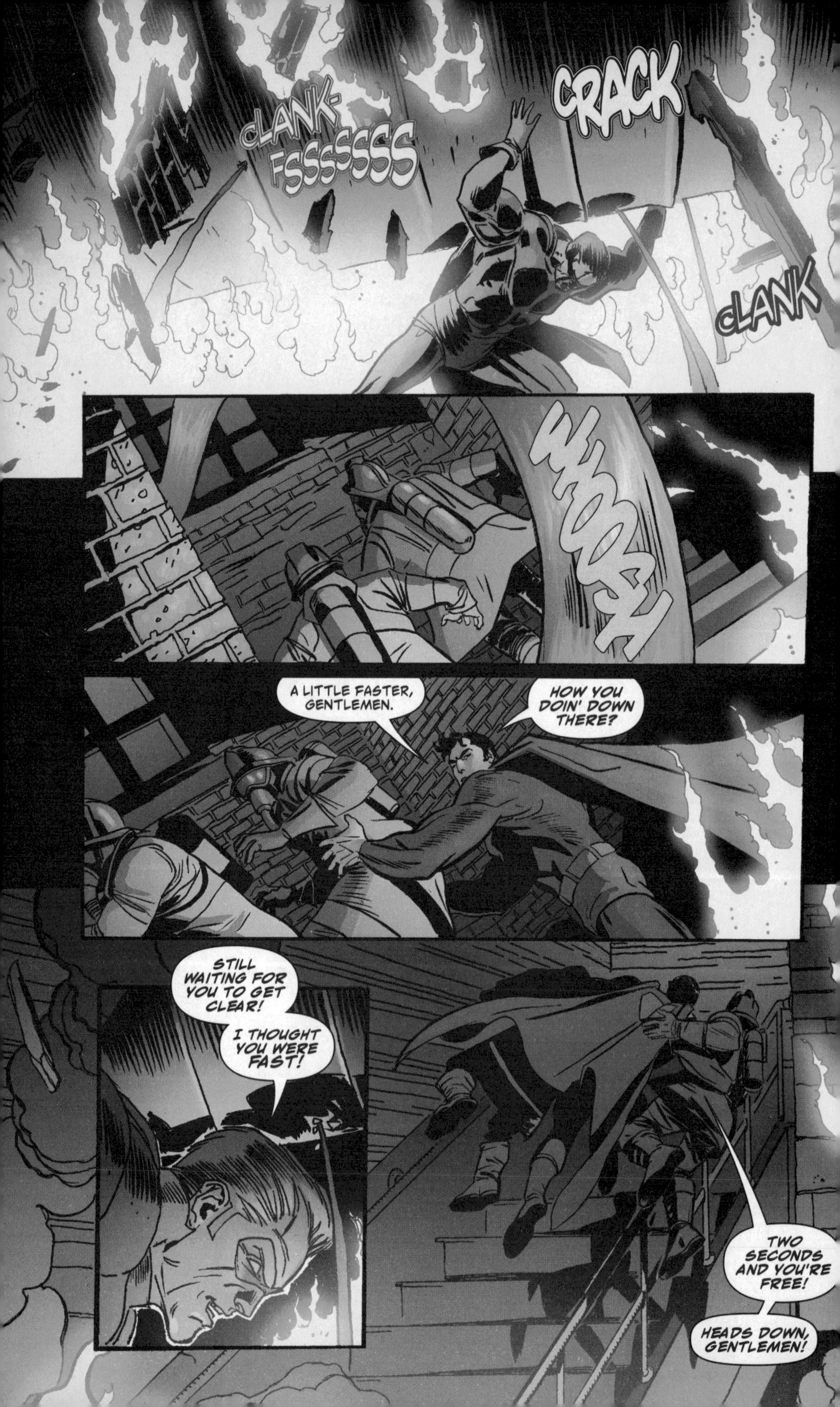
CLANK-FSSSSSSS
CRACK
CLANK
WHOOSH
A LITTLE FASTER, GENTLEMEN.
HOW YOU DOIN' DOWN THERE?
STILL WAITING FOR YOU TO GET CLEAR!
I THOUGHT YOU WERE FAST!
TWO SECONDS AND YOU'RE FREE!
HEADS DOWN, GENTLEMEN!

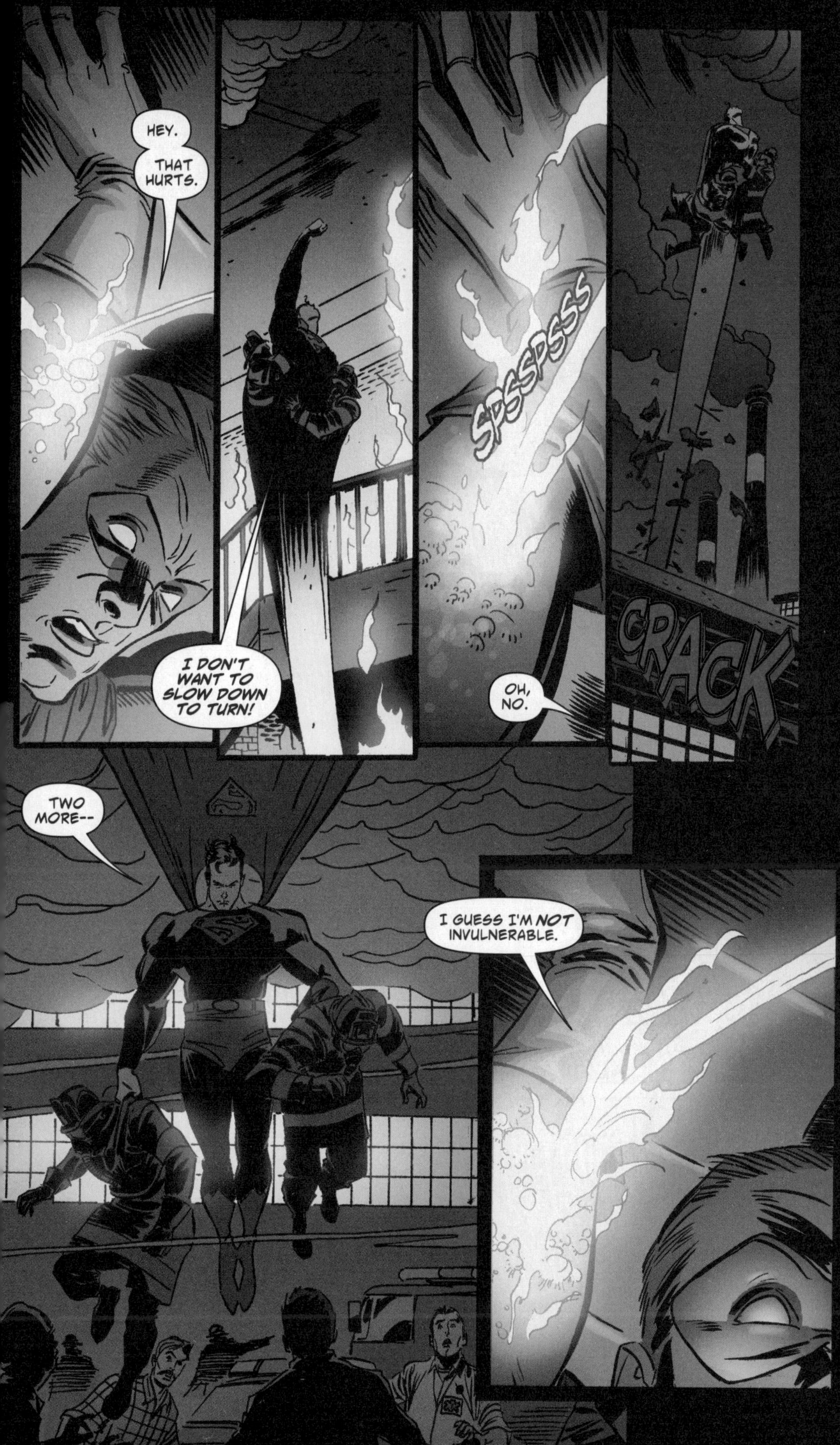
HEY.
THAT HURTS.
I DON'T WANT TO SLOW DOWN TO TURN!
SPSSPSSS
OH, NO.
CRACK
TWO MORE--
I GUESS I'M NOT INVULNERABLE.

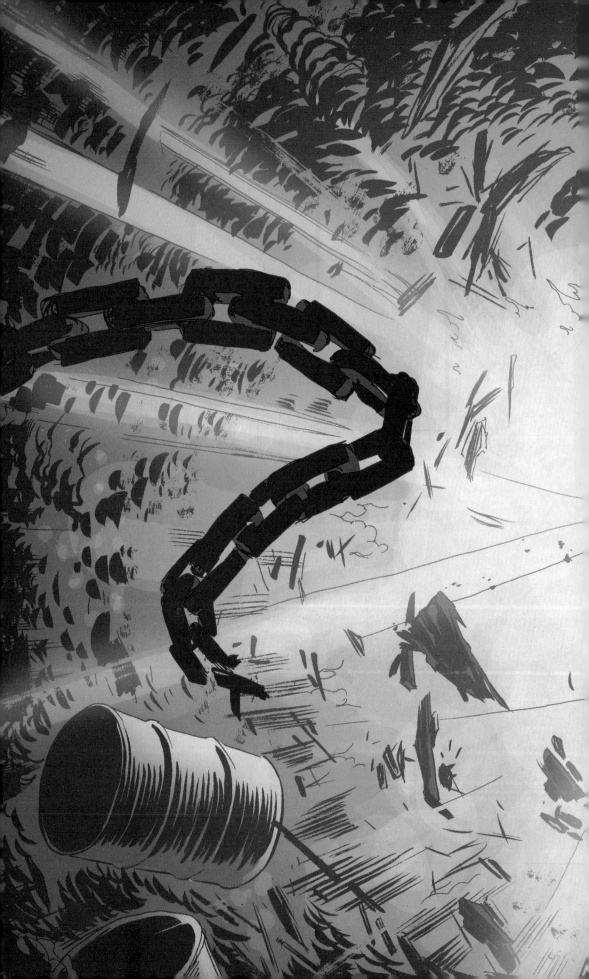

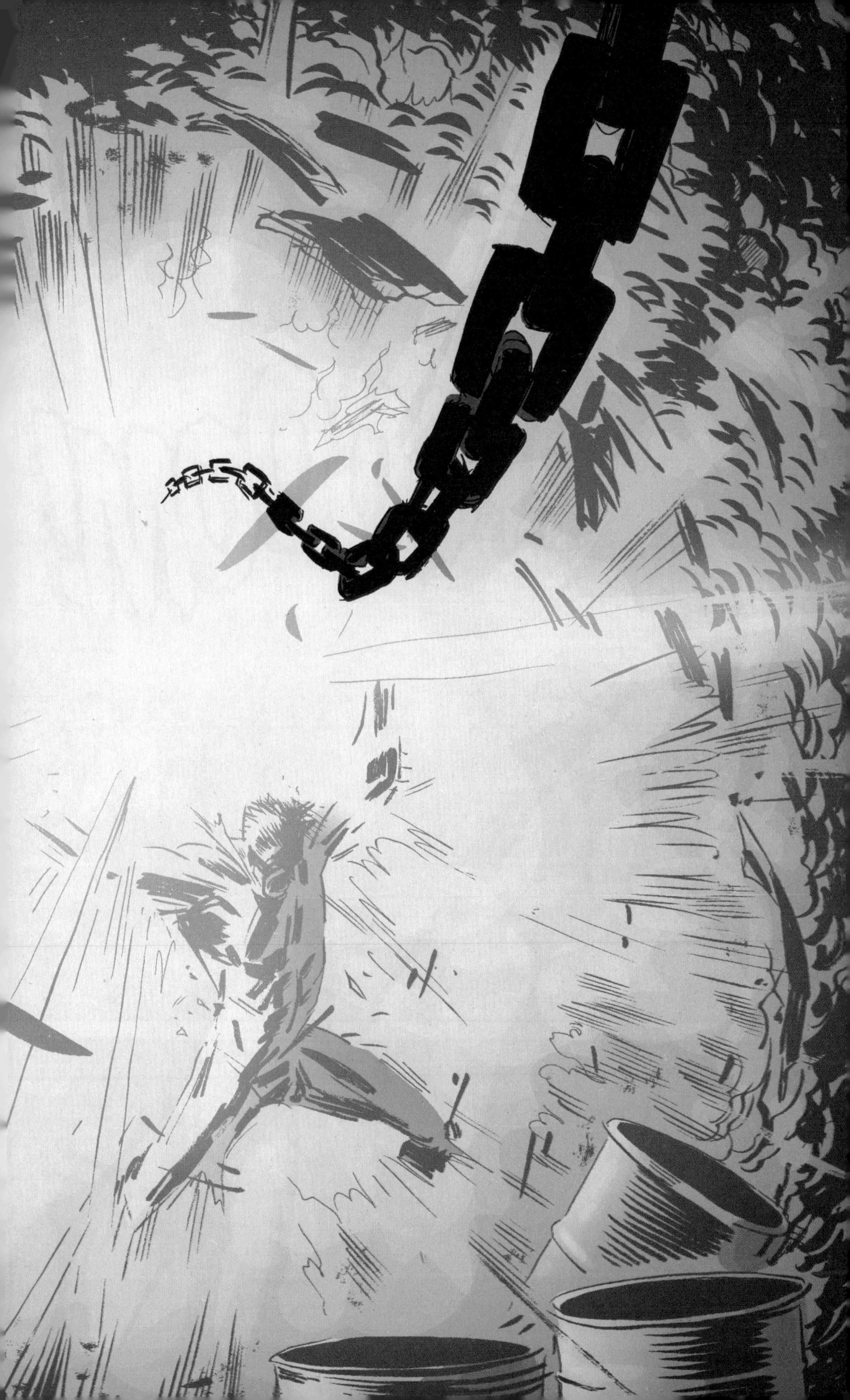

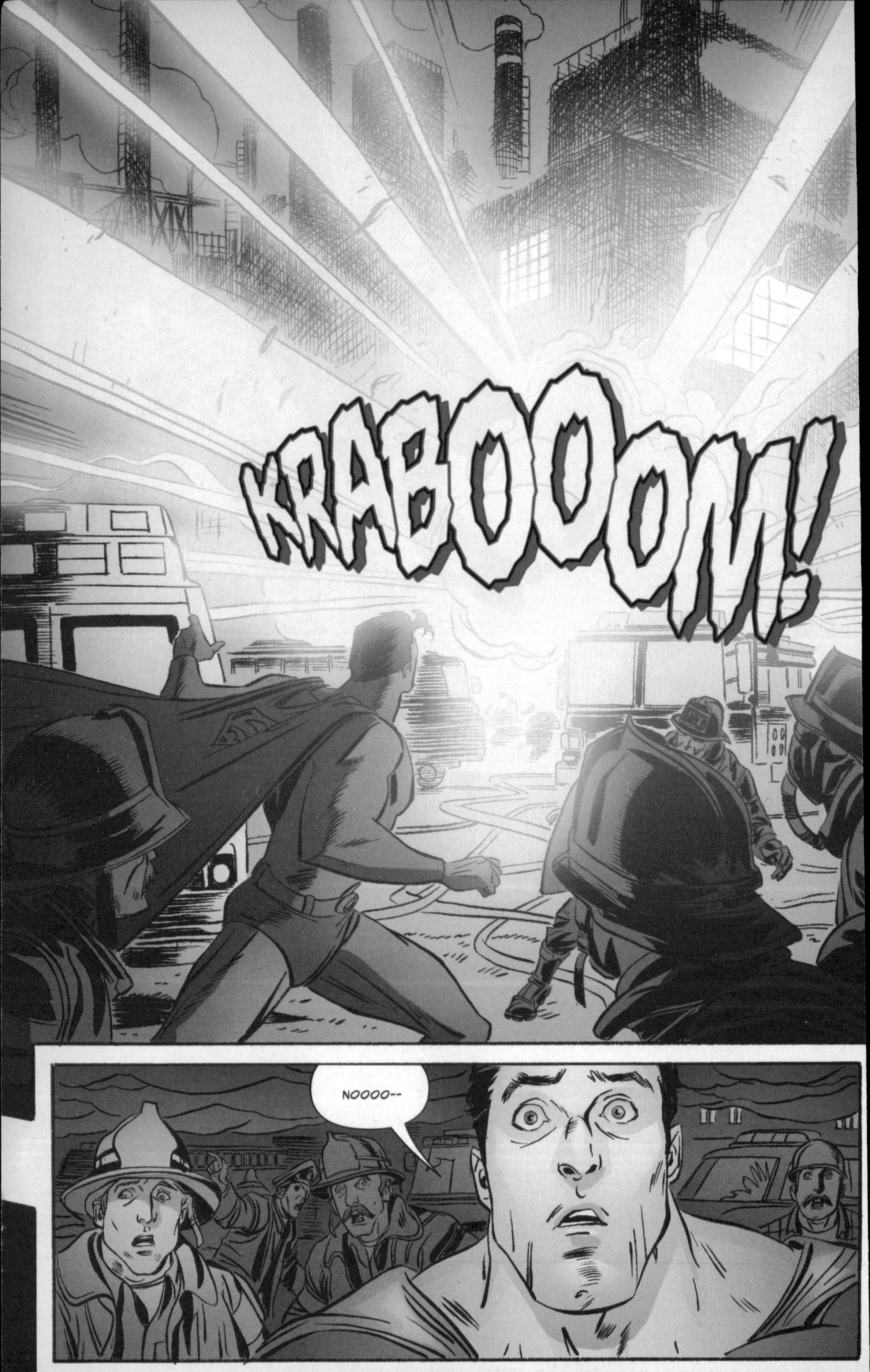
KRABOOOM!
NOOOO--

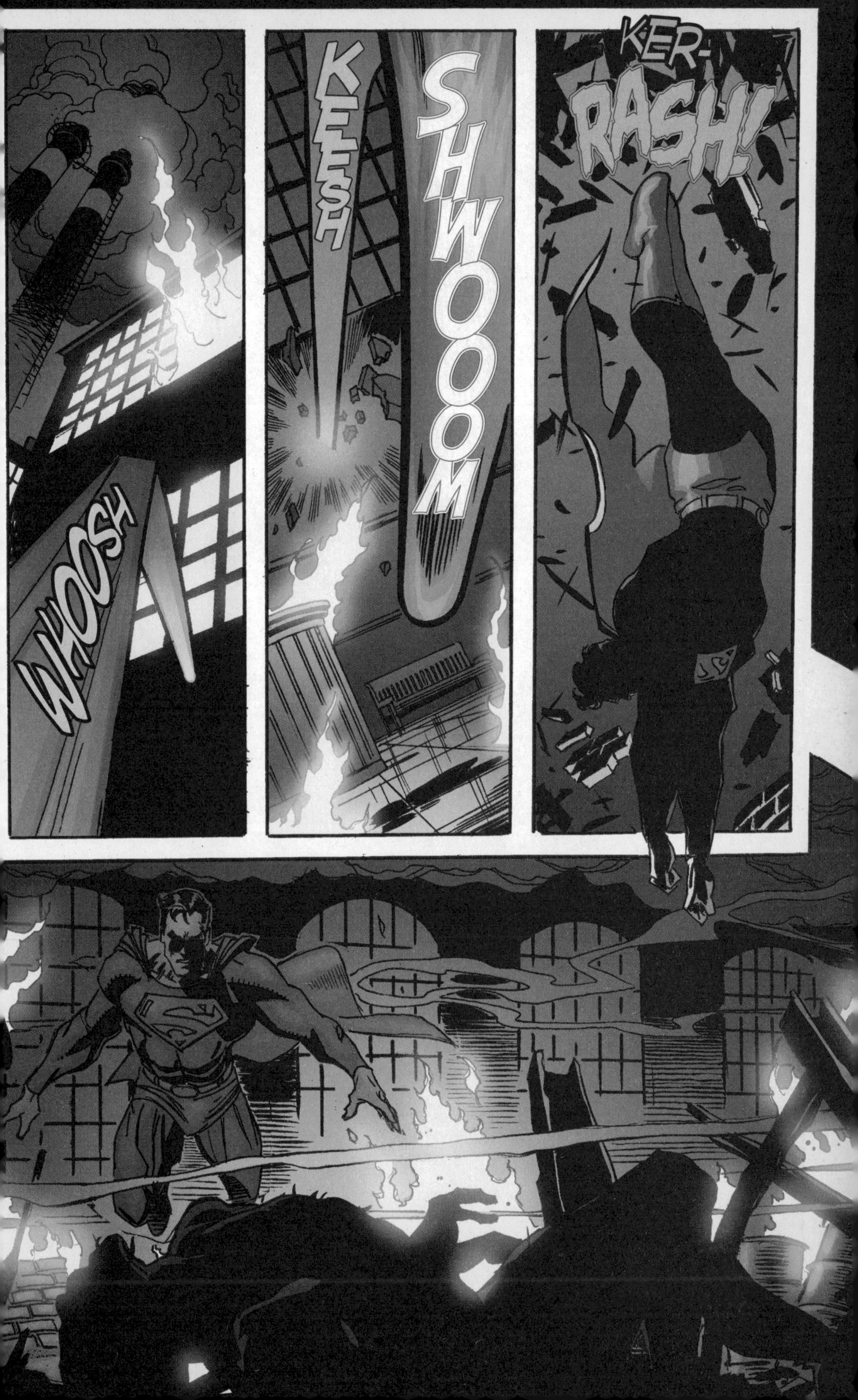
WHOOSH
KEESH
SHWOOOM
KER-
RASH!

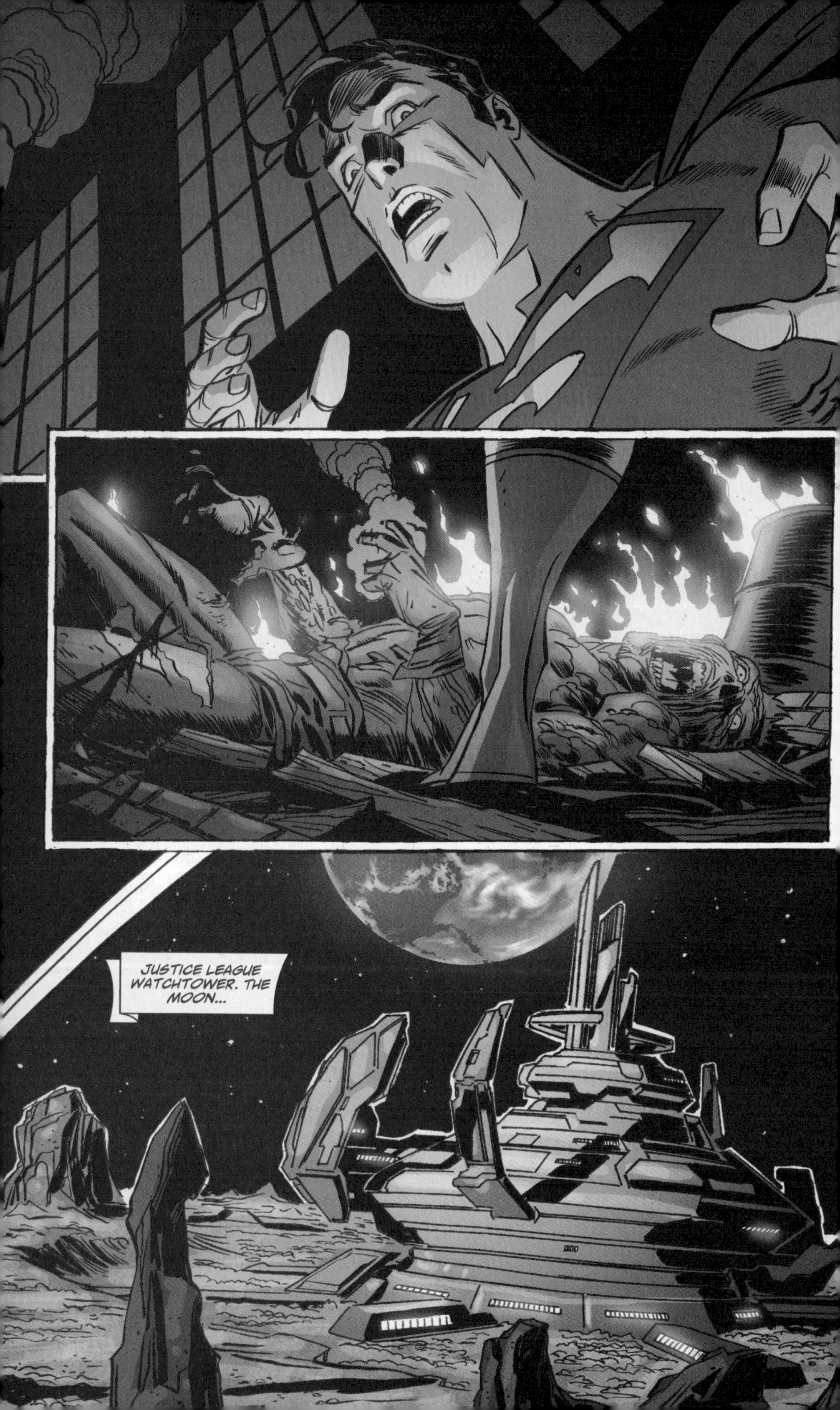
JUSTICE LEAGUE WATCHTOWER. THE MOON...

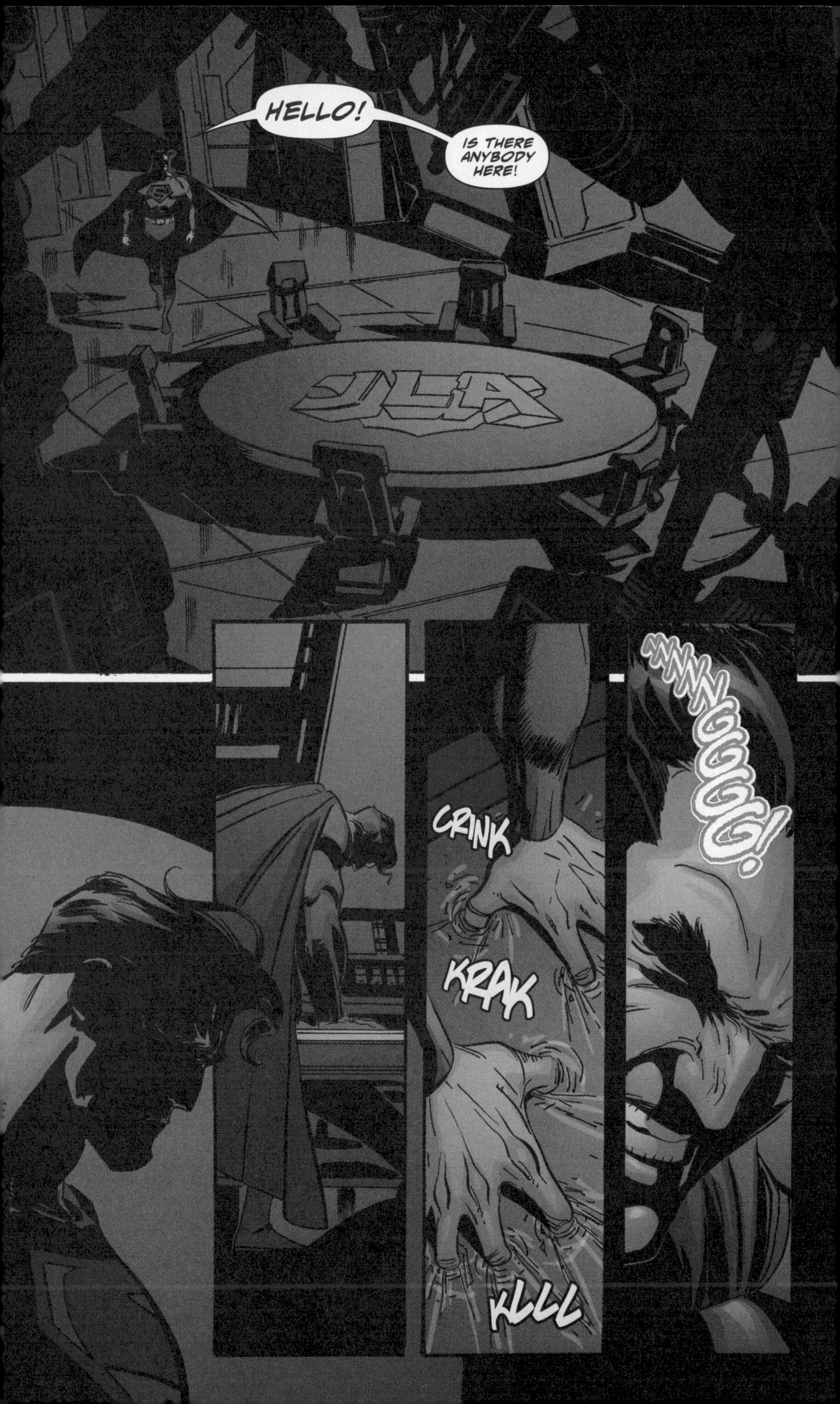
HELLO!
IS THERE ANYBODY HERE!
JLA
CRINK
KRAK
KLLL
NNNNGGGG!

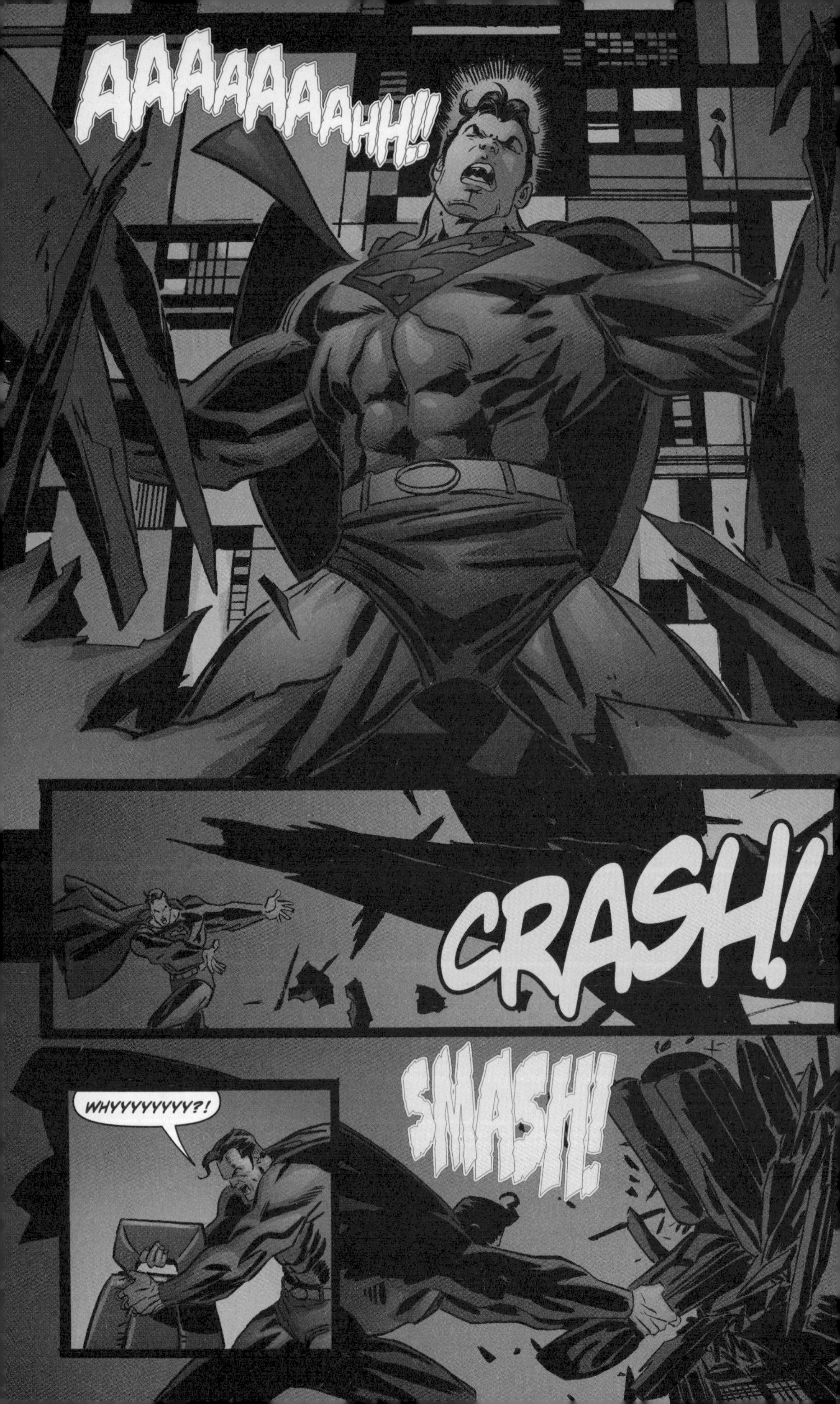
AAAAAAAAHH!!
CRASH!
WHYYYYYYYY?!
SMASH!

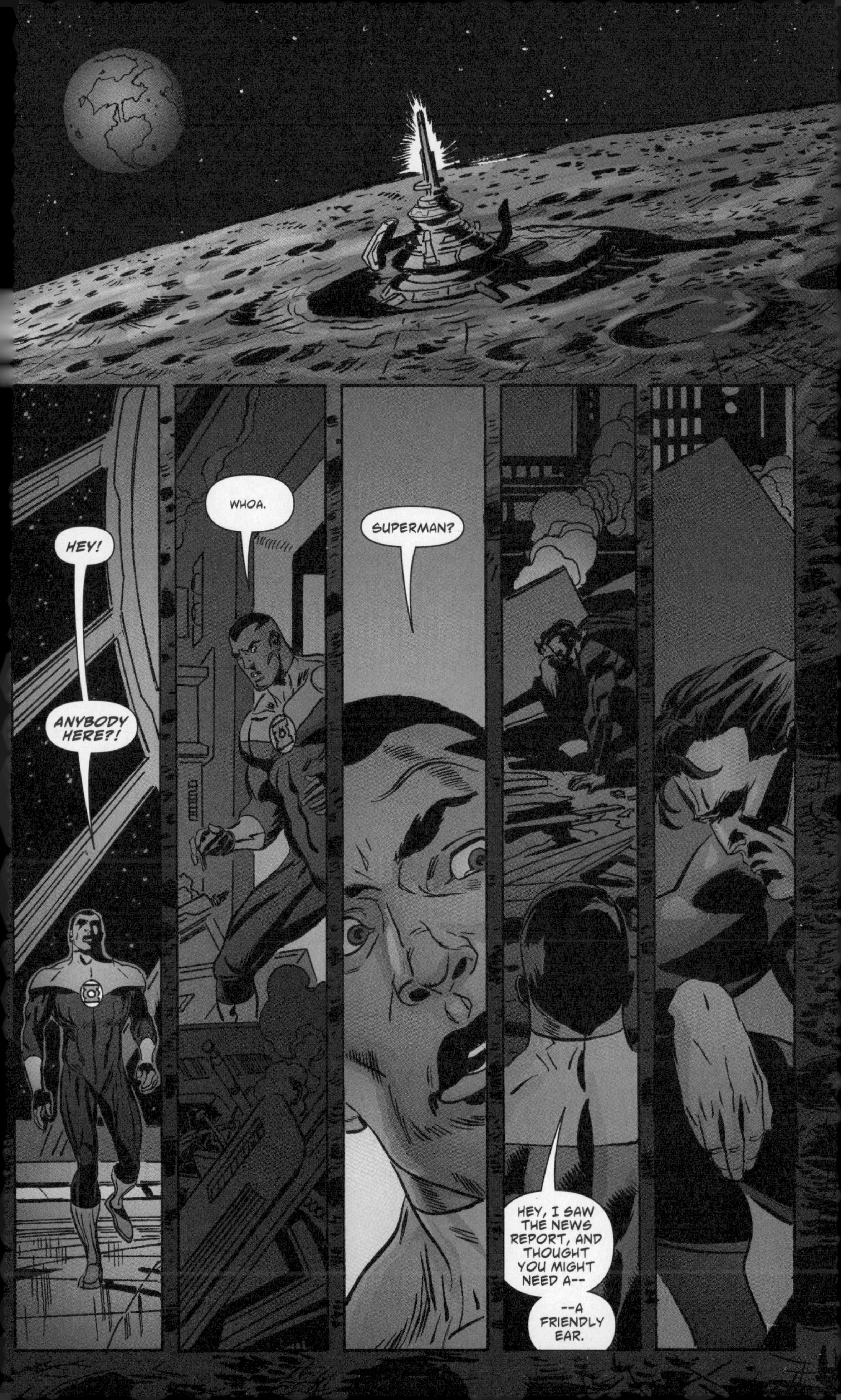
HEY!
ANYBODY HERE?!
WHOA.
SUPERMAN?
HEY, I SAW THE NEWS REPORT, AND THOUGHT YOU MIGHT NEED A--
--A FRIENDLY EAR.

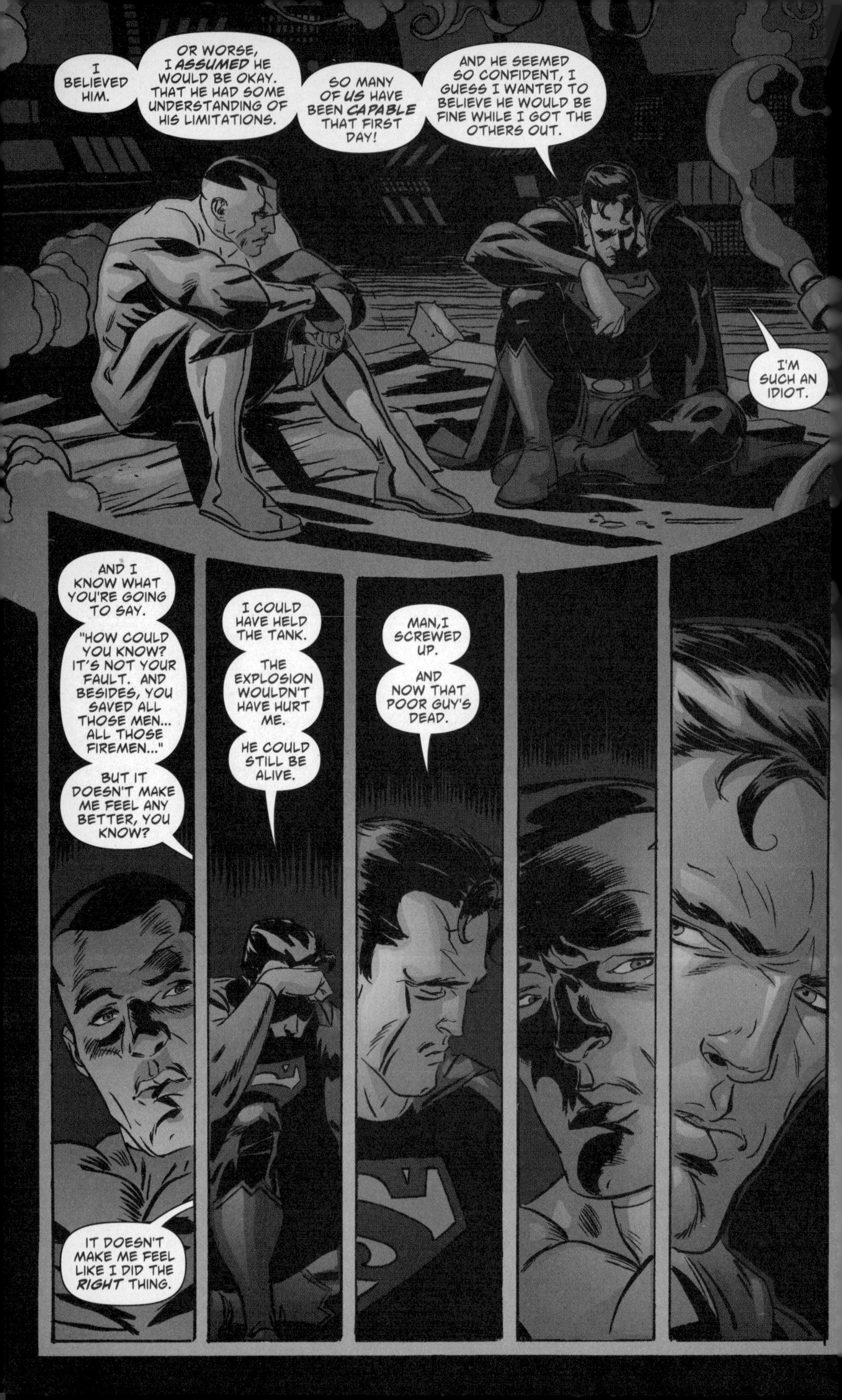

I BELIEVED HIM.
OR WORSE, I ASSUMED HE WOULD BE OKAY. THAT HE HAD SOME UNDERSTANDING OF HIS LIMITATIONS.
SO MANY OF US HAVE BEEN CAPABLE THAT FIRST DAY!
AND HE SEEMED SO CONFIDENT, I GUESS I WANTED TO BELIEVE HE WOULD BE FINE WHILE I GOT THE OTHERS OUT.
I'M SUCH AN IDIOT.
AND I KNOW WHAT YOU'RE GOING TO SAY.
"HOW COULD YOU KNOW? IT'S NOT YOUR FAULT. AND BESIDES, YOU SAVED ALL THOSE MEN... ALL THOSE FIREMEN..."
BUT IT DOESN'T MAKE ME FEEL ANY BETTER, YOU KNOW?
IT DOESN'T MAKE ME FEEL LIKE I DID THE RIGHT THING.
I COULD HAVE HELD THE TANK.
THE EXPLOSION WOULDN'T HAVE HURT ME.
HE COULD STILL BE ALIVE.
MAN, I SCREWED UP.
AND NOW THAT POOR GUY'S DEAD.

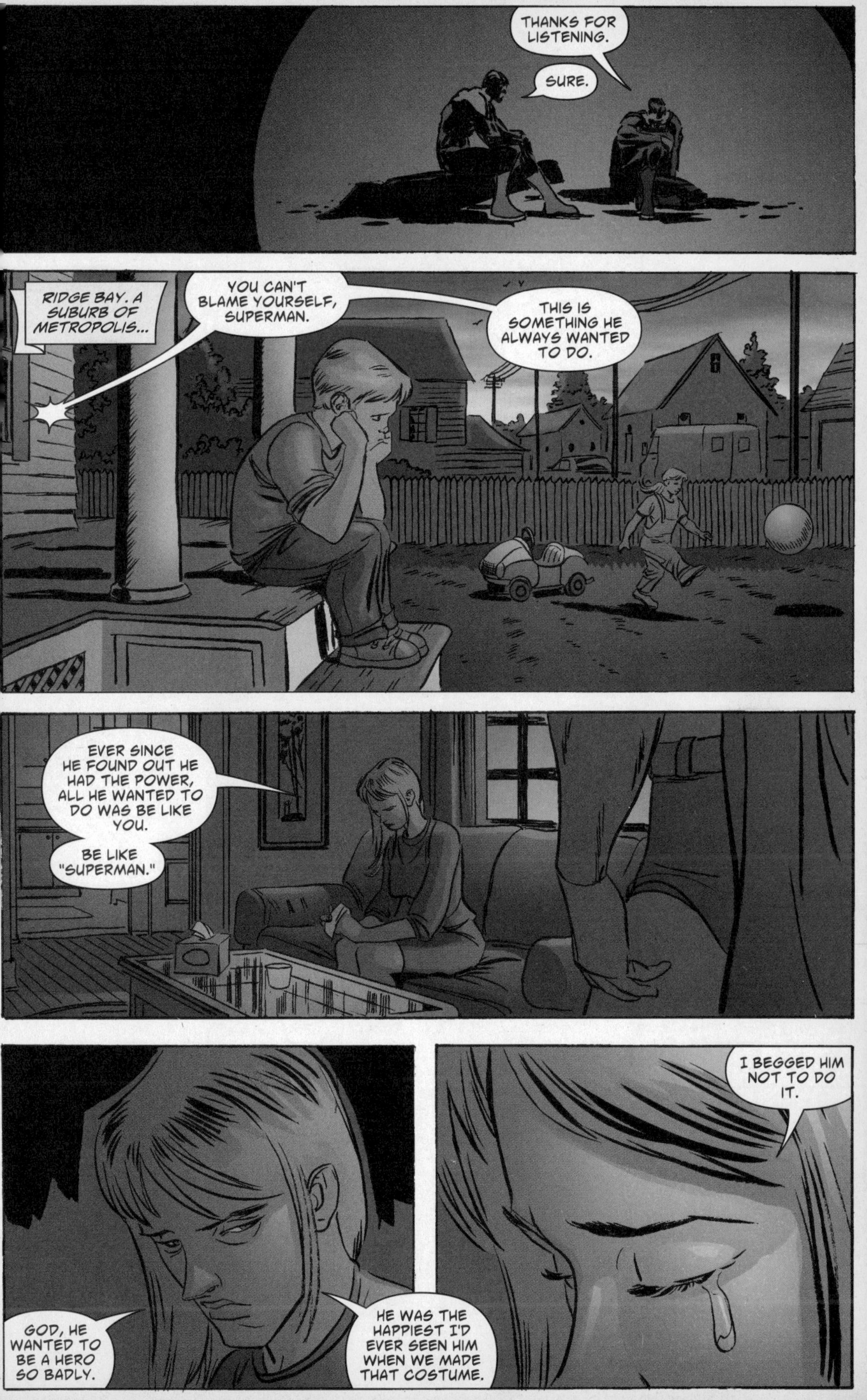
THANKS FOR LISTENING.
SURE.
RIDGE BAY. A SUBURB OF METROPOLIS...
YOU CAN'T BLAME YOURSELF, SUPERMAN.
THIS IS SOMETHING HE ALWAYS WANTED TO DO.
EVER SINCE HE FOUND OUT HE HAD THE POWER, ALL HE WANTED TO DO WAS BE LIKE YOU.
BE LIKE "SUPERMAN."
GOD, HE WANTED TO BE A HERO SO BADLY.
HE WAS THE HAPPIEST I'D EVER SEEN HIM WHEN WE MADE THAT COSTUME.
I BEGGED HIM NOT TO DO IT.

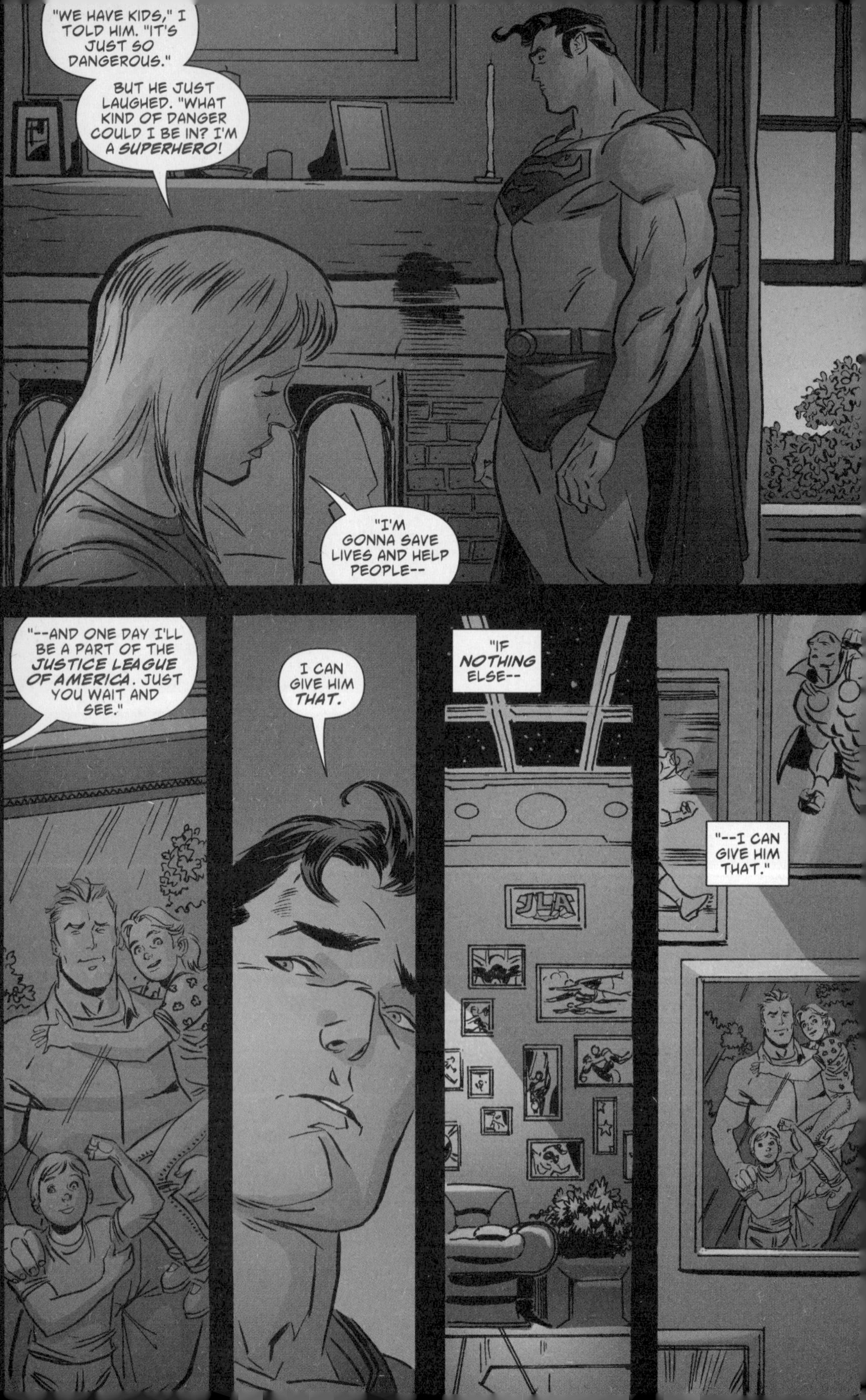
"WE HAVE KIDS," I TOLD HIM. "IT'S JUST SO DANGEROUS."
BUT HE JUST LAUGHED. "WHAT KIND OF DANGER COULD I BE IN? I'M A *SUPERHERO*!
"I'M GONNA SAVE LIVES AND HELP PEOPLE--
"--AND ONE DAY I'LL BE A PART OF THE *JUSTICE LEAGUE OF AMERICA*. JUST YOU WAIT AND SEE."
I CAN GIVE HIM *THAT.*
"IF *NOTHING* ELSE--
JLA
"--I CAN GIVE HIM THAT."

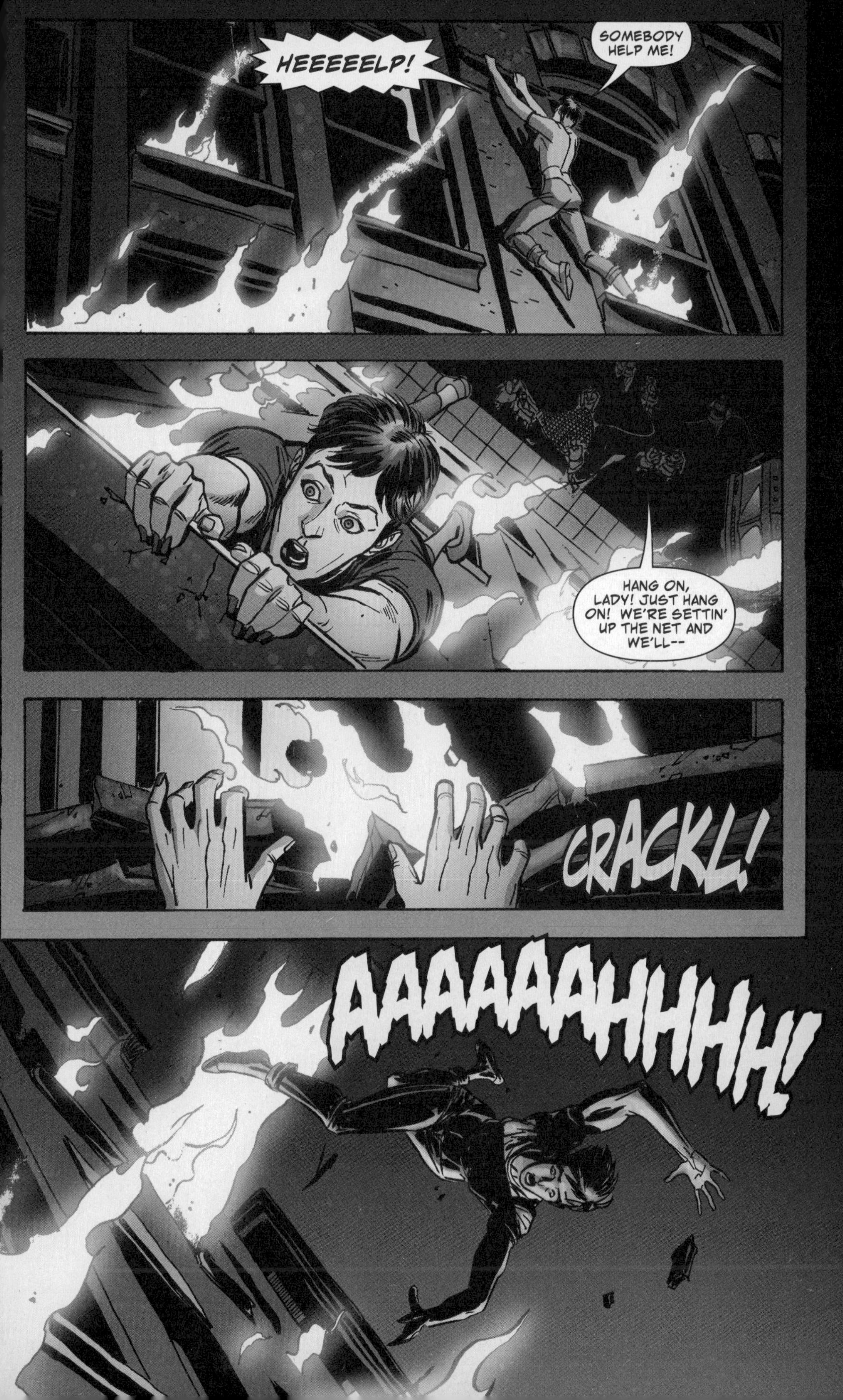
HEEEEELP!
SOMEBODY HELP ME!
HANG ON, LADY! JUST HANG ON! WE'RE SETTIN' UP THE NET AND WE'LL--
CRACKL!
AAAAAHHHH!

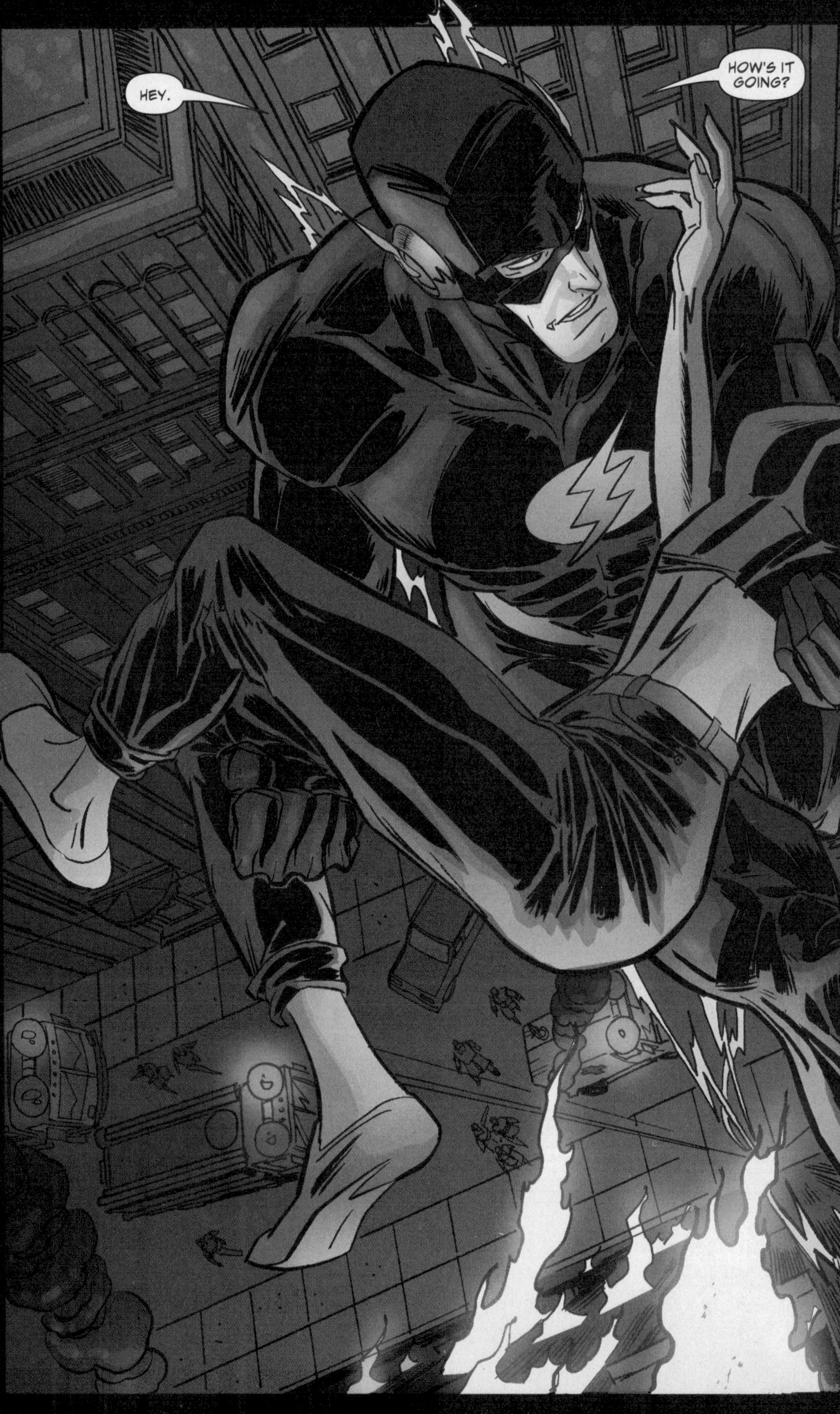
HEY.
HOW'S IT GOING?

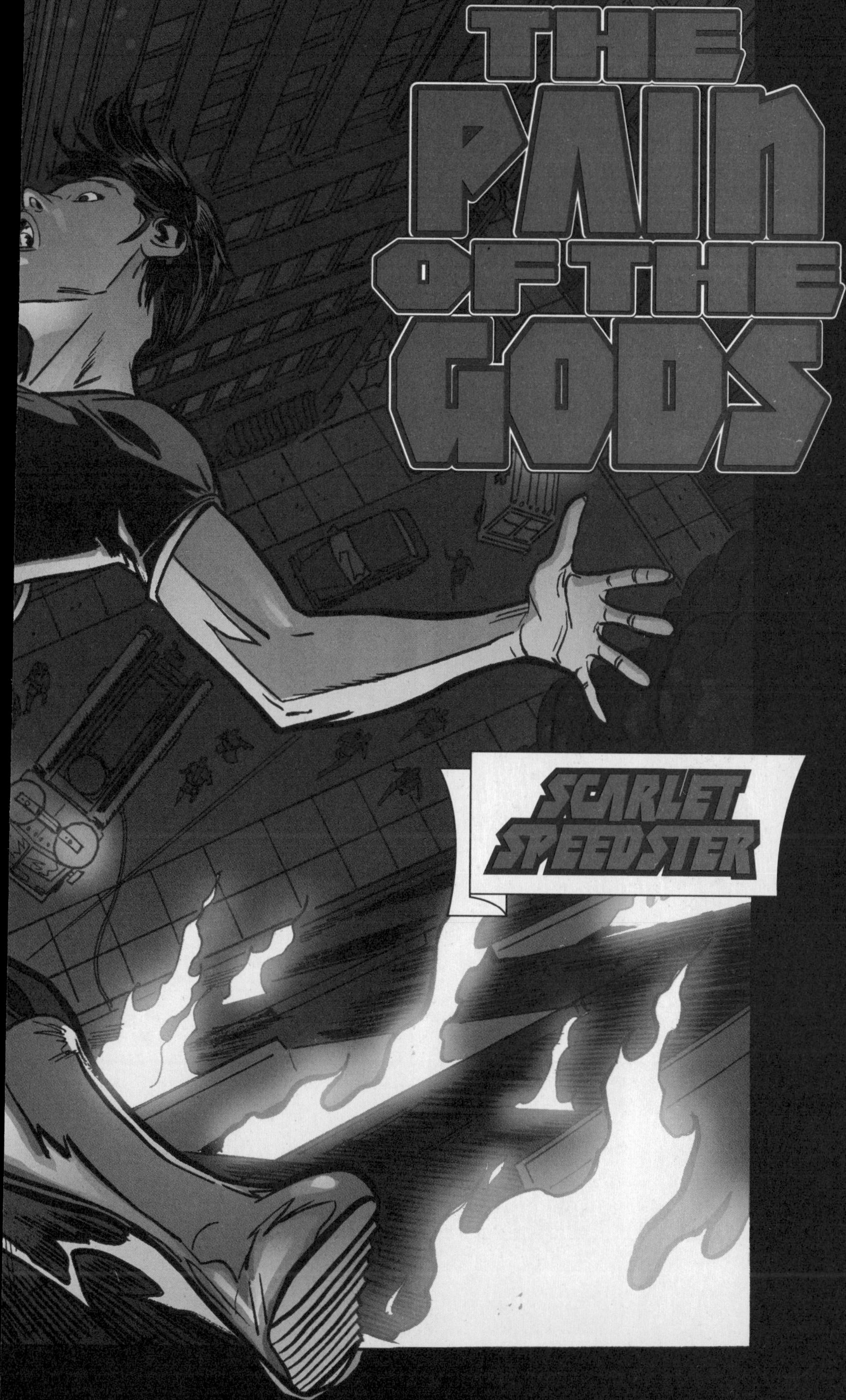
THE PAIN OF THE GODS
SCARLET SPEEDSTER

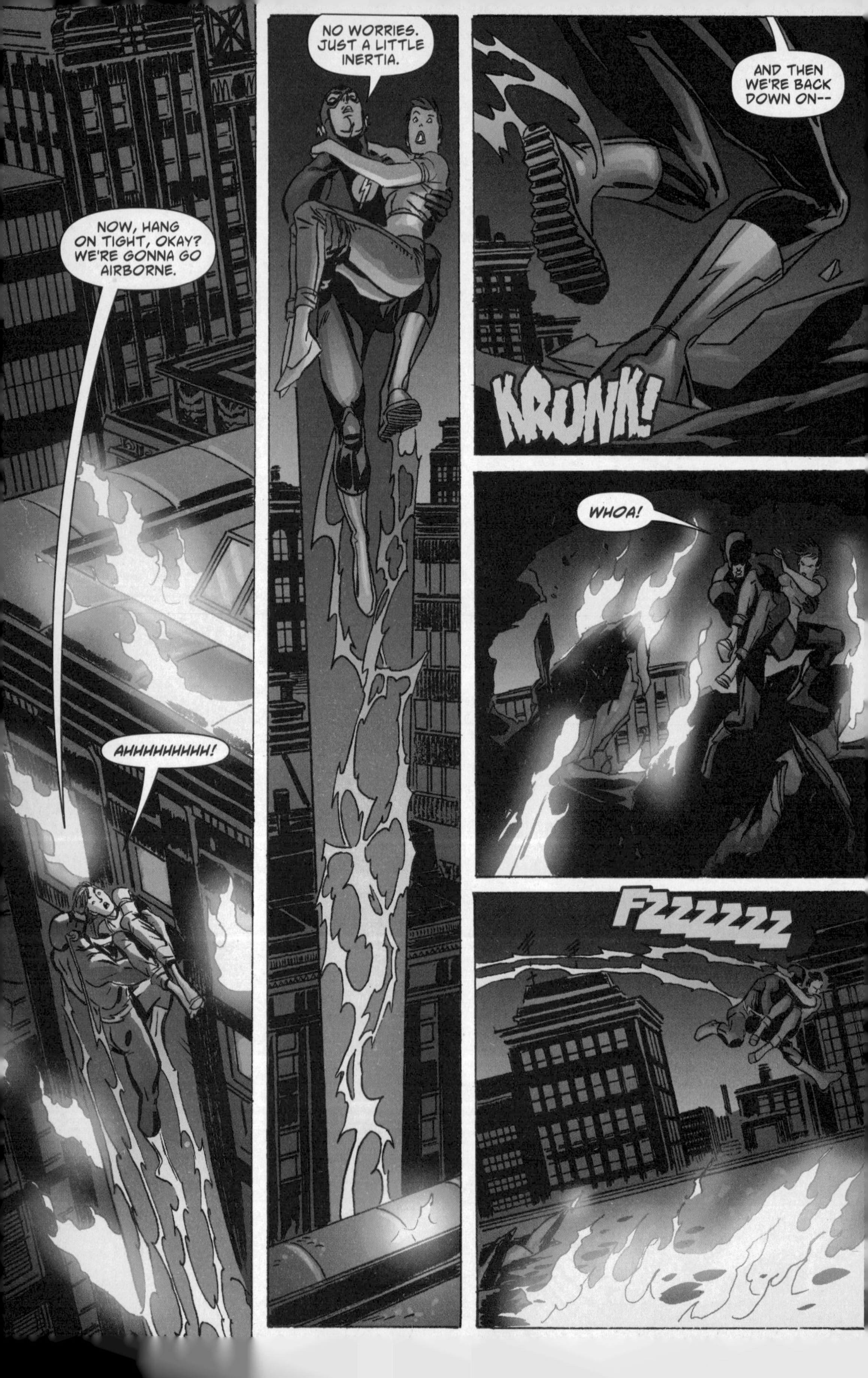
NOW, HANG ON TIGHT, OKAY? WE'RE GONNA GO AIRBORNE.
AHHHHHHHHH!
NO WORRIES. JUST A LITTLE INERTIA.
AND THEN WE'RE BACK DOWN ON--
KRUNK!
WHOA!
FZZZZZZ

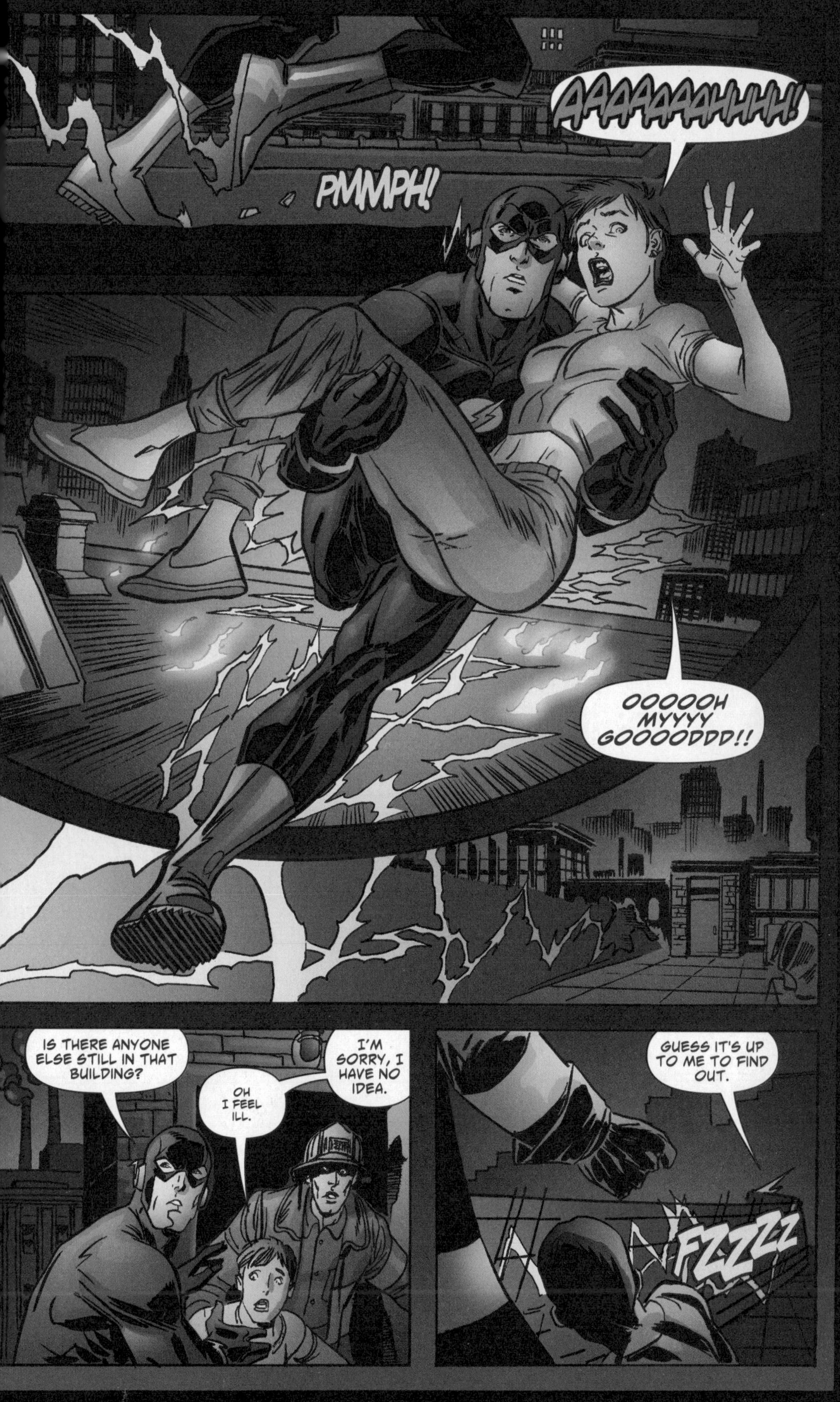

PMMPH!
AAAAAAAHHHH!
OOOOOH MYYYY GOOOODDD!!
IS THERE ANYONE ELSE STILL IN THAT BUILDING?
OH I FEEL ILL.
I'M SORRY, I HAVE NO IDEA.
GUESS IT'S UP TO ME TO FIND OUT.
FZZZZ

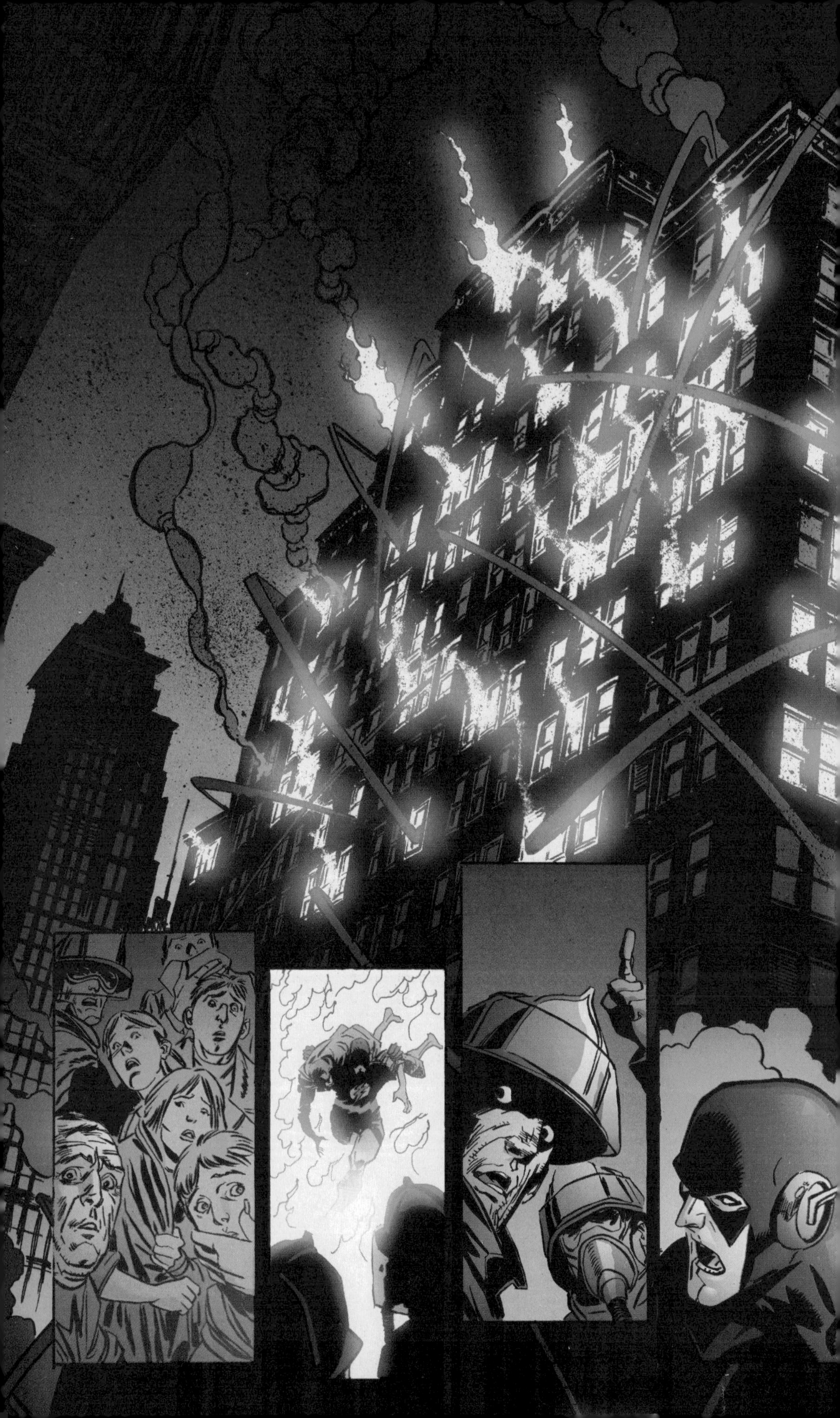

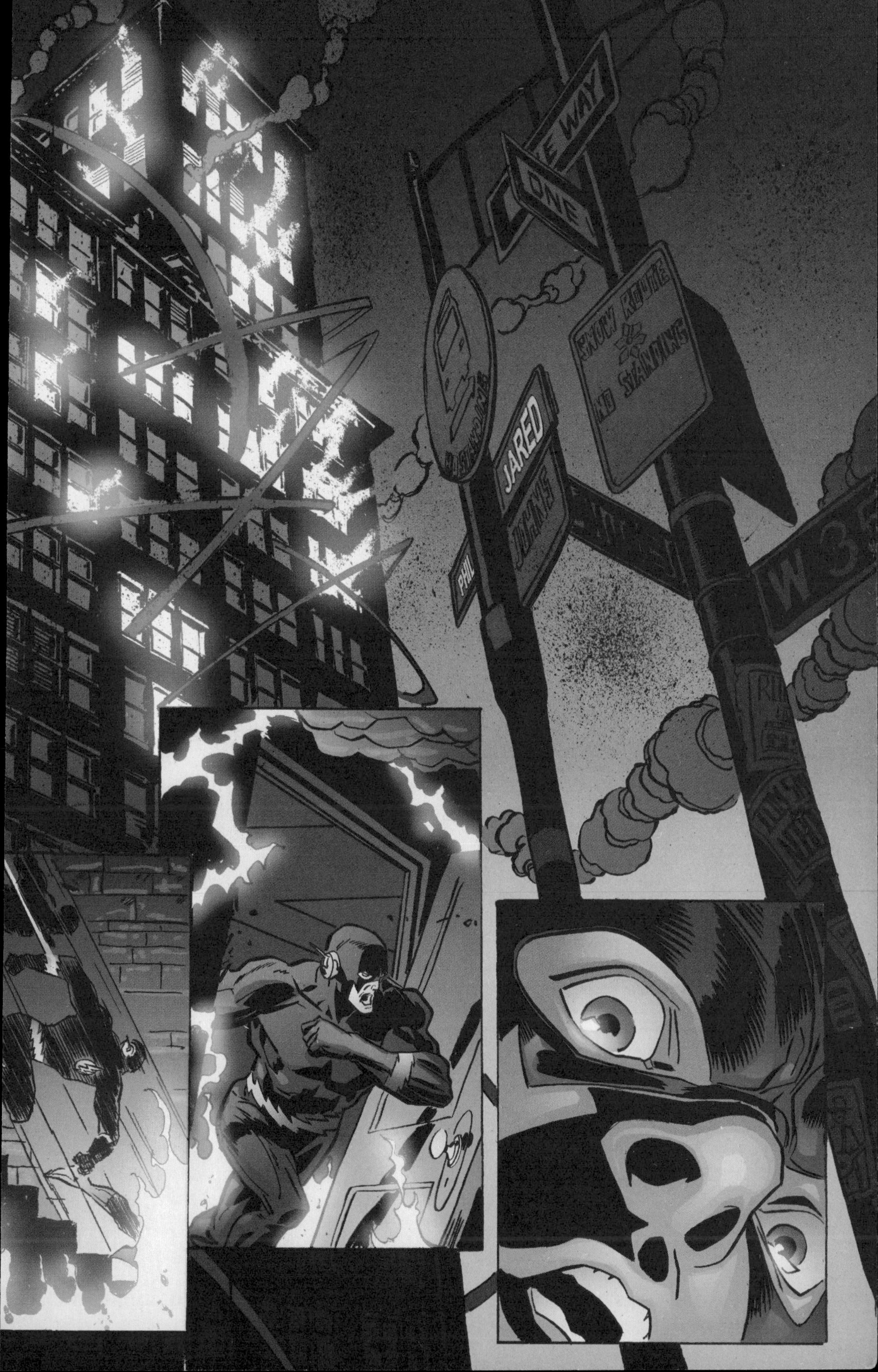
ONE
SNOW ROUTE
NO STANDING
JARED
JOHNS
PHIL

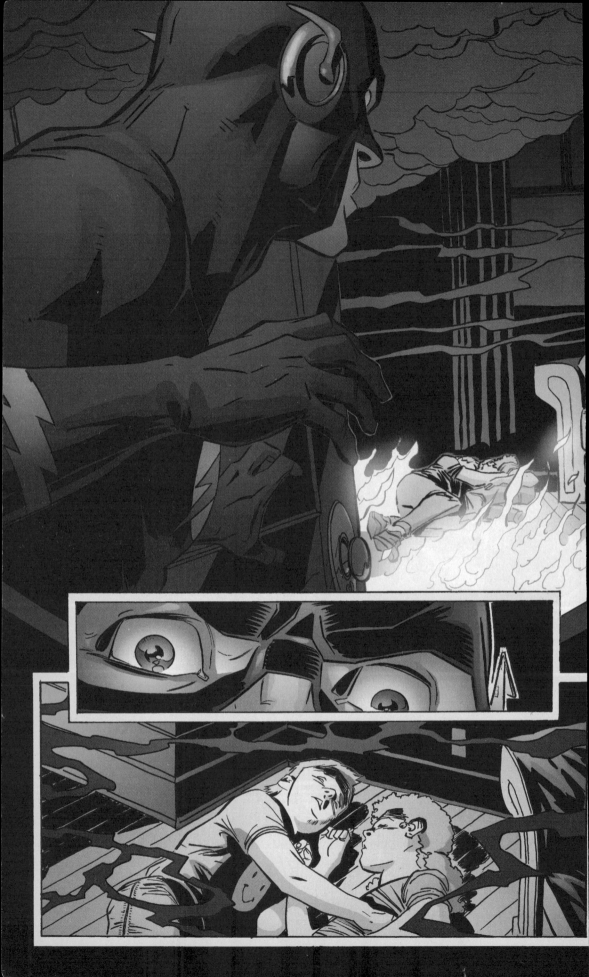

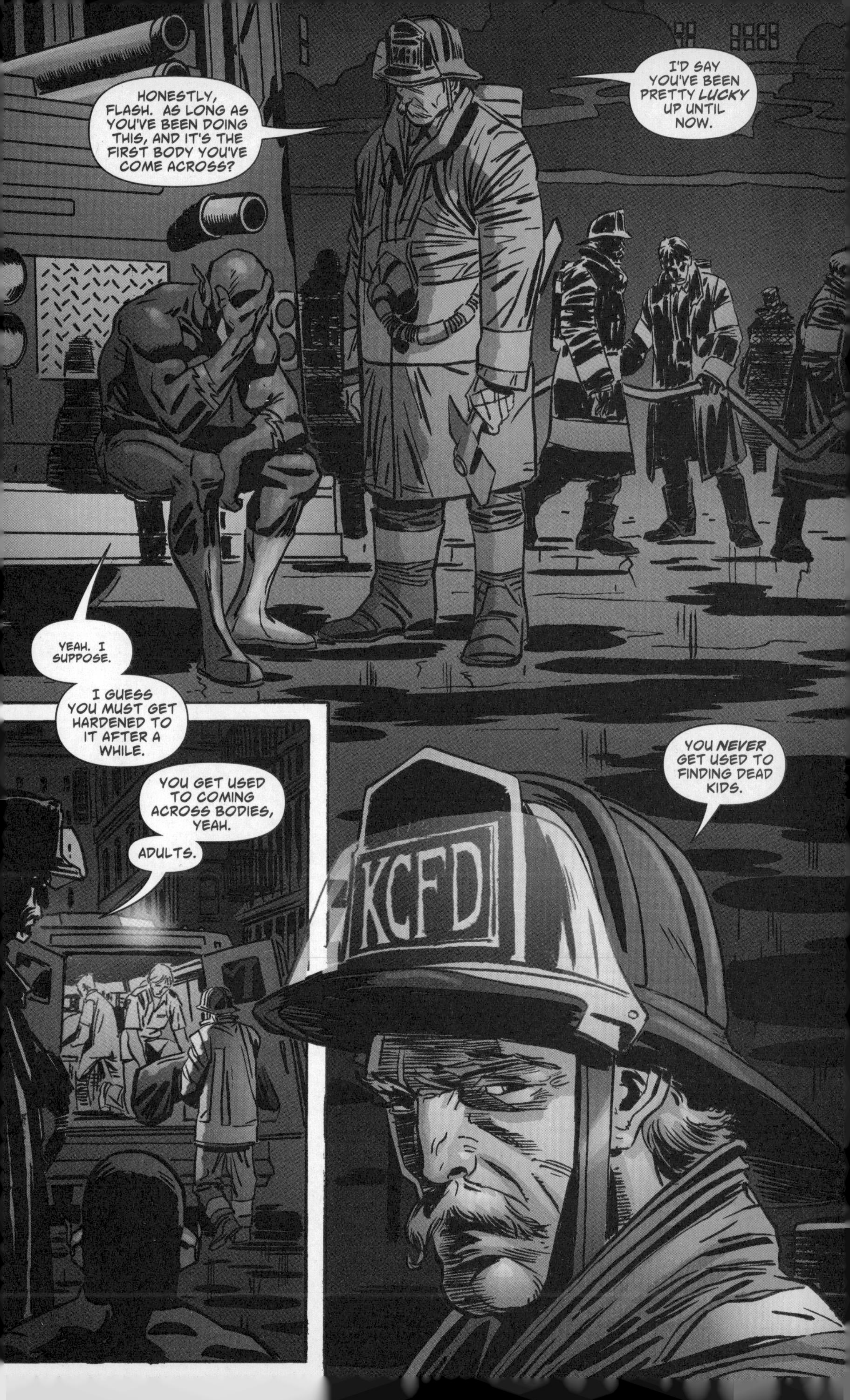
HONESTLY, FLASH. AS LONG AS YOU'VE BEEN DOING THIS, AND IT'S THE FIRST BODY YOU'VE COME ACROSS?
I'D SAY YOU'VE BEEN PRETTY LUCKY UP UNTIL NOW.
YEAH. I SUPPOSE.
I GUESS YOU MUST GET HARDENED TO IT AFTER A WHILE.
YOU GET USED TO COMING ACROSS BODIES, YEAH.
ADULTS.
YOU NEVER GET USED TO FINDING DEAD KIDS.
KCFD

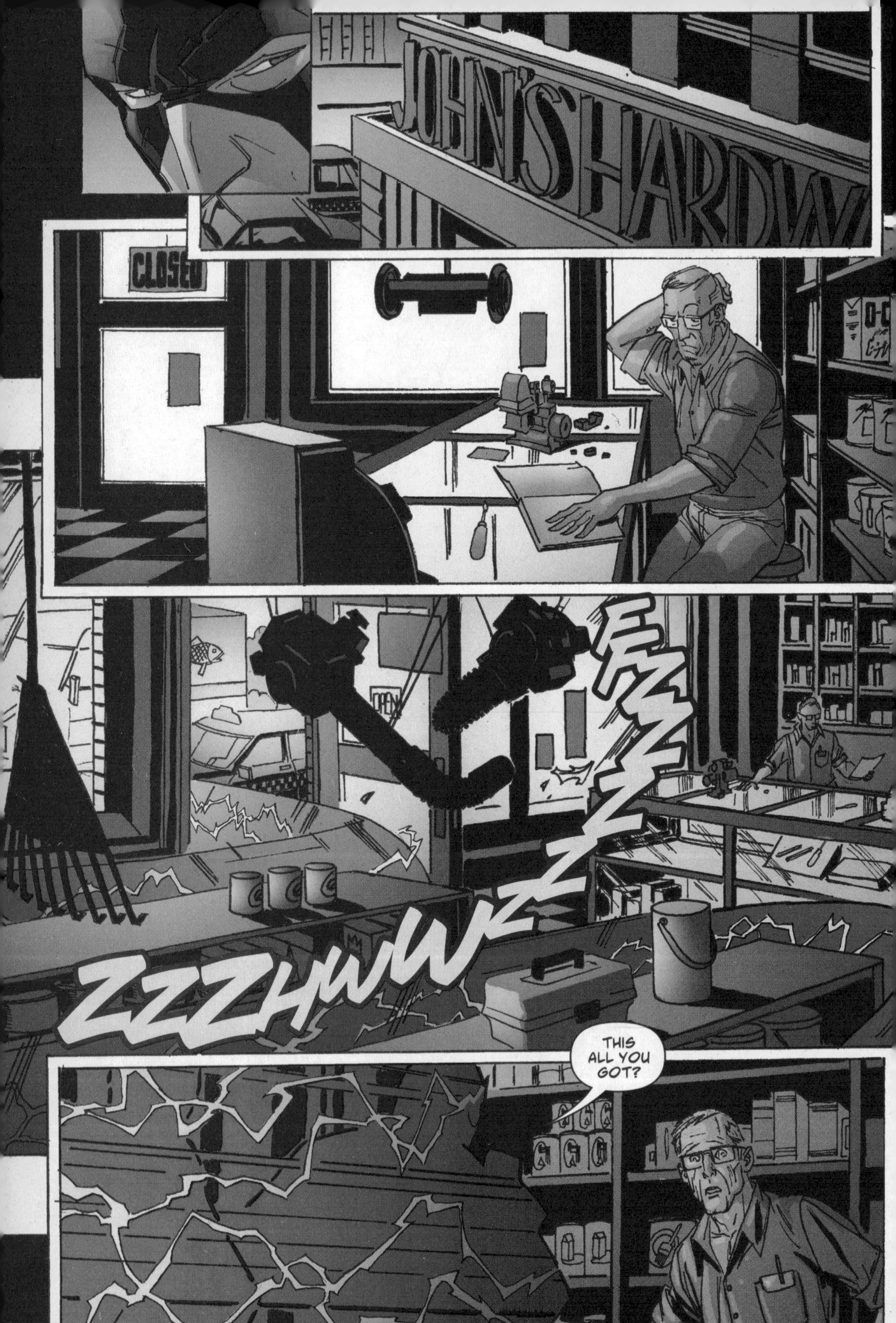
JOHN'S HARDW
CLOSED
OPEN
FZZZZZ
ZZZHWWZ
THIS ALL YOU GOT?

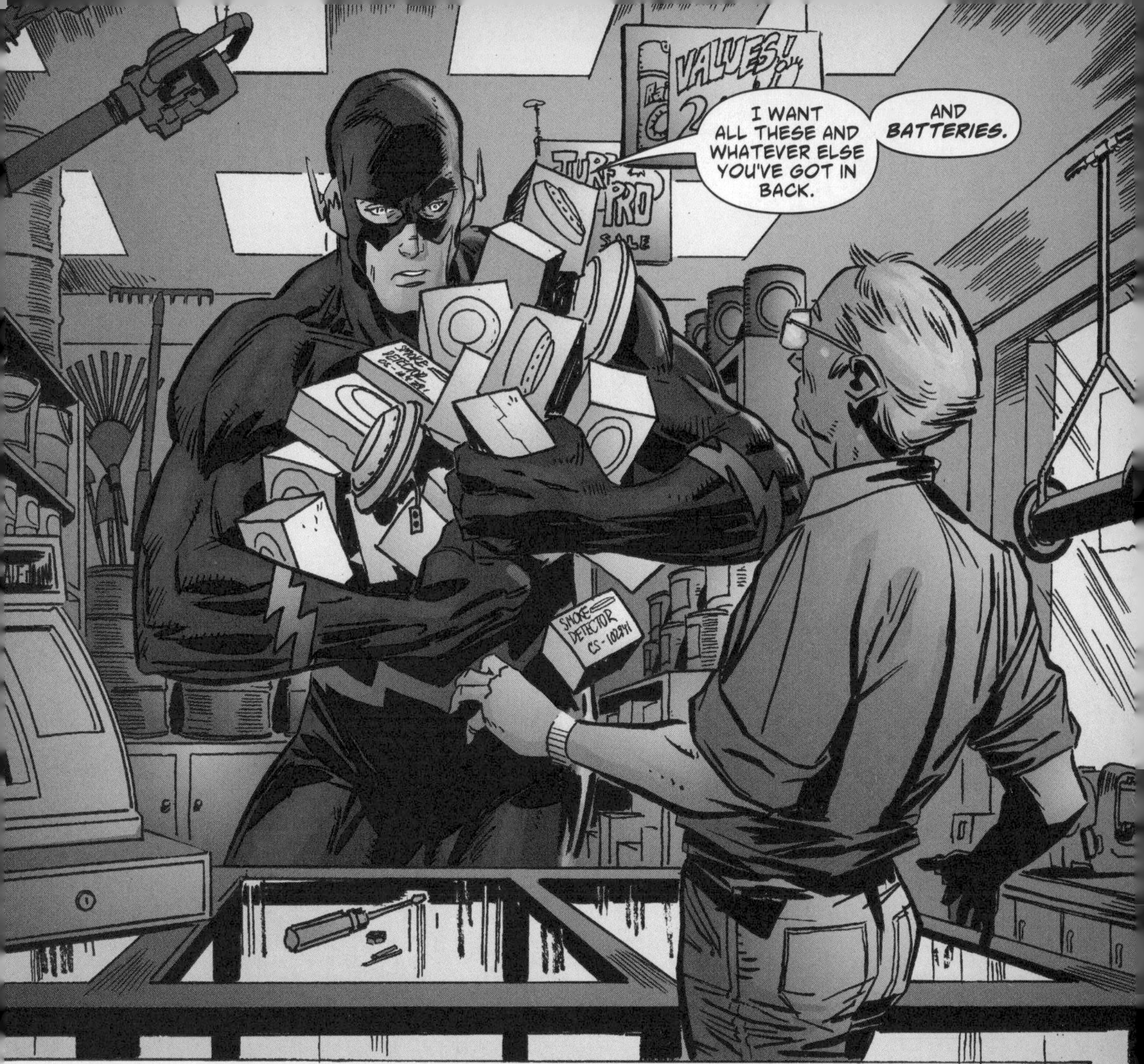
VALUES!
I WANT ALL THESE AND WHATEVER ELSE YOU'VE GOT IN BACK.
AND BATTERIES.
SALE
SMOKE DETECTOR CS-102341

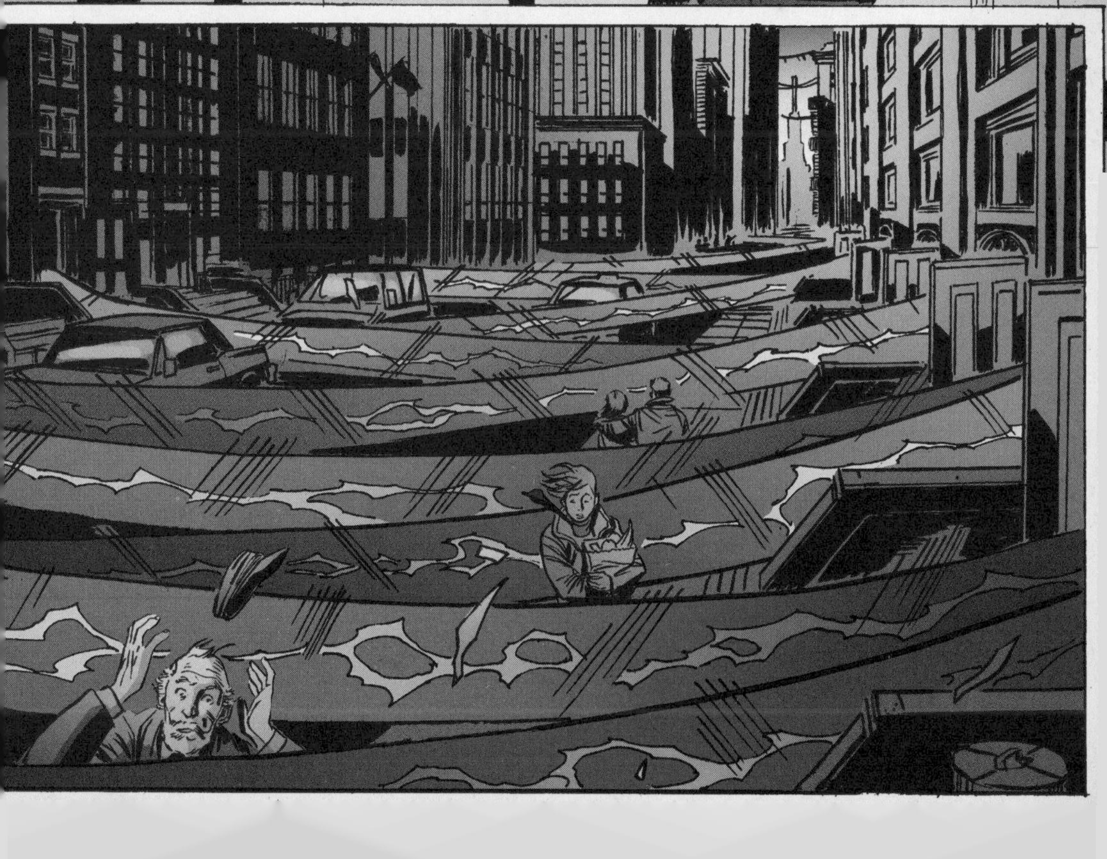

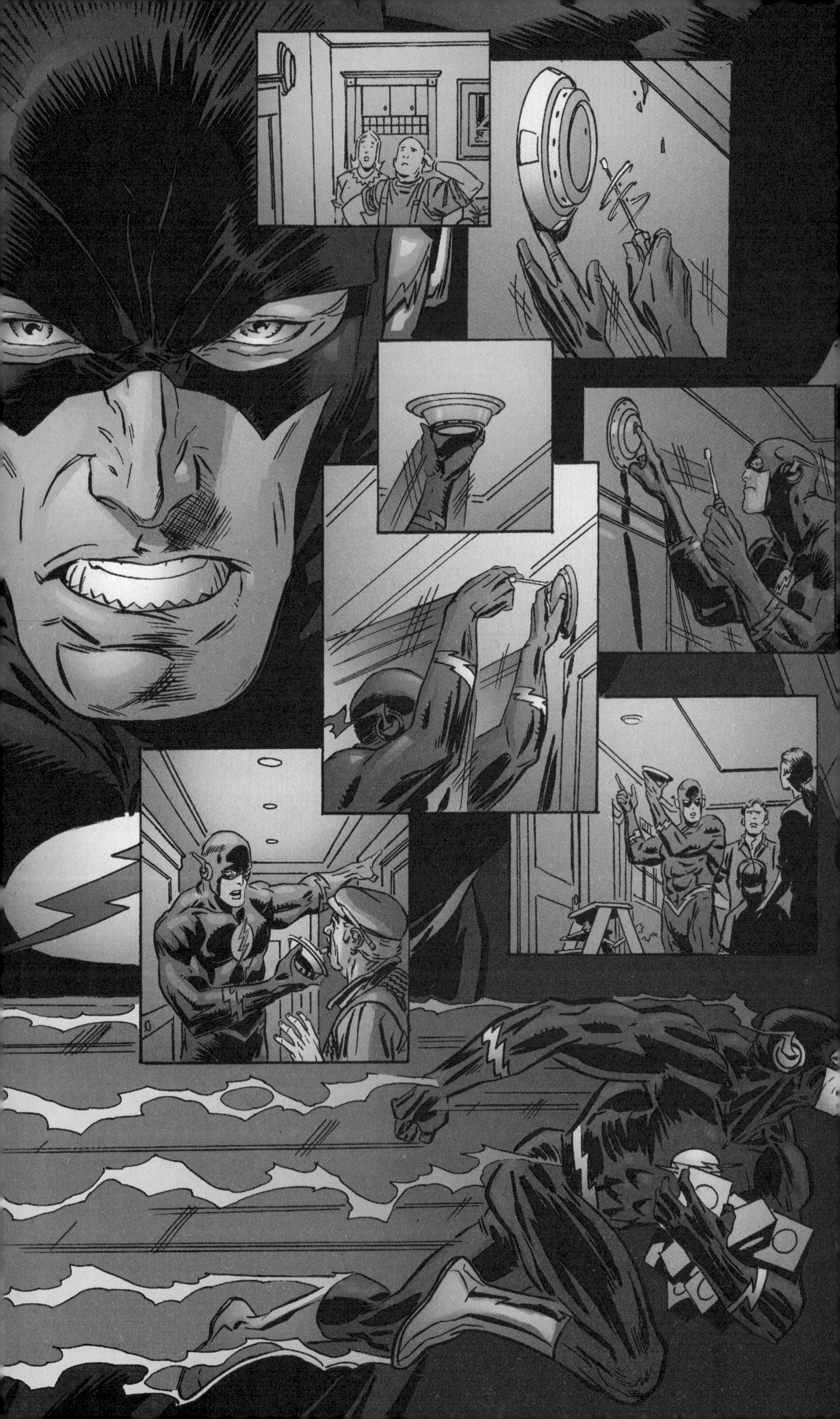

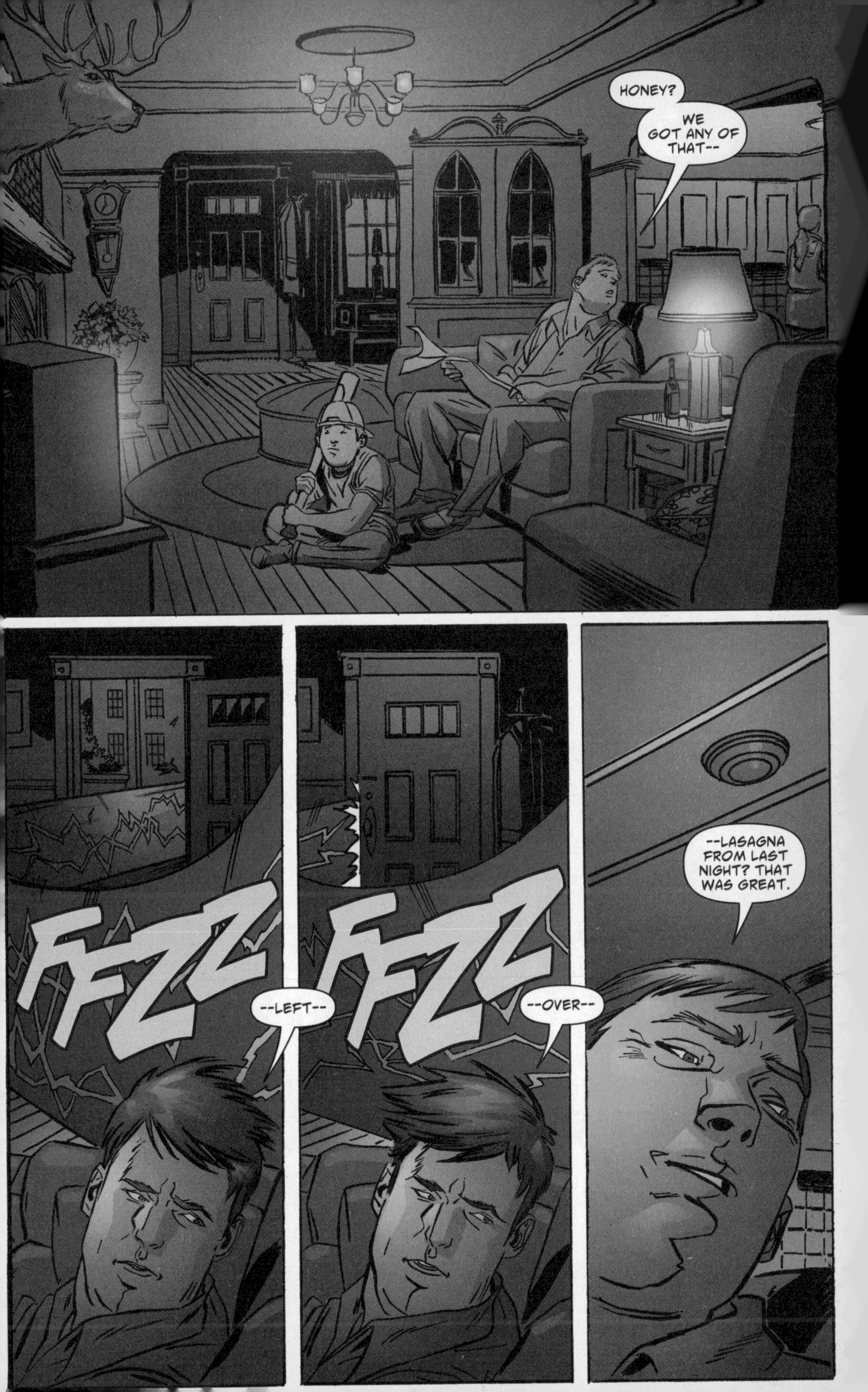
HONEY?
WE GOT ANY OF THAT--
FFZZ
--LEFT--
FFZZ
--OVER--
--LASAGNA FROM LAST NIGHT? THAT WAS GREAT.

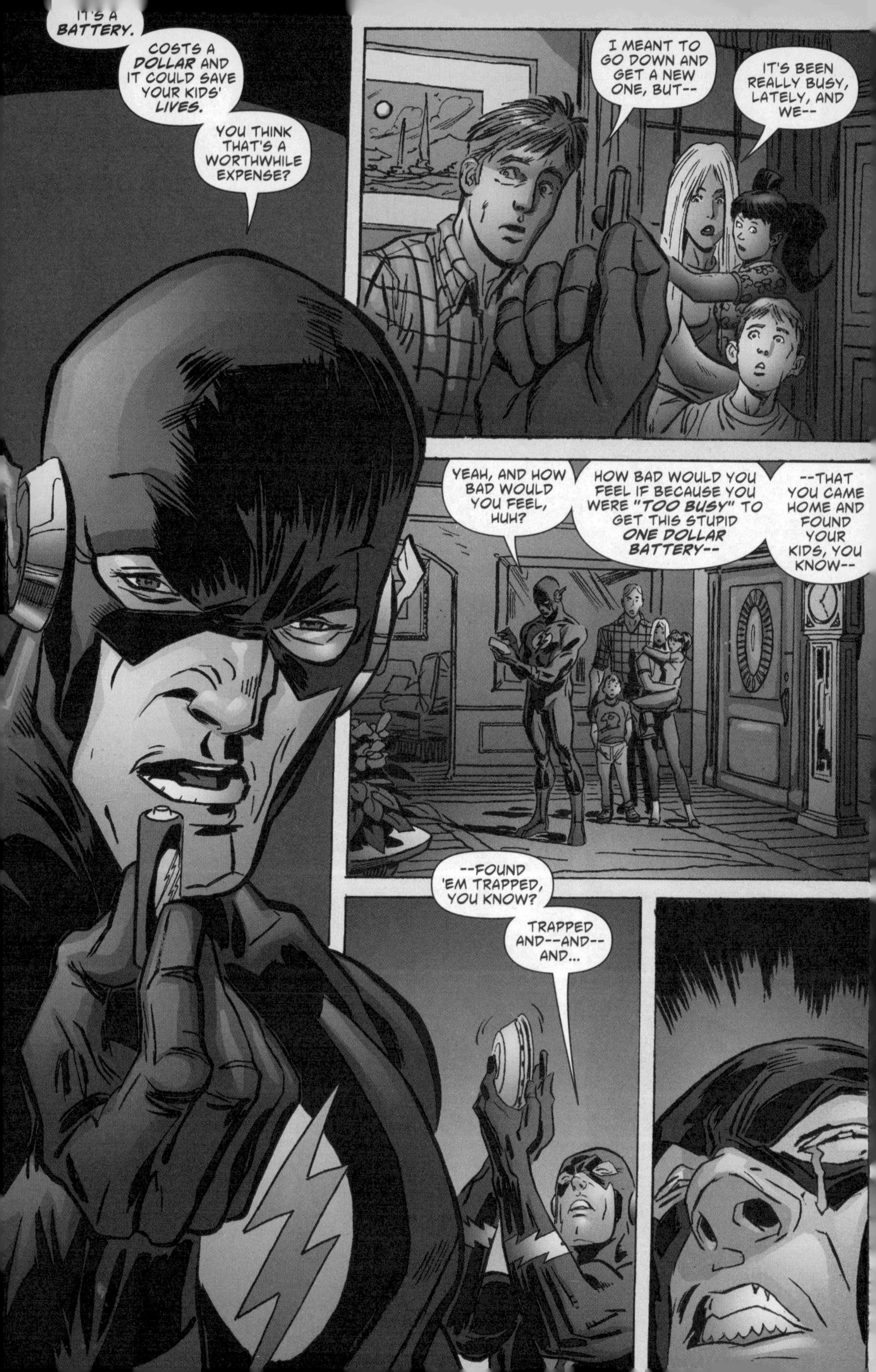
IT'S A BATTERY.
COSTS A DOLLAR AND IT COULD SAVE YOUR KIDS' LIVES.
YOU THINK THAT'S A WORTHWHILE EXPENSE?
I MEANT TO GO DOWN AND GET A NEW ONE, BUT--
IT'S BEEN REALLY BUSY, LATELY, AND WE--
YEAH, AND HOW BAD WOULD YOU FEEL, HUH?
HOW BAD WOULD YOU FEEL IF BECAUSE YOU WERE "TOO BUSY" TO GET THIS STUPID ONE DOLLAR BATTERY--
--THAT YOU CAME HOME AND FOUND YOUR KIDS, YOU KNOW--
--FOUND 'EM TRAPPED, YOU KNOW?
TRAPPED AND--AND--AND...

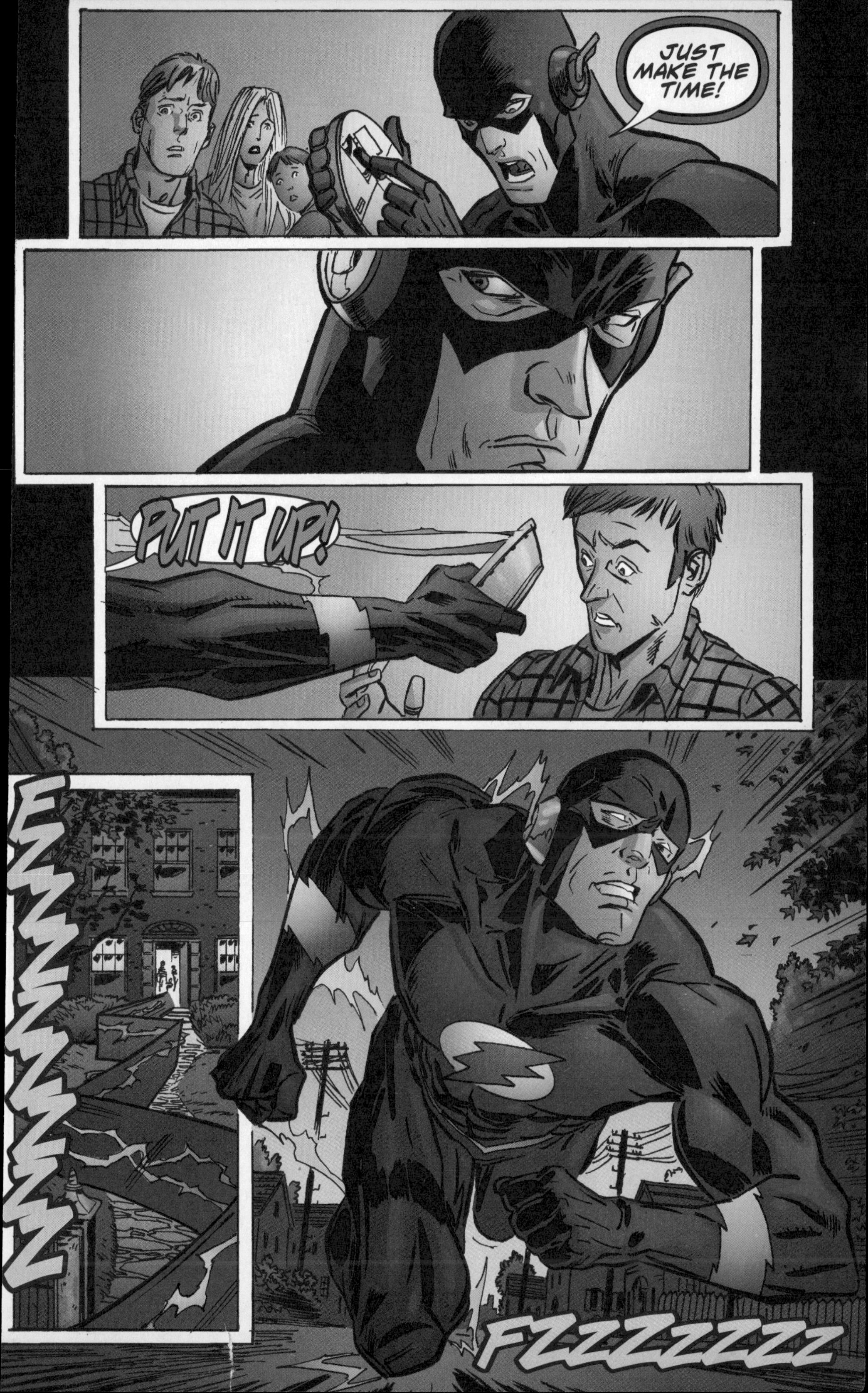
JUST MAKE THE TIME!
PUT IT UP!
FZZZZZZZZ
FZZZZZZZZ

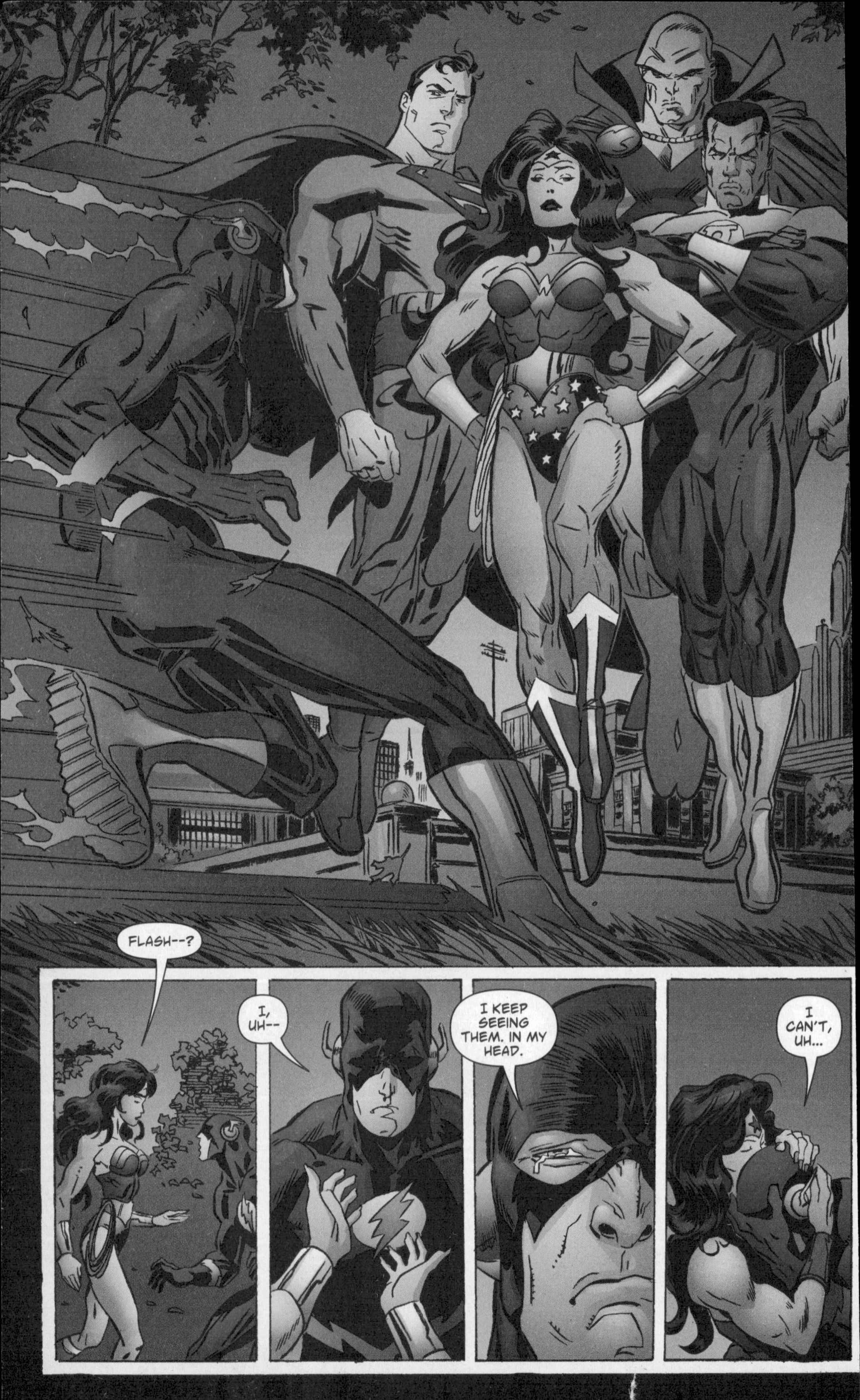
FLASH--?
I, UH--
I KEEP SEEING THEM. IN MY HEAD.
I CAN'T, UH...

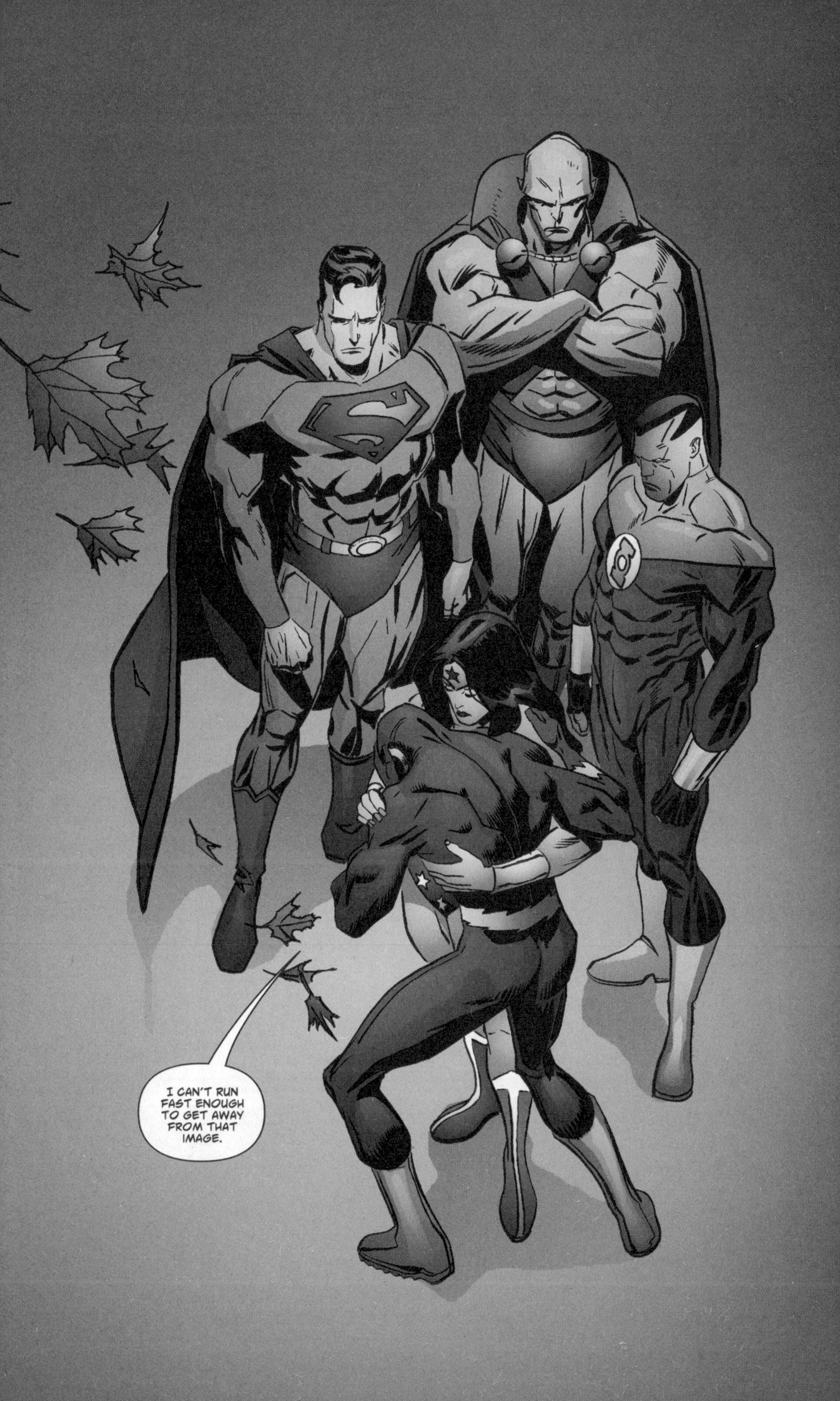
I CAN'T RUN FAST ENOUGH TO GET AWAY FROM THAT IMAGE.

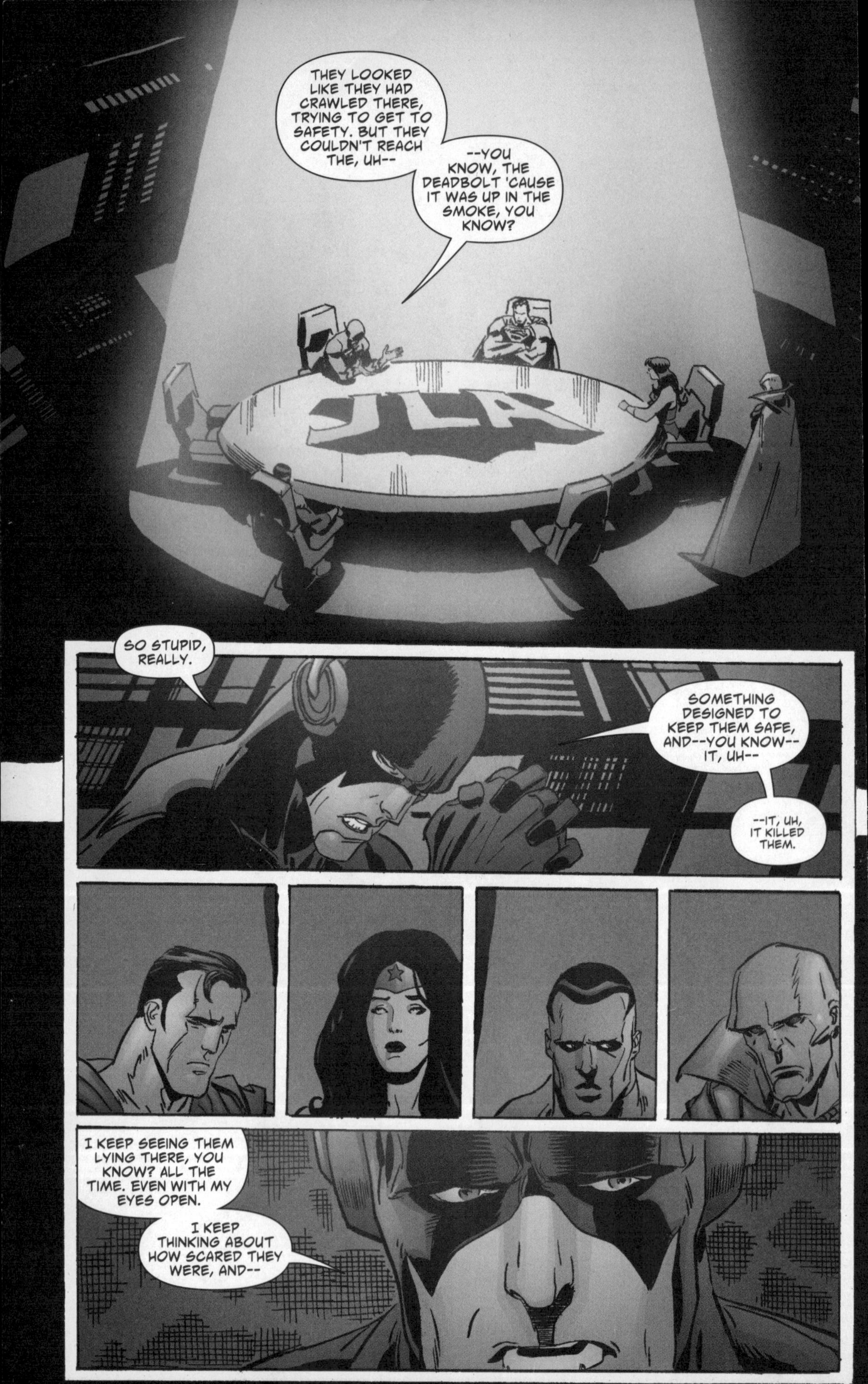
THEY LOOKED LIKE THEY HAD CRAWLED THERE, TRYING TO GET TO SAFETY. BUT THEY COULDN'T REACH THE, UH--
--YOU KNOW, THE DEADBOLT 'CAUSE IT WAS UP IN THE SMOKE, YOU KNOW?
SO STUPID, REALLY.
SOMETHING DESIGNED TO KEEP THEM SAFE, AND--YOU KNOW--IT, UH--
--IT, UH, IT KILLED THEM.
I KEEP SEEING THEM LYING THERE, YOU KNOW? ALL THE TIME. EVEN WITH MY EYES OPEN.
I KEEP THINKING ABOUT HOW SCARED THEY WERE, AND--

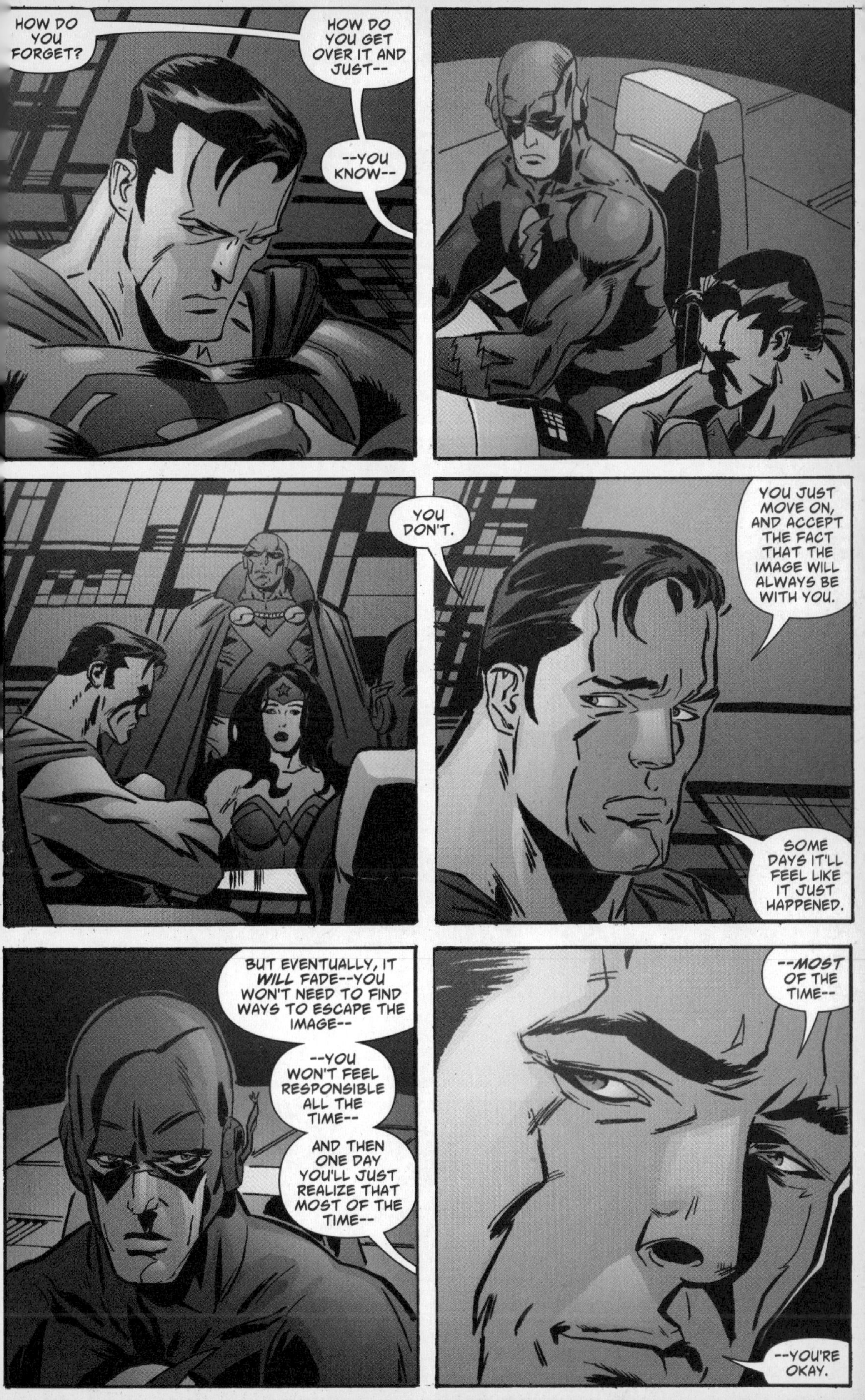
HOW DO YOU FORGET?
HOW DO YOU GET OVER IT AND JUST--
--YOU KNOW--
YOU DON'T.
YOU JUST MOVE ON, AND ACCEPT THE FACT THAT THE IMAGE WILL ALWAYS BE WITH YOU.
SOME DAYS IT'LL FEEL LIKE IT JUST HAPPENED.
BUT EVENTUALLY, IT *WILL* FADE--YOU WON'T NEED TO FIND WAYS TO ESCAPE THE IMAGE--
--YOU WON'T FEEL RESPONSIBLE ALL THE TIME--
AND THEN ONE DAY YOU'LL JUST REALIZE THAT MOST OF THE TIME--
--*MOST* OF THE TIME--
--YOU'RE OKAY.

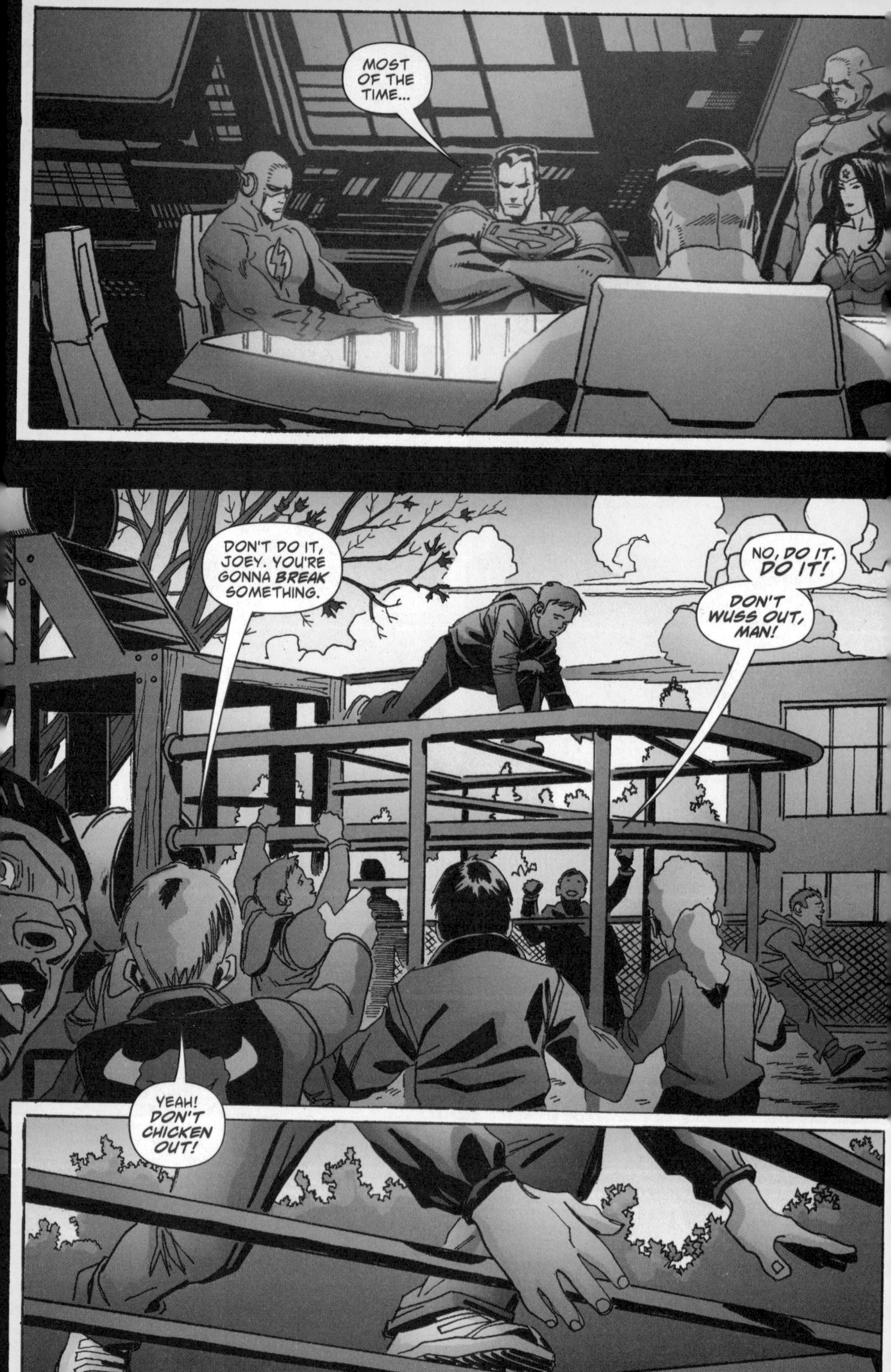
MOST OF THE TIME...
DON'T DO IT, JOEY. YOU'RE GONNA BREAK SOMETHING.
NO, DO IT. DO IT!
DON'T WUSS OUT, MAN!
YEAH! DON'T CHICKEN OUT!

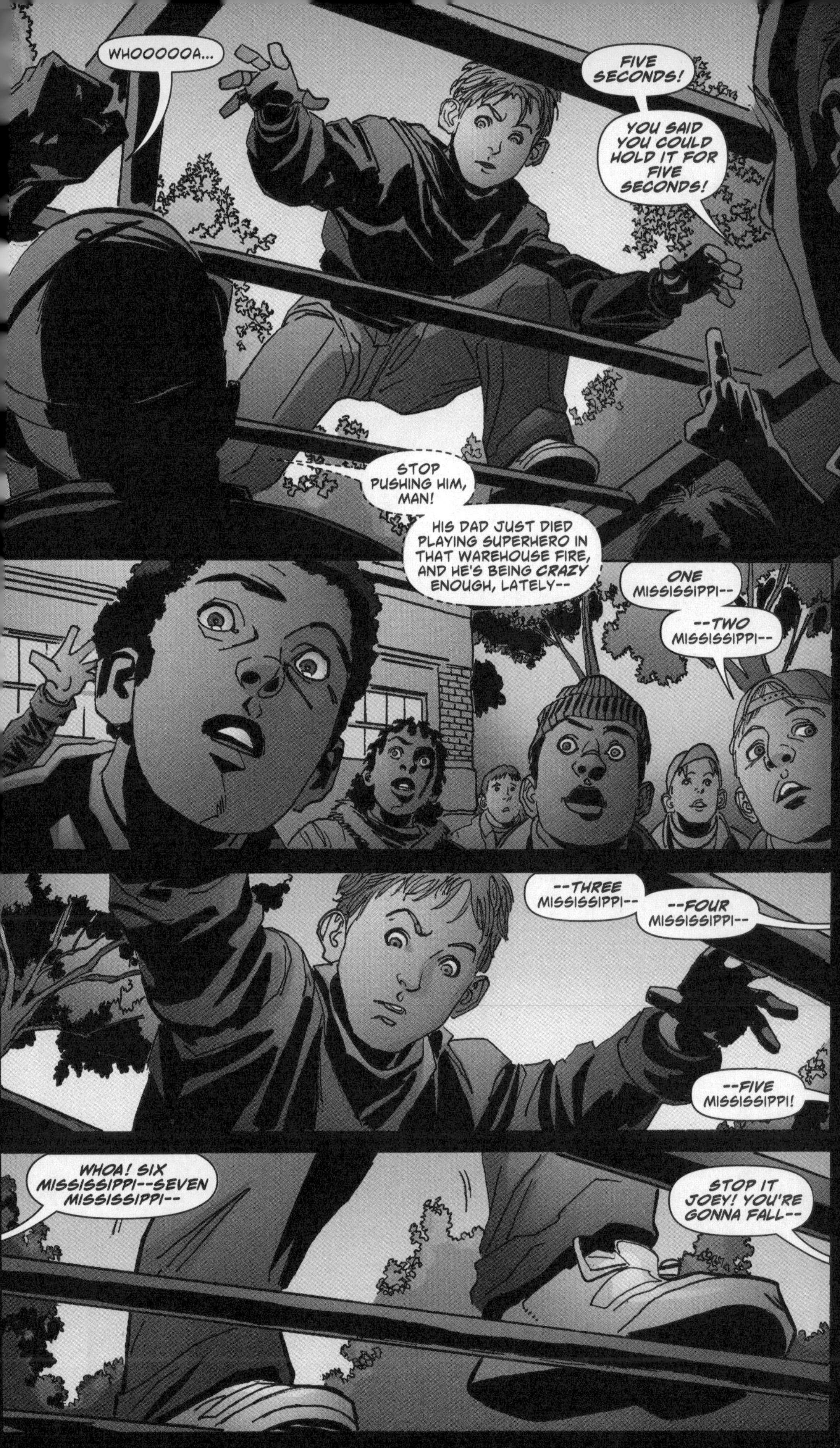
WHOOOOOA...
FIVE SECONDS!
YOU SAID YOU COULD HOLD IT FOR FIVE SECONDS!
STOP PUSHING HIM, MAN!
HIS DAD JUST DIED PLAYING SUPERHERO IN THAT WAREHOUSE FIRE, AND HE'S BEING CRAZY ENOUGH, LATELY--
ONE MISSISSIPPI--
--TWO MISSISSIPPI--
--THREE MISSISSIPPI--
--FOUR MISSISSIPPI--
--FIVE MISSISSIPPI!
WHOA! SIX MISSISSIPPI--SEVEN MISSISSIPPI--
STOP IT JOEY! YOU'RE GONNA FALL--

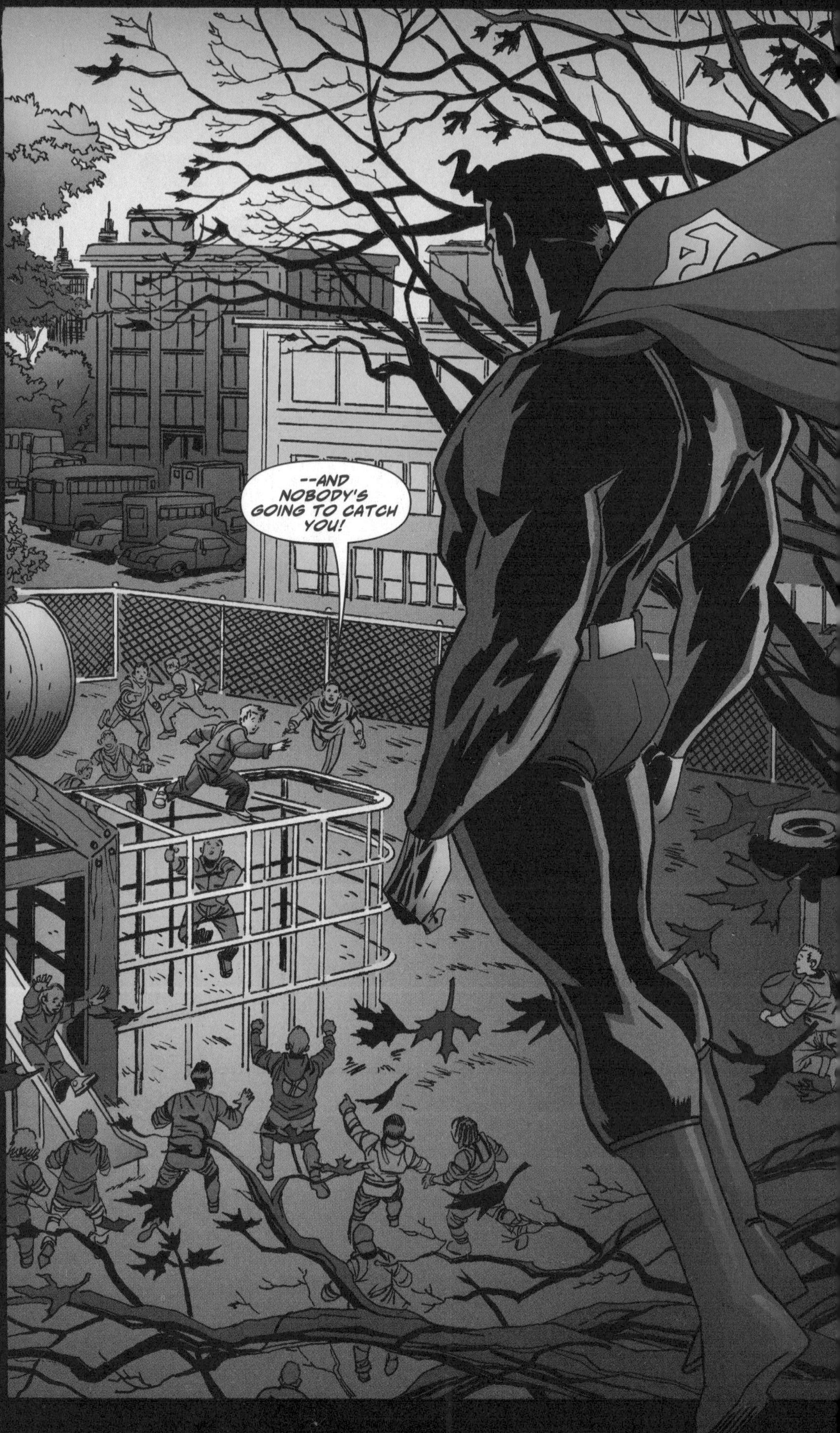
--AND NOBODY'S GOING TO CATCH YOU!

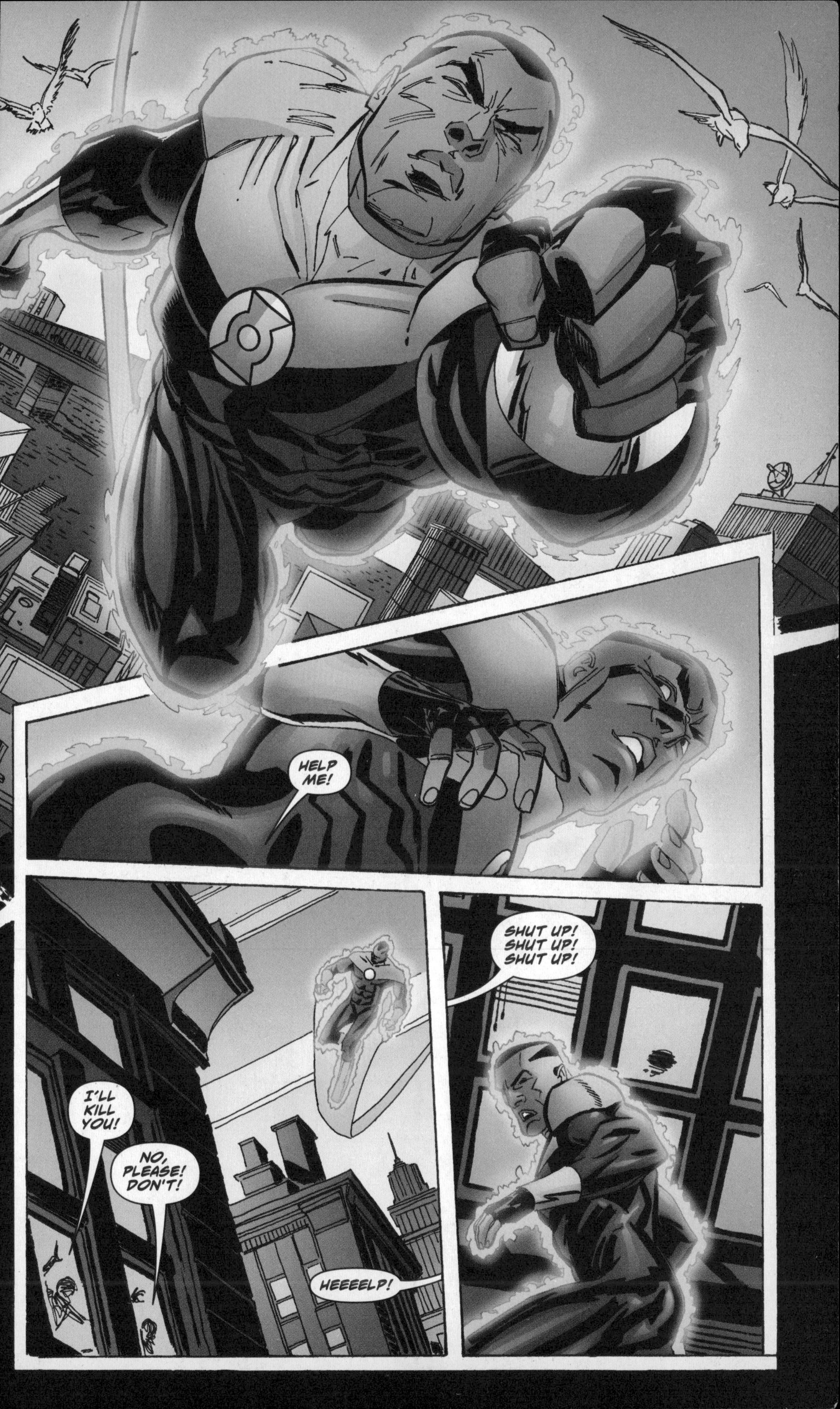
HELP ME!
SHUT UP! SHUT UP! SHUT UP!
I'LL KILL YOU!
NO, PLEASE! DON'T!
HEEEELP!

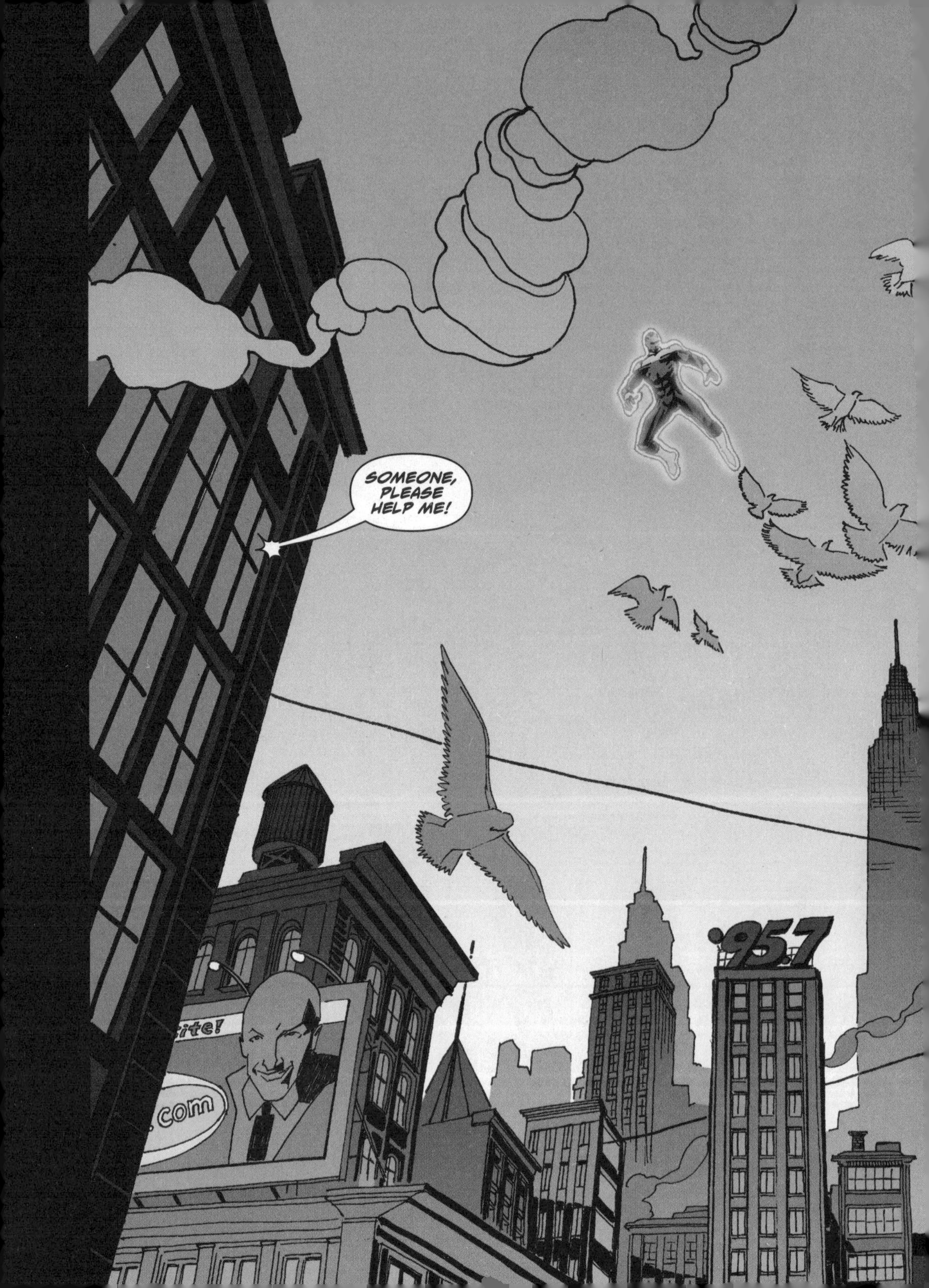
SOMEONE, PLEASE HELP ME!
95.7

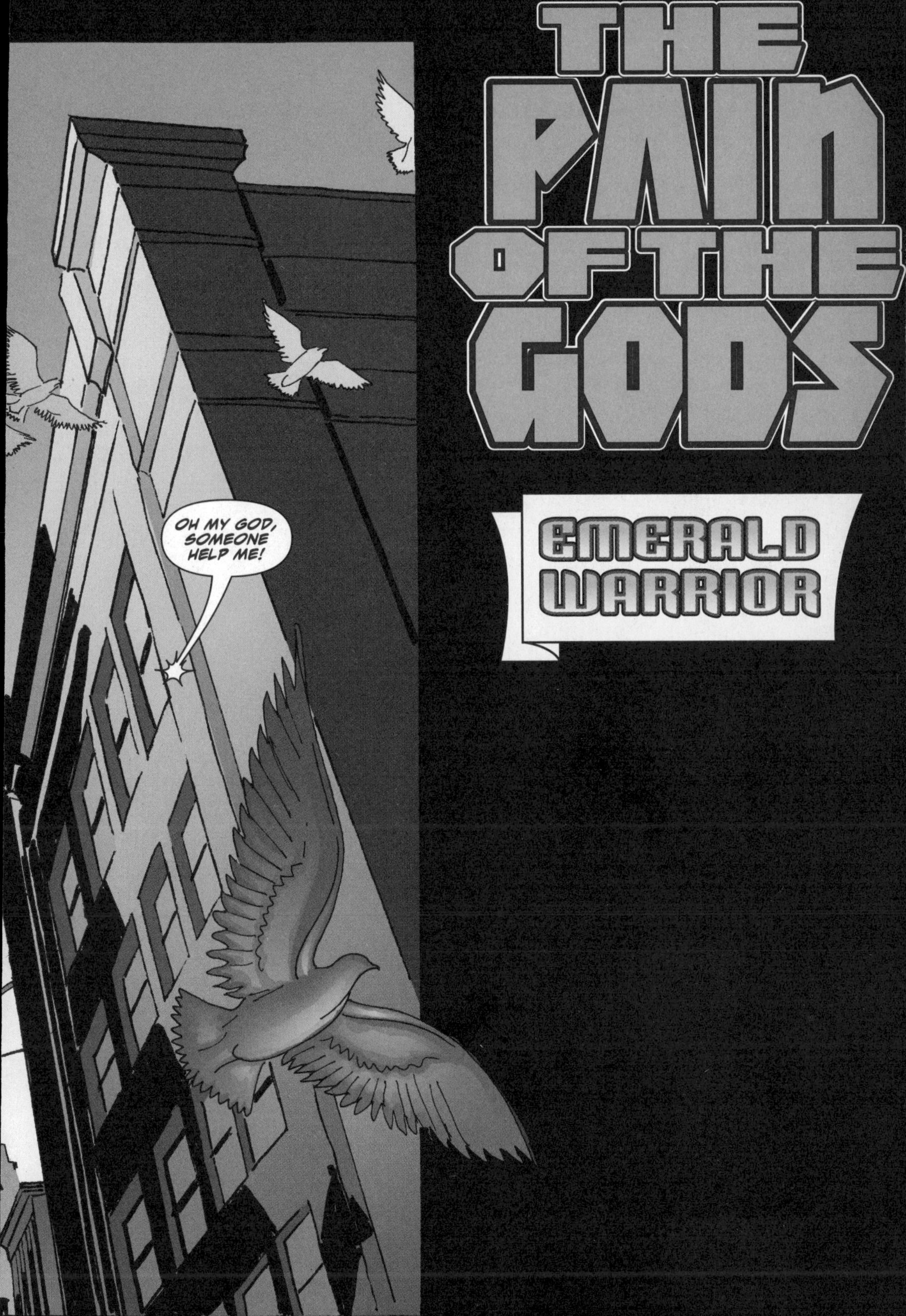

OH MY GOD, SOMEONE HELP ME!
THE PAIN OF THE GODS
EMERALD WARRIOR

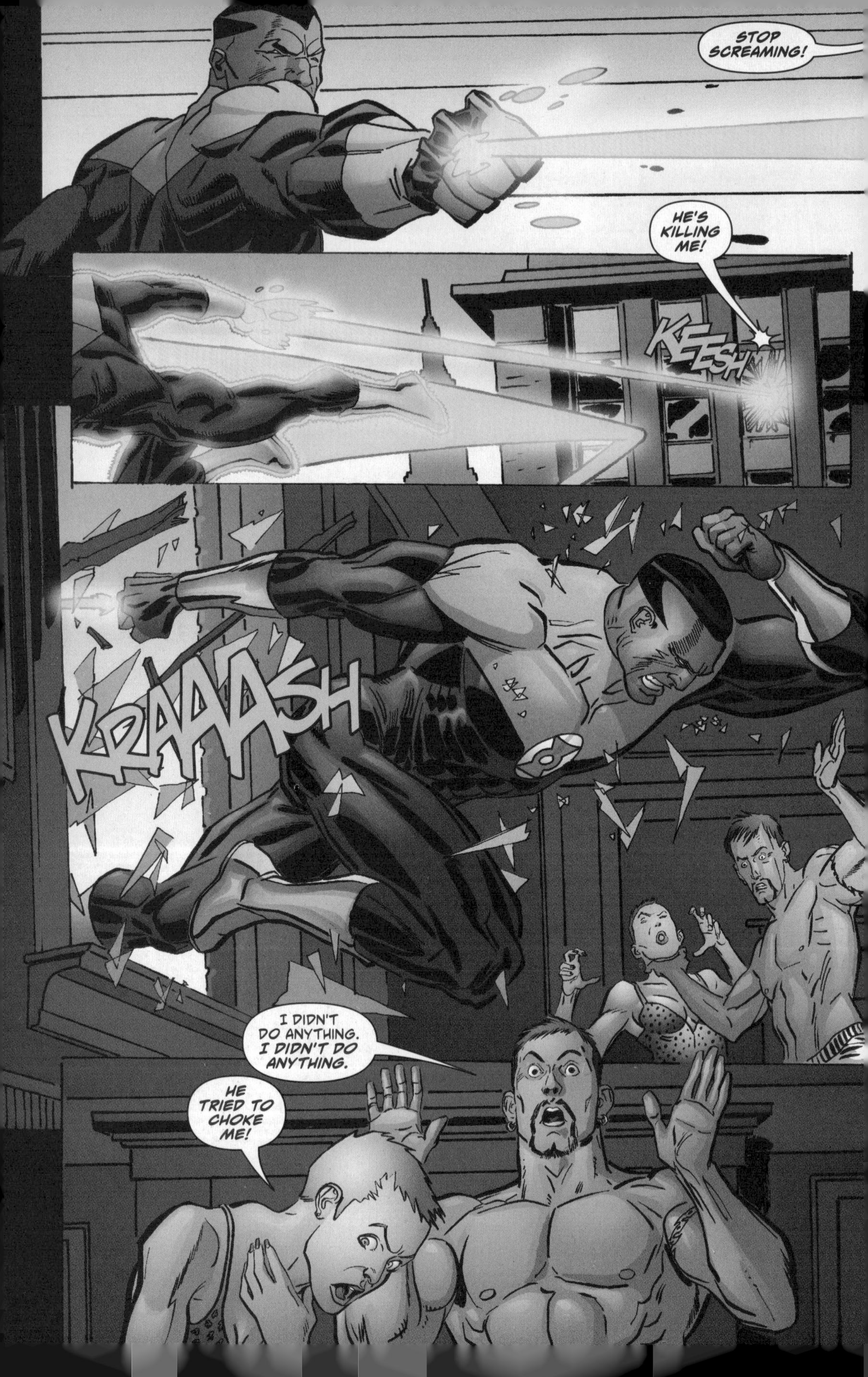
STOP SCREAMING!
HE'S KILLING ME!
KEESH
KRAAASH
I DIDN'T DO ANYTHING. I DIDN'T DO ANYTHING.
HE TRIED TO CHOKE ME!

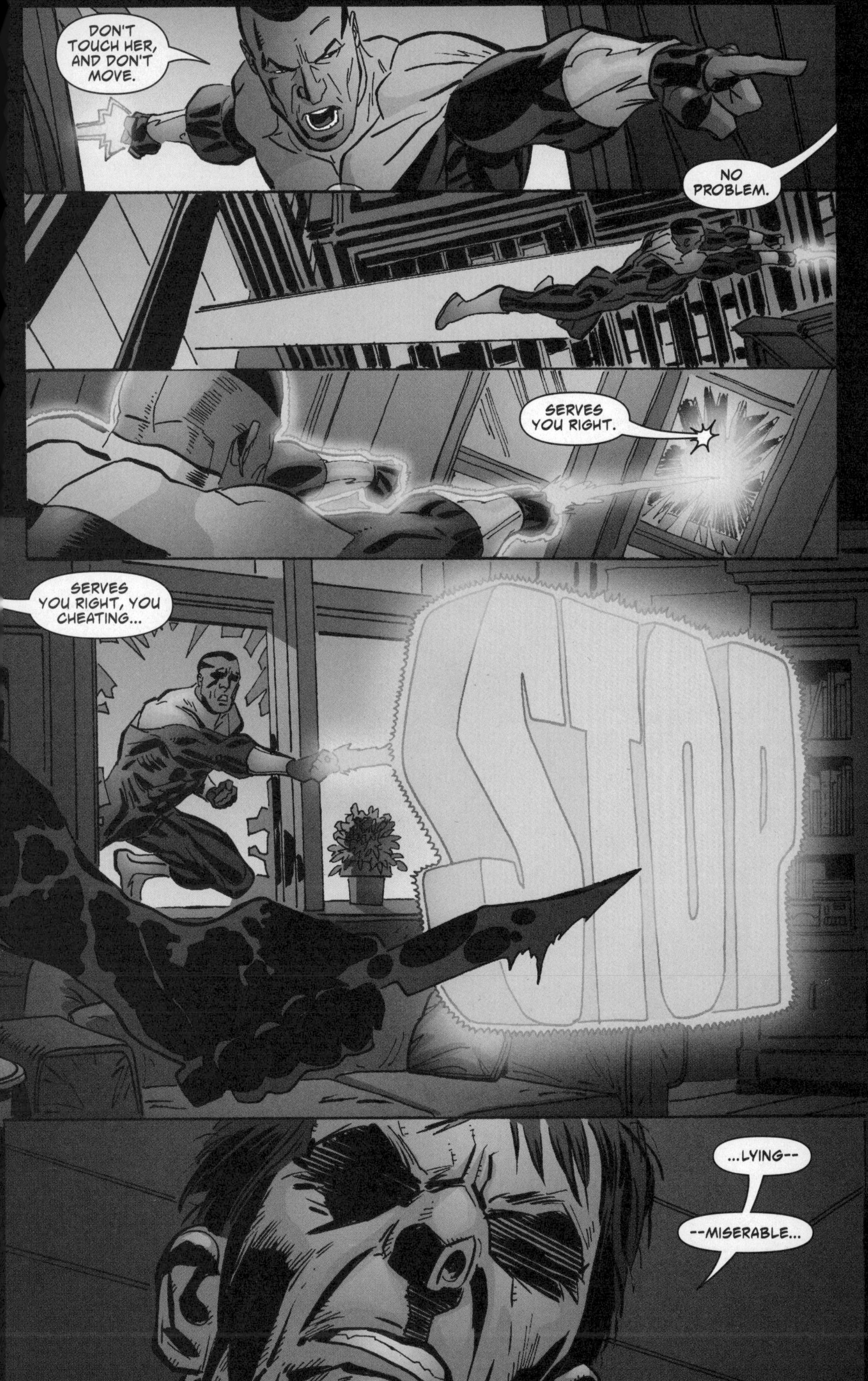
DON'T TOUCH HER, AND DON'T MOVE.
NO PROBLEM.
SERVES YOU RIGHT.
SERVES YOU RIGHT, YOU CHEATING...
STOP
...LYING--
--MISERABLE...

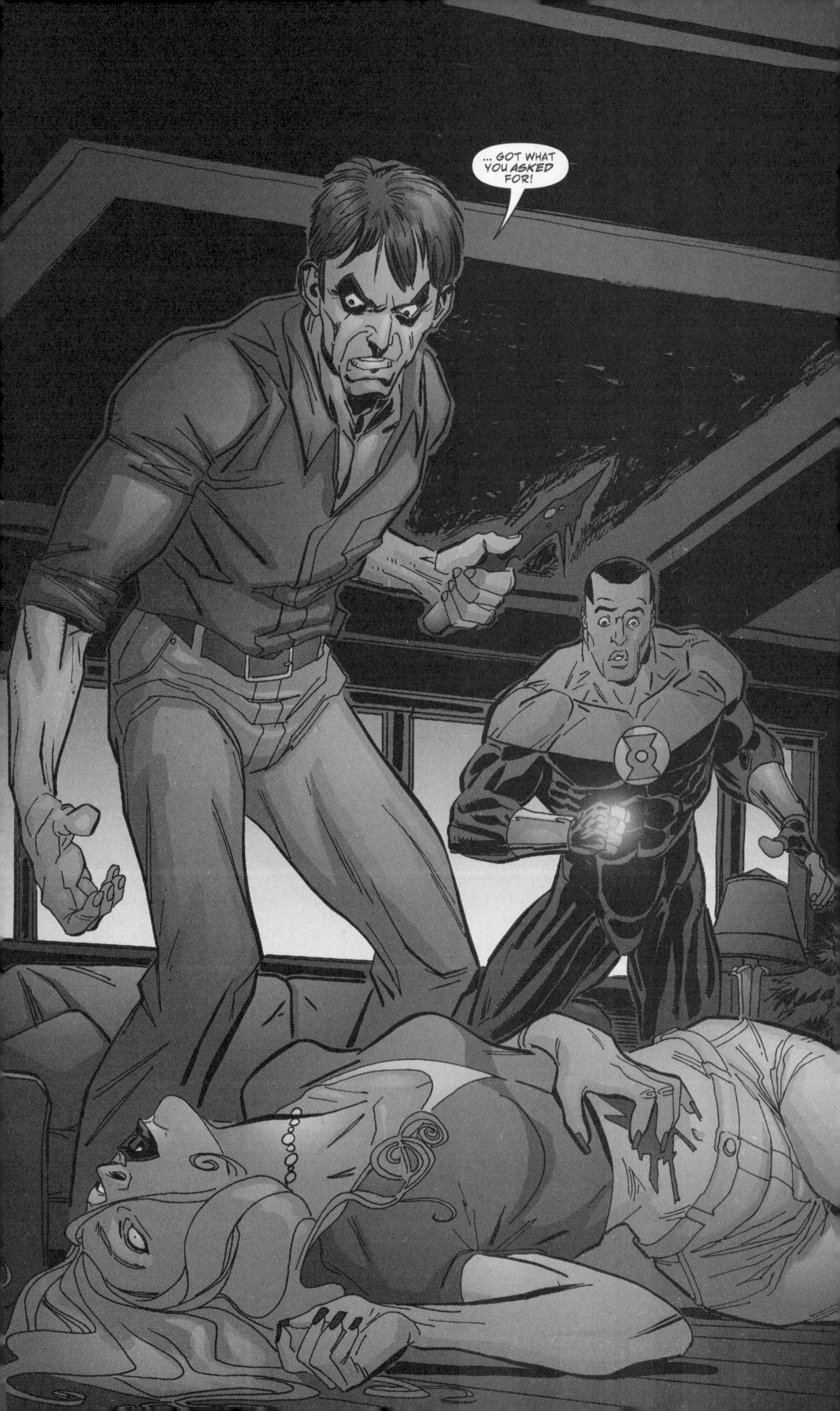
... GOT WHAT YOU ASKED FOR!

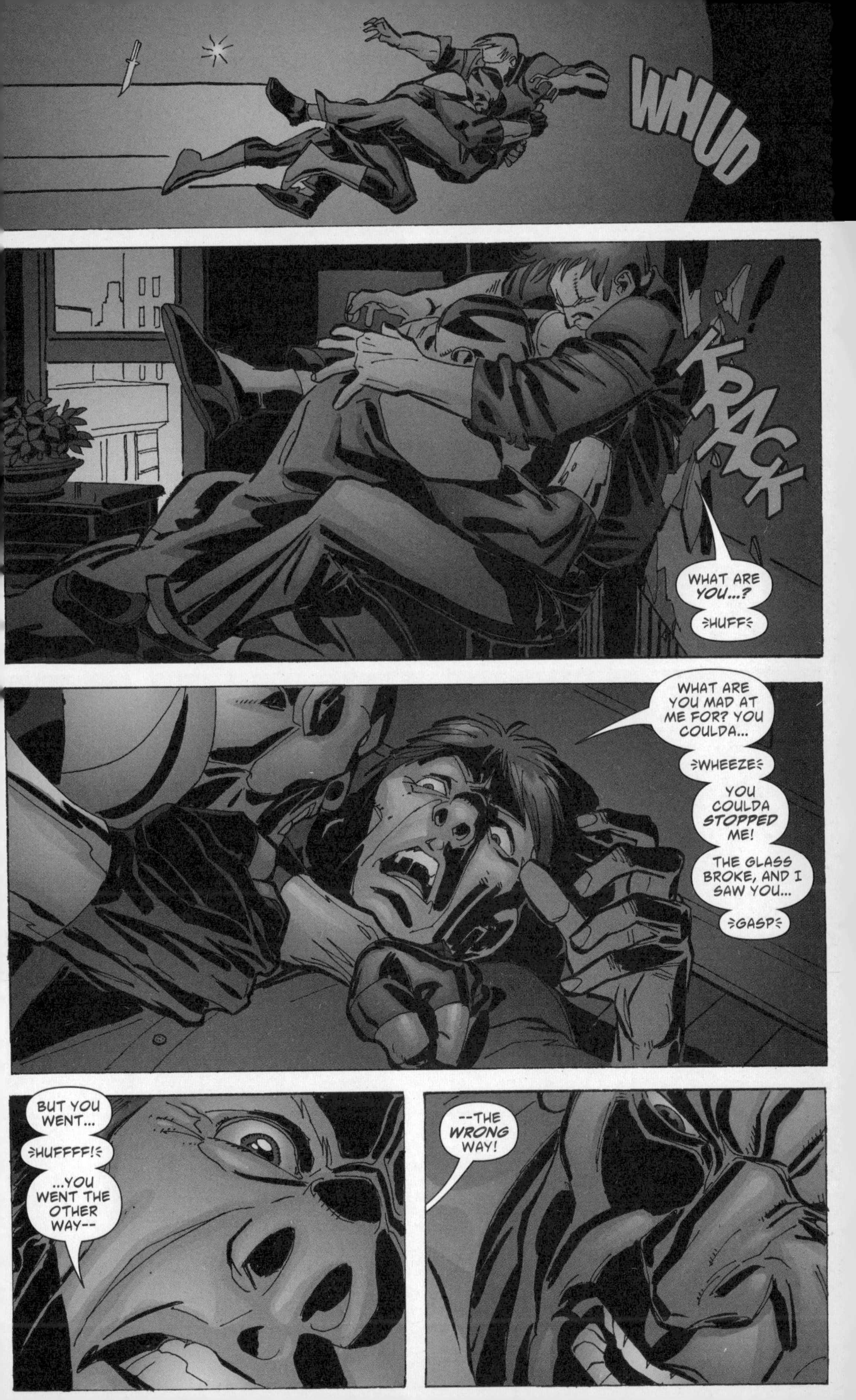
WHUD
KRACK
WHAT ARE YOU...?
HUFF
WHAT ARE YOU MAD AT ME FOR? YOU COULDA...
WHEEZE
YOU COULDA STOPPED ME!
THE GLASS BROKE, AND I SAW YOU...
GASP
BUT YOU WENT...
HUFFFF!
...YOU WENT THE OTHER WAY--
--THE WRONG WAY!

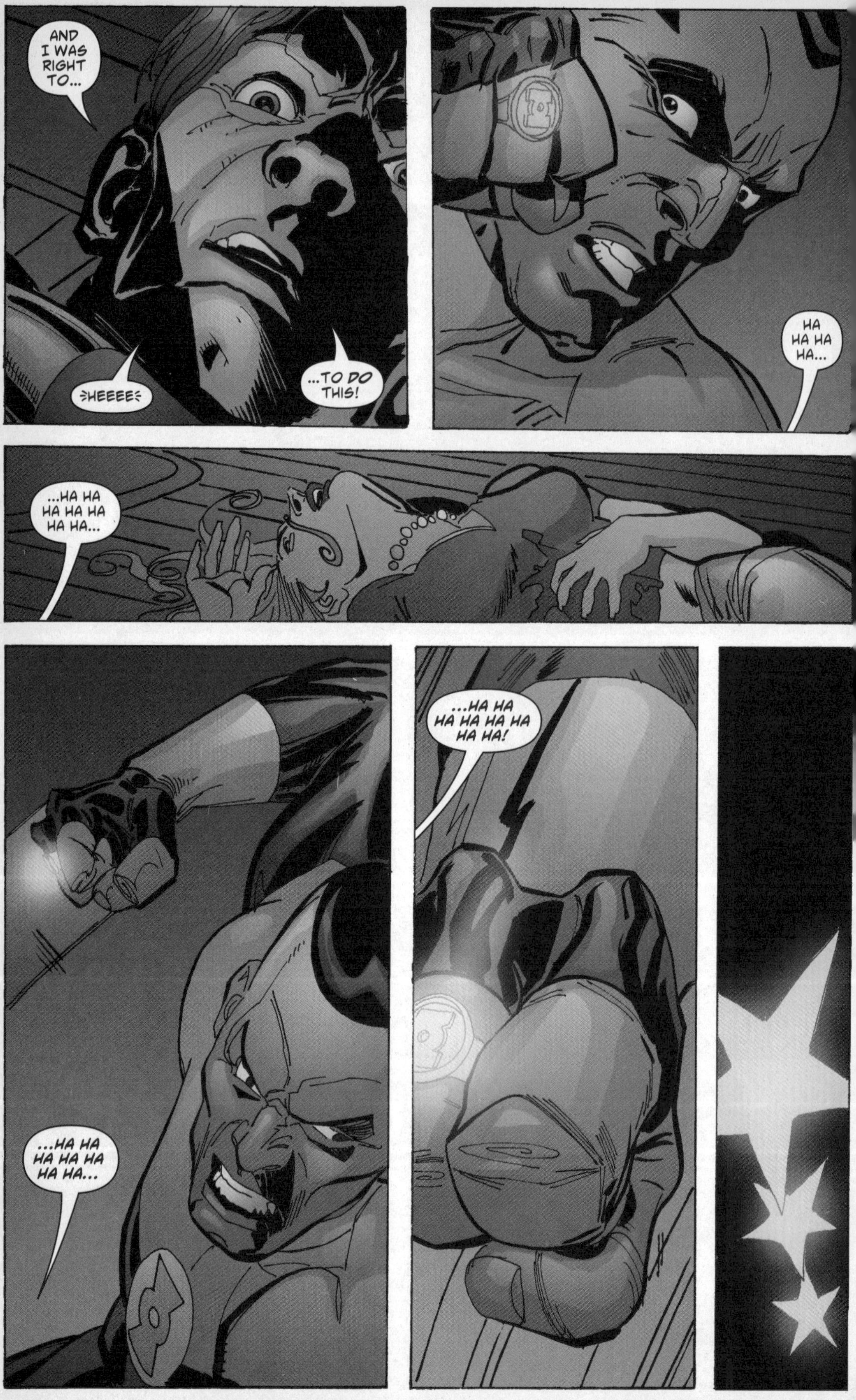
AND I WAS RIGHT TO...
HEEEE
...TO DO THIS!
HA HA HA HA...
...HA HA HA HA HA HA HA...
...HA HA HA HA HA HA HA...
...HA HA HA HA HA HA HA HA!

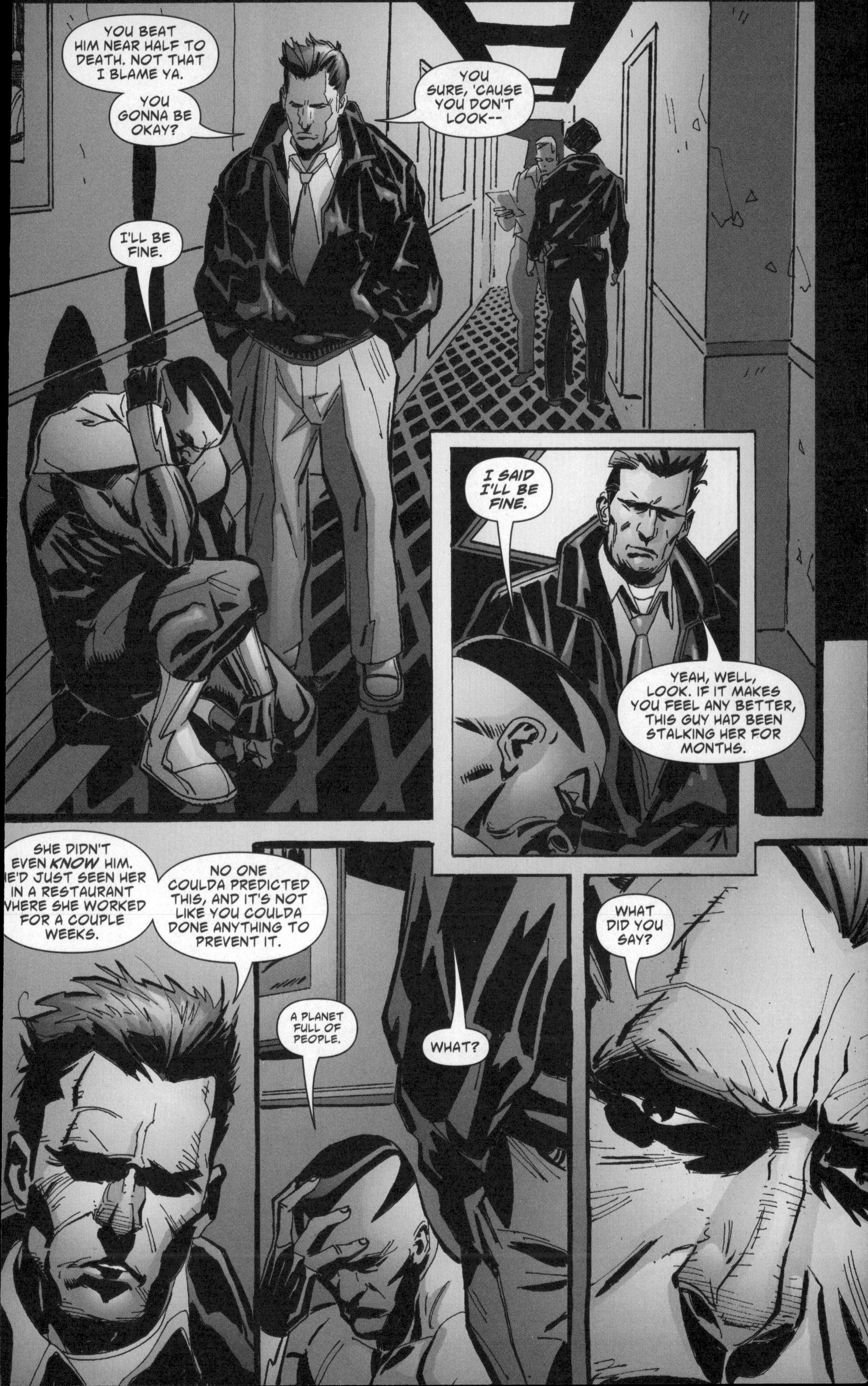
YOU BEAT HIM NEAR HALF TO DEATH. NOT THAT I BLAME YA.
YOU GONNA BE OKAY?
I'LL BE FINE.
YOU SURE, 'CAUSE YOU DON'T LOOK--
I SAID I'LL BE *FINE.*
YEAH, WELL, LOOK. IF IT MAKES YOU FEEL ANY BETTER, THIS GUY HAD BEEN STALKING HER FOR MONTHS.
SHE DIDN'T EVEN ***KNOW*** HIM. HE'D JUST SEEN HER IN A RESTAURANT WHERE SHE WORKED FOR A COUPLE WEEKS.
NO ONE COULDA PREDICTED THIS, AND IT'S NOT LIKE YOU COULDA DONE ANYTHING TO PREVENT IT.
A PLANET FULL OF PEOPLE.
WHAT?
WHAT DID YOU SAY?

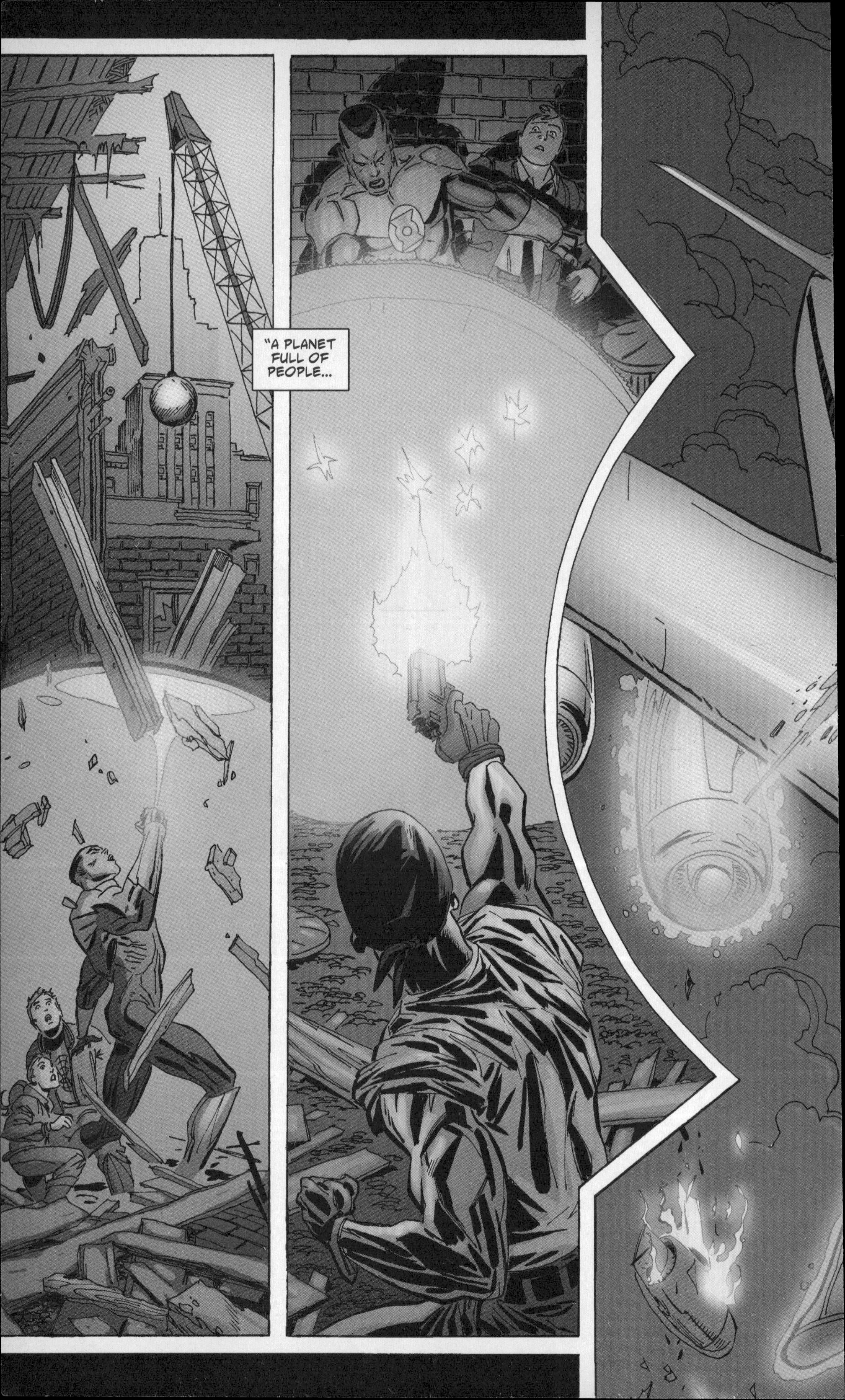
"A PLANET FULL OF PEOPLE...

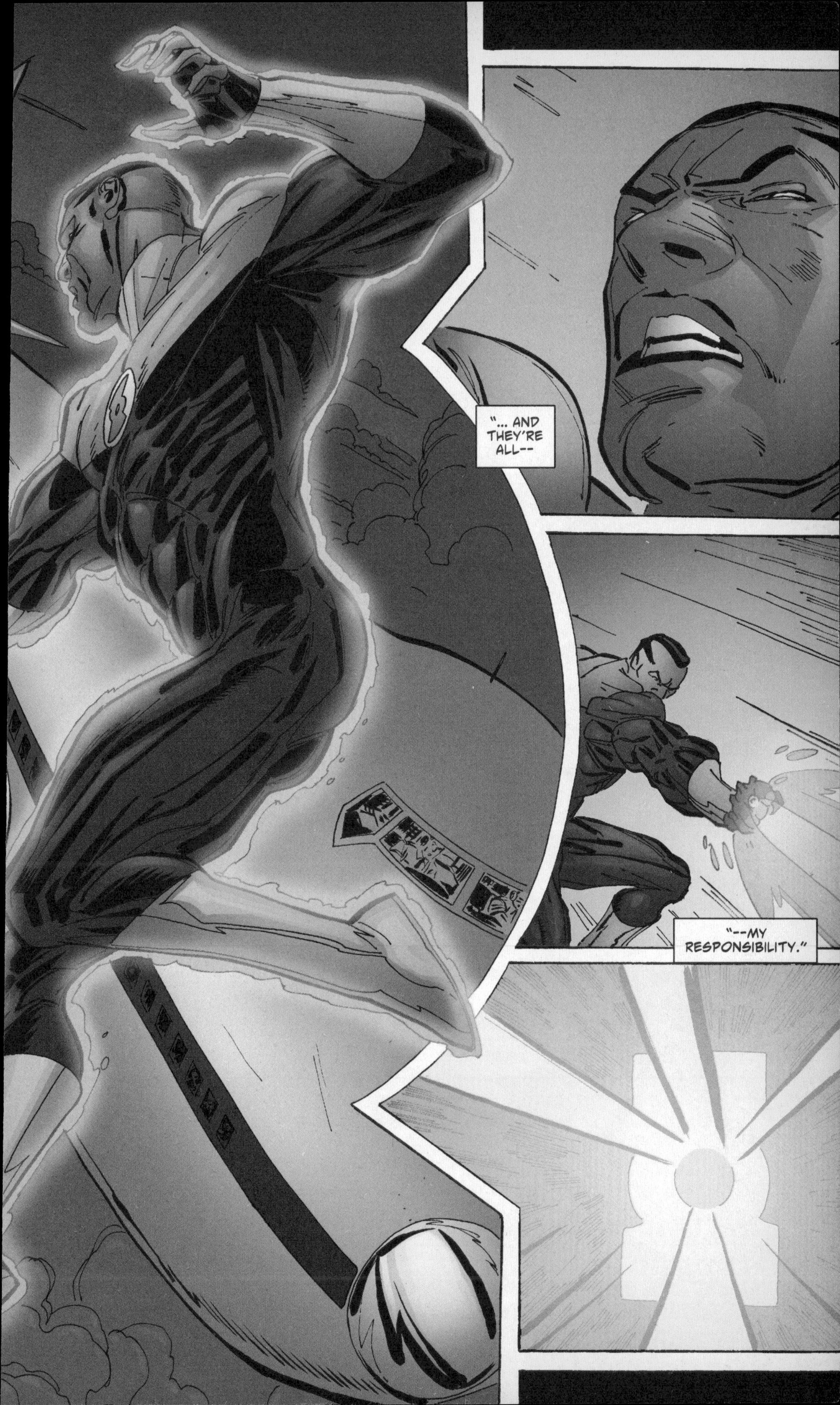
"... AND THEY'RE ALL--
"--MY RESPONSIBILITY."

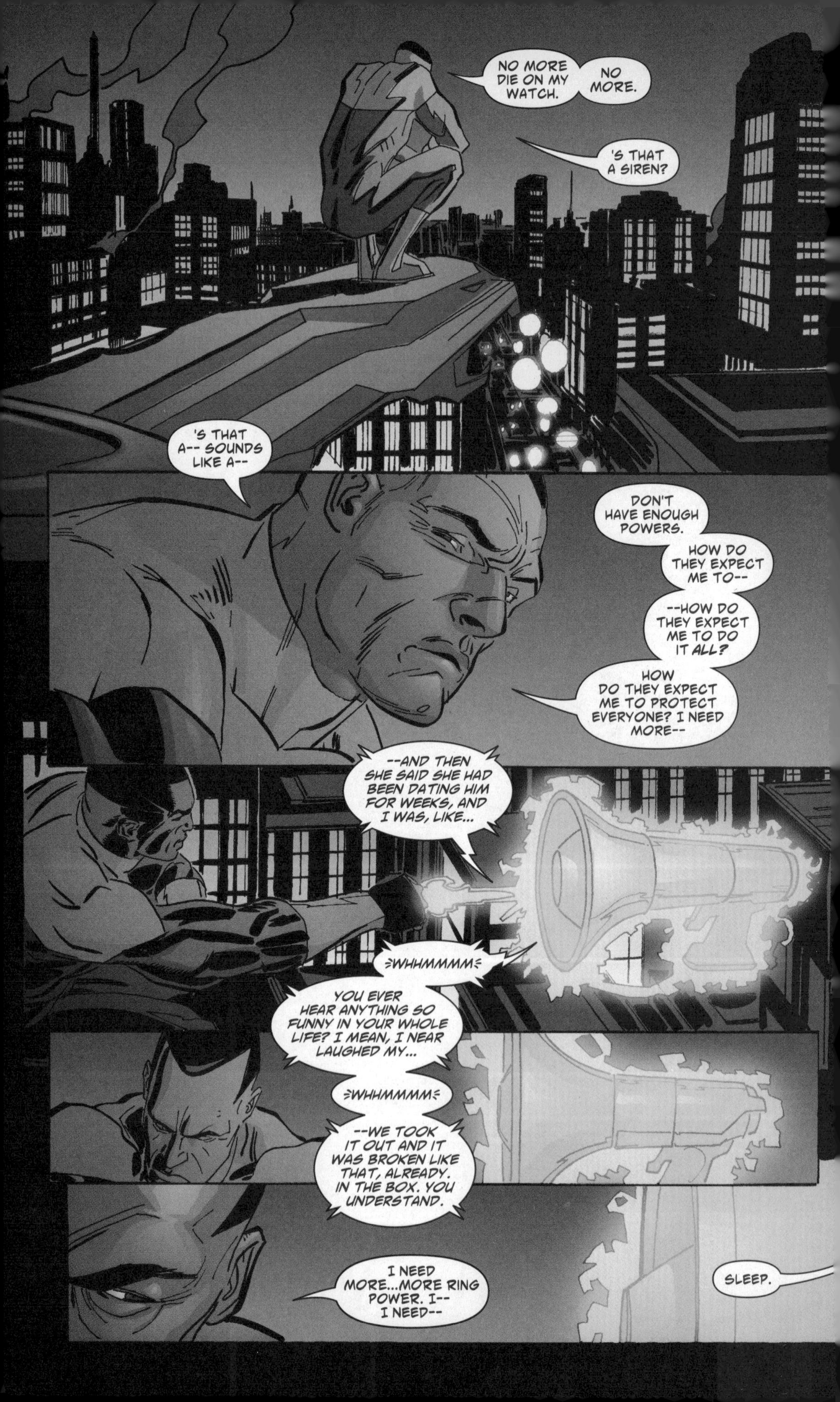
NO MORE DIE ON MY WATCH.
NO MORE.
'S THAT A SIREN?
'S THAT A-- SOUNDS LIKE A--
DON'T HAVE ENOUGH POWERS.
HOW DO THEY EXPECT ME TO--
--HOW DO THEY EXPECT ME TO DO IT ALL?
HOW DO THEY EXPECT ME TO PROTECT EVERYONE? I NEED MORE--
--AND THEN SHE SAID SHE HAD BEEN DATING HIM FOR WEEKS, AND I WAS, LIKE...
WHHMMMM
YOU EVER HEAR ANYTHING SO FUNNY IN YOUR WHOLE LIFE? I MEAN, I NEAR LAUGHED MY...
WHHMMMM
--WE TOOK IT OUT AND IT WAS BROKEN LIKE THAT, ALREADY. IN THE BOX. YOU UNDERSTAND.
I NEED MORE...MORE RING POWER. I-- I NEED--
SLEEP.

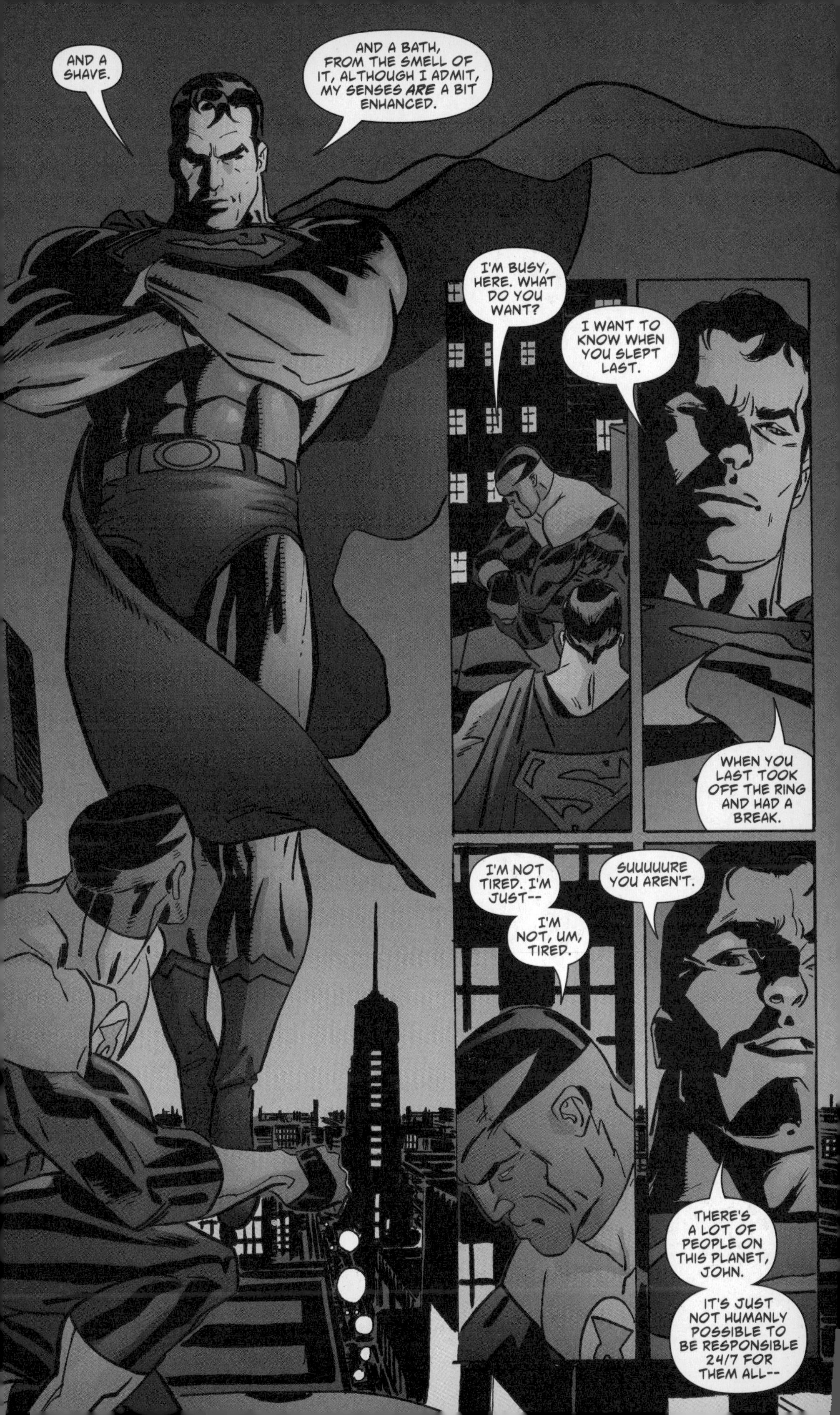
AND A SHAVE.
AND A BATH, FROM THE SMELL OF IT, ALTHOUGH I ADMIT, MY SENSES *ARE* A BIT ENHANCED.
I'M BUSY, HERE. WHAT DO YOU WANT?
I WANT TO KNOW WHEN YOU SLEPT LAST.
WHEN YOU LAST TOOK OFF THE RING AND HAD A BREAK.
I'M NOT TIRED. I'M JUST--
I'M NOT, UM, TIRED.
SUUUUURE YOU AREN'T.
THERE'S A LOT OF PEOPLE ON THIS PLANET, JOHN.
IT'S JUST NOT HUMANLY POSSIBLE TO BE RESPONSIBLE 24/7 FOR THEM ALL--

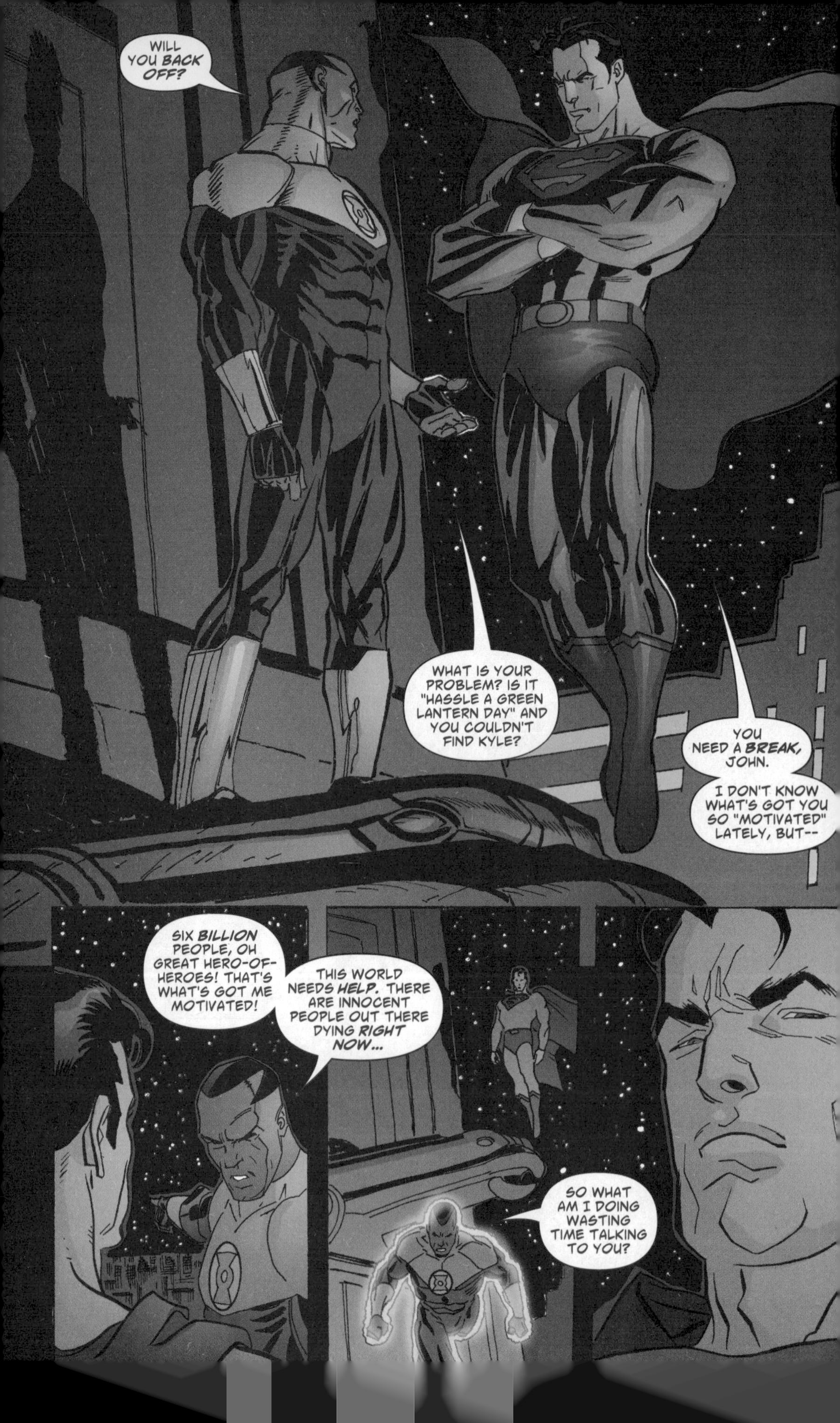
WILL YOU BACK OFF?
WHAT IS YOUR PROBLEM? IS IT "HASSLE A GREEN LANTERN DAY" AND YOU COULDN'T FIND KYLE?
YOU NEED A BREAK, JOHN.
I DON'T KNOW WHAT'S GOT YOU SO "MOTIVATED" LATELY, BUT--
SIX BILLION PEOPLE, OH GREAT HERO-OF-HEROES! THAT'S WHAT'S GOT ME MOTIVATED!
THIS WORLD NEEDS HELP. THERE ARE INNOCENT PEOPLE OUT THERE DYING RIGHT NOW...
SO WHAT AM I DOING WASTING TIME TALKING TO YOU?

KRACK-
RMMMMMMMMM
GOTCHA. I GOTCHA.
NOBODY'S DYING TODAY.
PAF
OH MY GOD!
OH MY GOD, I DON'T BELIEVE IT! I THINK MY HUSBAND'S HAD A HEART ATTACK.
NOT A PROBLEM. NOT A PROBLEM.

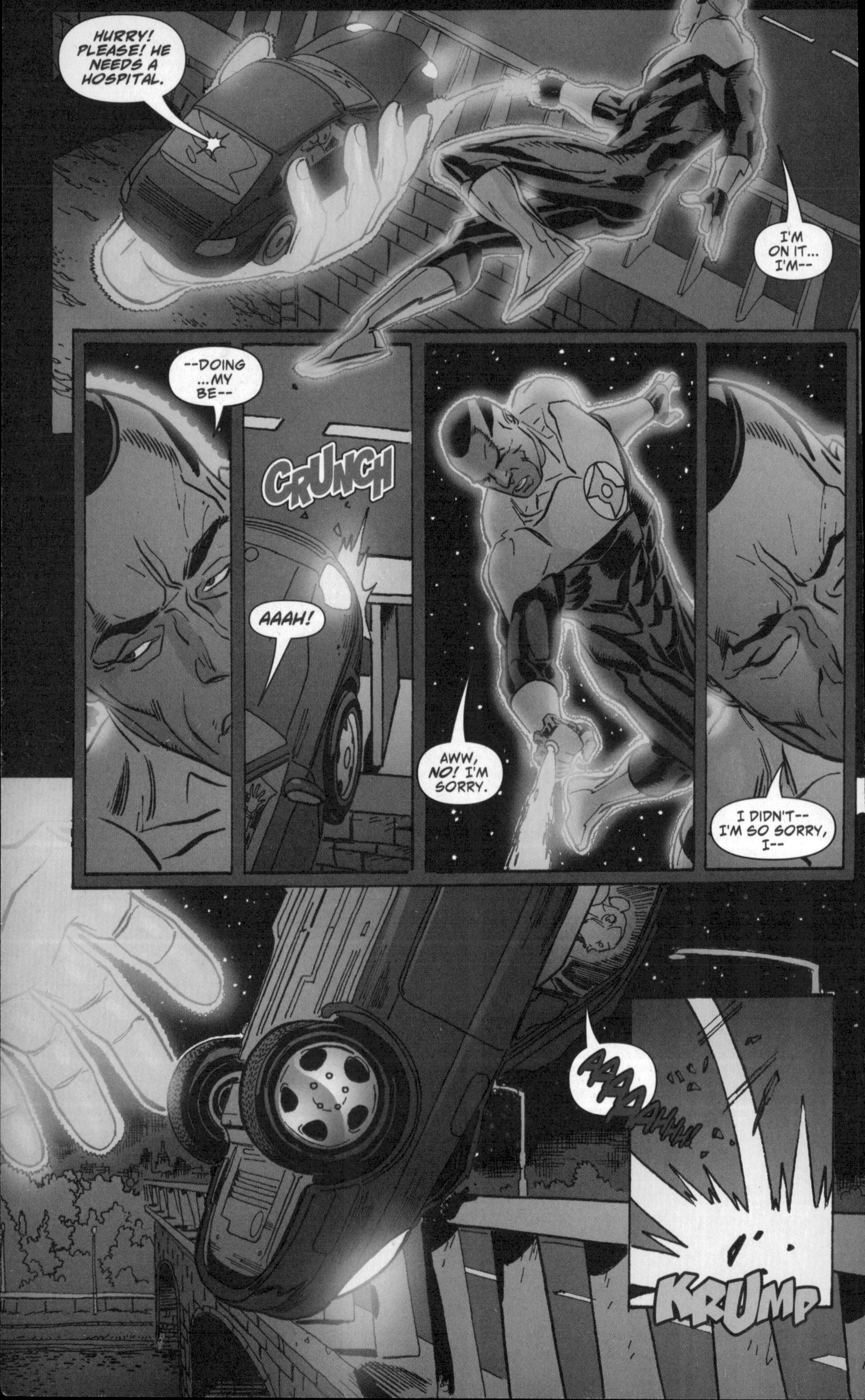
HURRY! PLEASE! HE NEEDS A HOSPITAL.
I'M ON IT... I'M--
--DOING ...MY BE--
CRUNCH
AAAH!
AWW, NO! I'M SORRY.
I DIDN'T-- I'M SO SORRY, I--
AAAAAHHH!
KRUMP

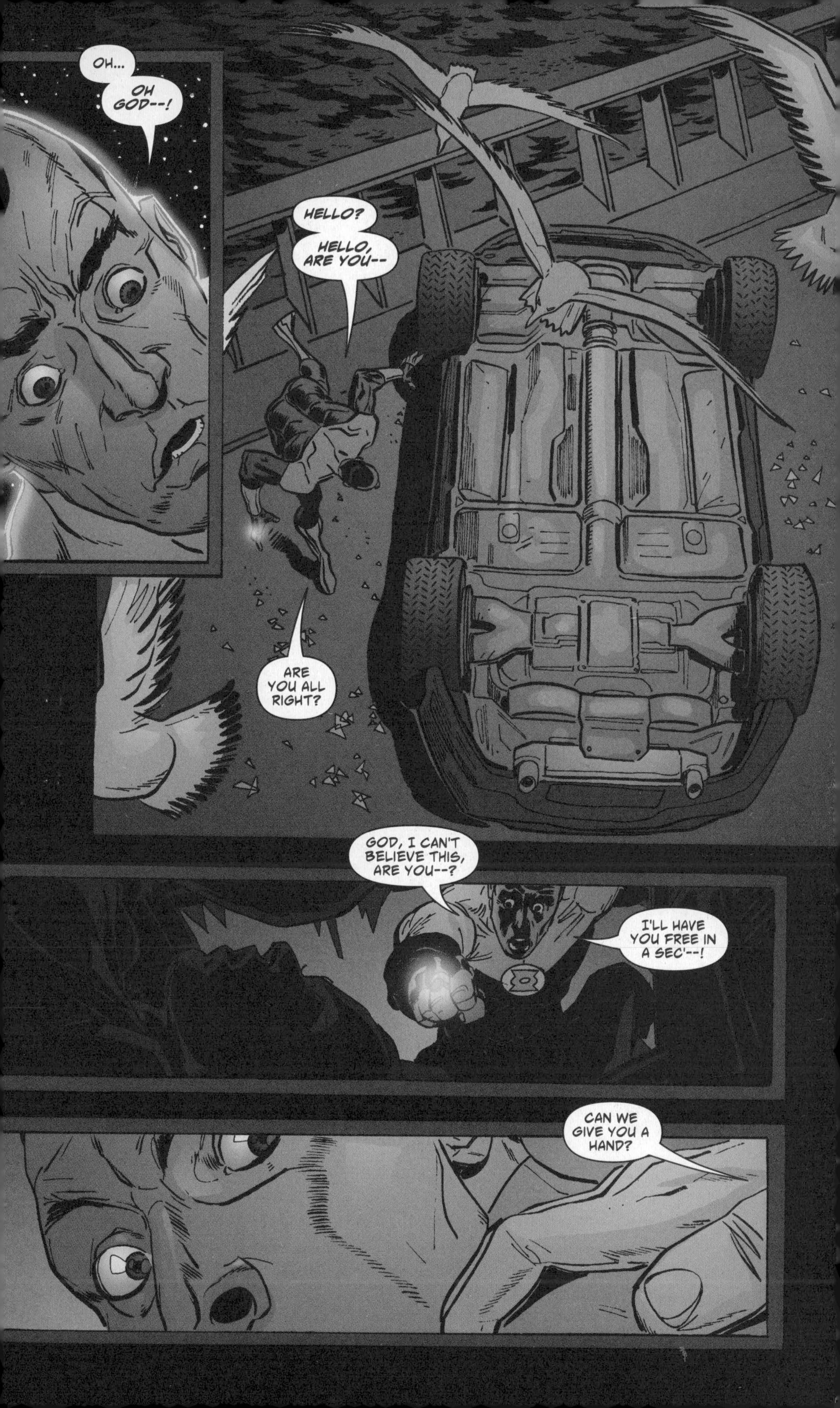

OH...
OH GOD--!
HELLO?
HELLO, ARE YOU--
ARE YOU ALL RIGHT?
GOD, I CAN'T BELIEVE THIS, ARE YOU--?
I'LL HAVE YOU FREE IN A SEC'--!
CAN WE GIVE YOU A HAND?

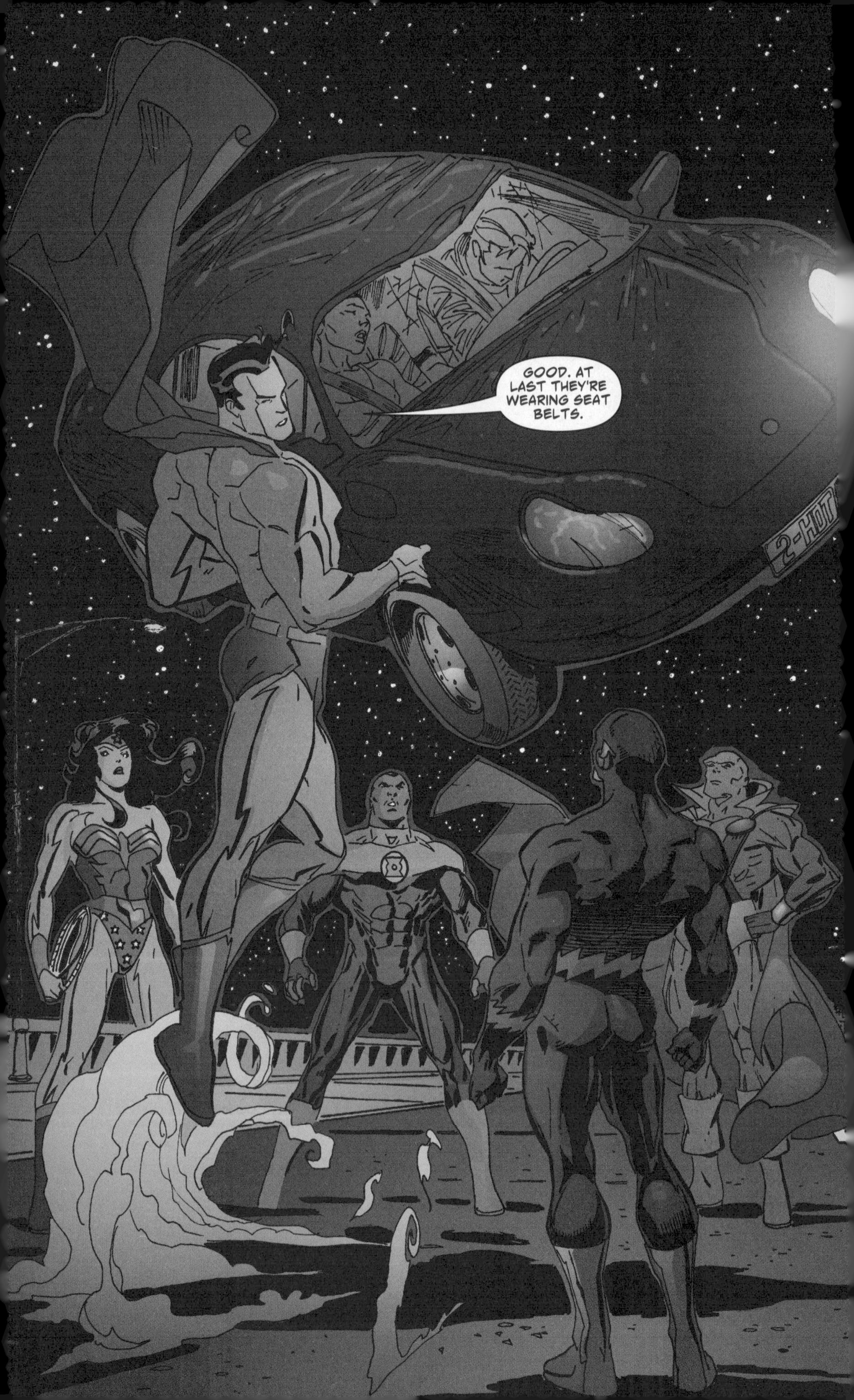
GOOD. AT LAST THEY'RE WEARING SEAT BELTS.
2-HOT

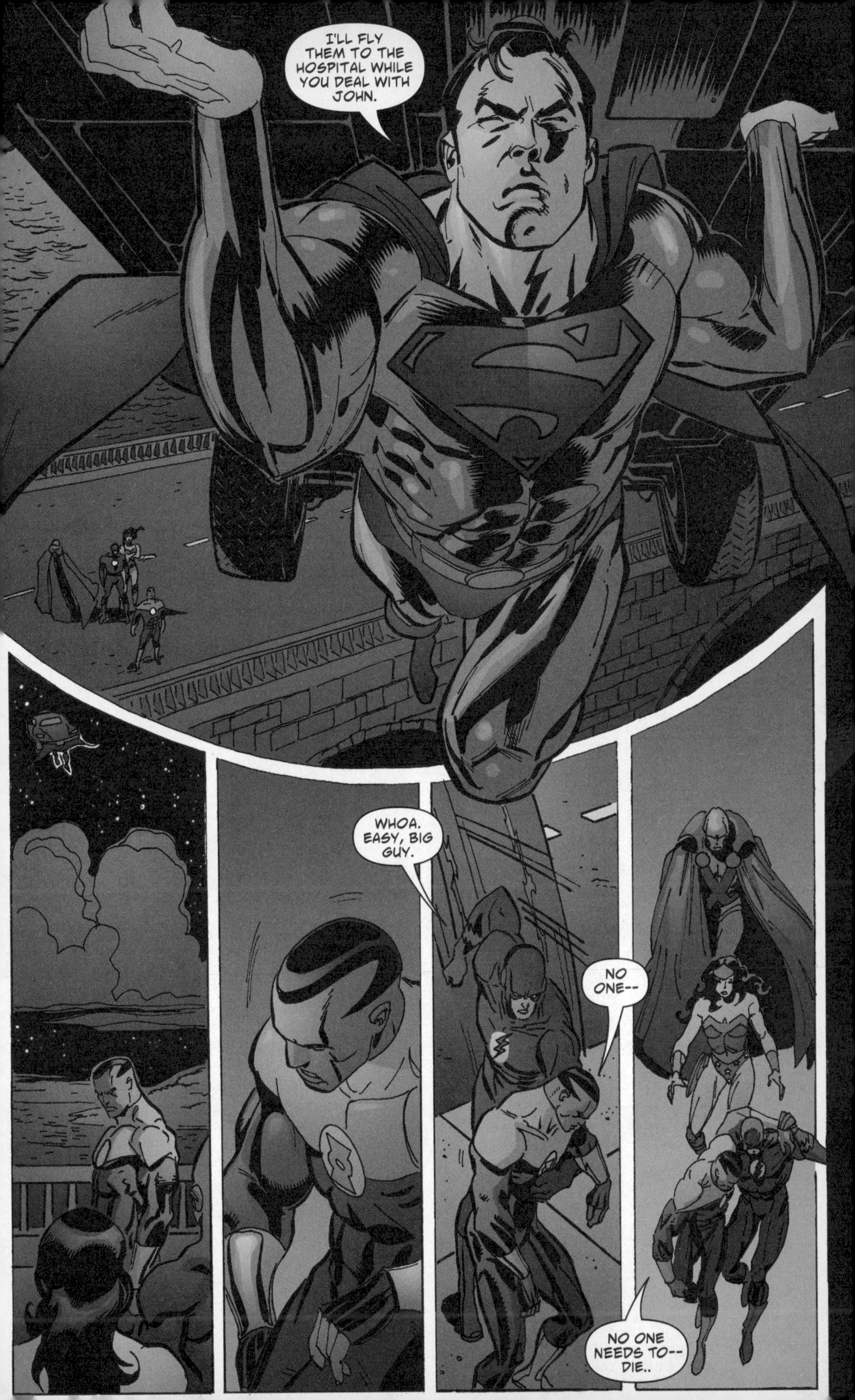
I'LL FLY THEM TO THE HOSPITAL WHILE YOU DEAL WITH JOHN.
WHOA. EASY, BIG GUY.
NO ONE--
NO ONE NEEDS TO-- DIE..

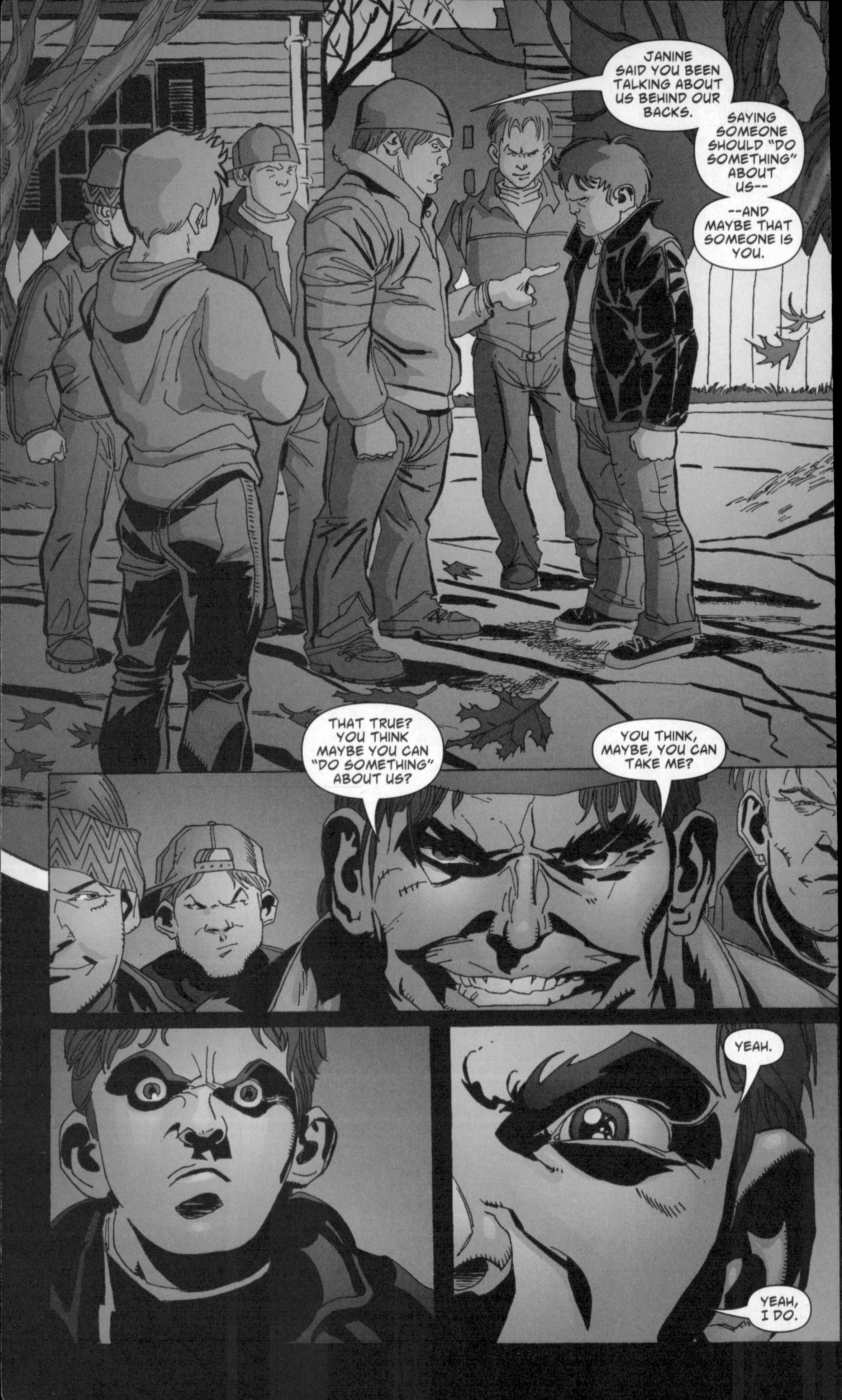
JANINE SAID YOU BEEN TALKING ABOUT US BEHIND OUR BACKS.
SAYING SOMEONE SHOULD "DO SOMETHING" ABOUT US--
--AND MAYBE THAT SOMEONE IS YOU.
THAT TRUE? YOU THINK MAYBE YOU CAN "DO SOMETHING" ABOUT US?
YOU THINK, MAYBE, YOU CAN TAKE ME?
YEAH.
YEAH, I DO.

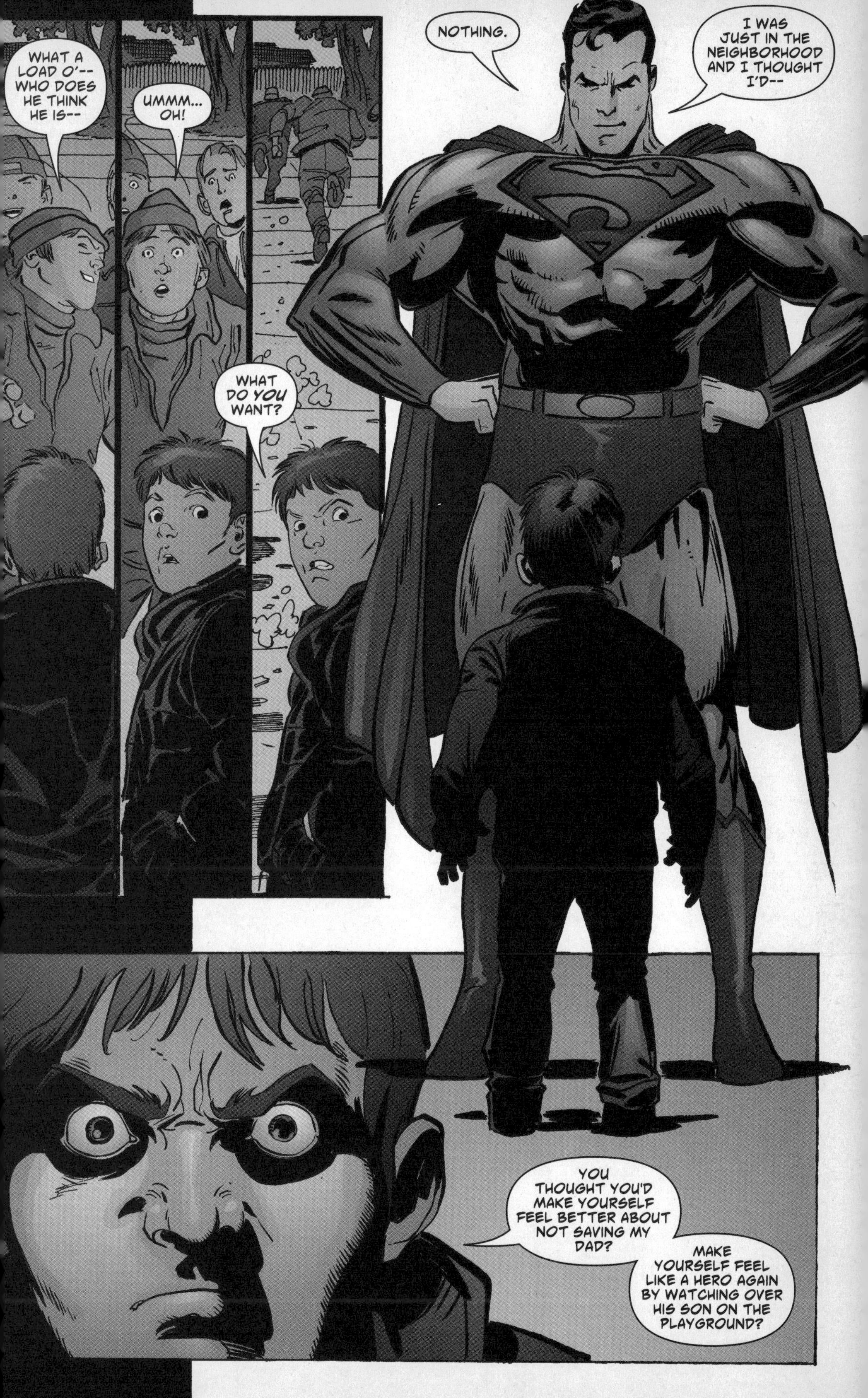
WHAT A LOAD O'-- WHO DOES HE THINK HE IS--
UMMM... OH!
WHAT DO YOU WANT?
NOTHING.
I WAS JUST IN THE NEIGHBORHOOD AND I THOUGHT I'D--
YOU THOUGHT YOU'D MAKE YOURSELF FEEL BETTER ABOUT NOT SAVING MY DAD?
MAKE YOURSELF FEEL LIKE A HERO AGAIN BY WATCHING OVER HIS SON ON THE PLAYGROUND?

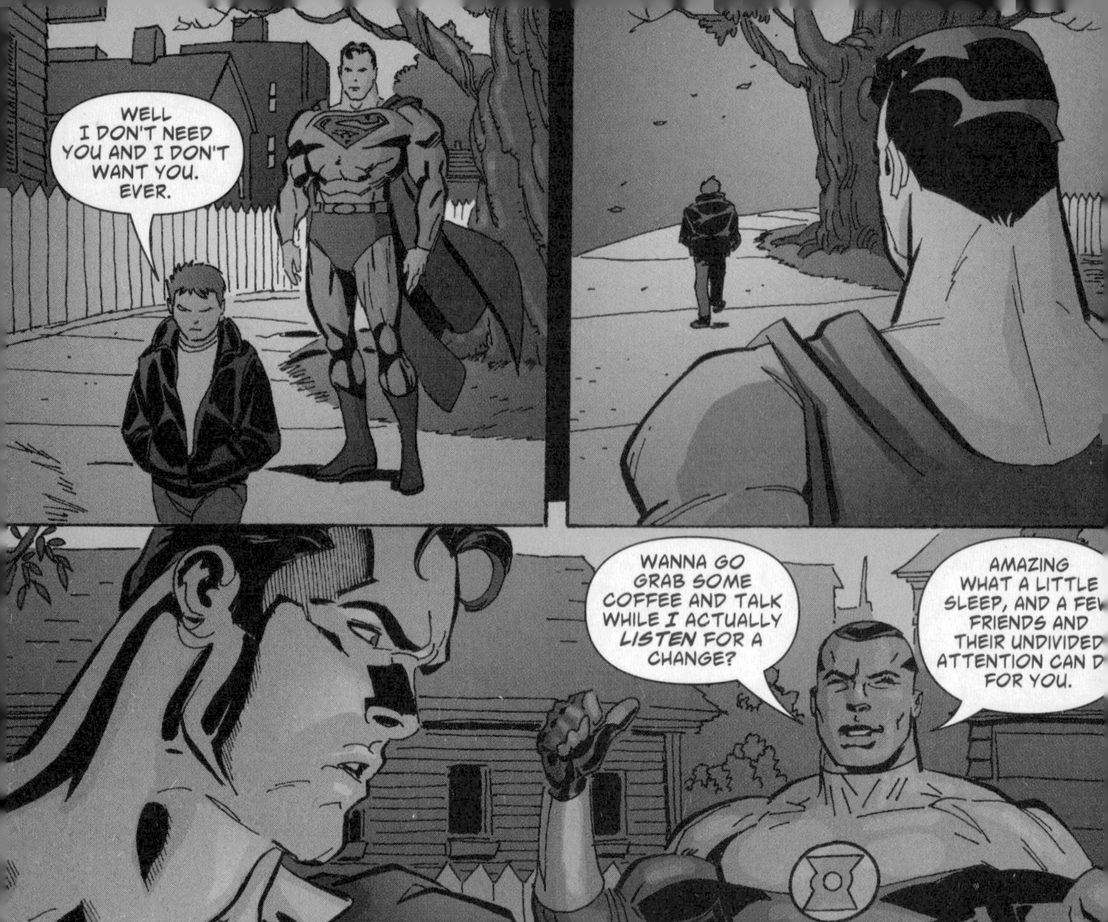
WELL I DON'T NEED YOU AND I DON'T WANT YOU. EVER.
WANNA GO GRAB SOME COFFEE AND TALK WHILE I ACTUALLY LISTEN FOR A CHANGE?
AMAZING WHAT A LITTLE SLEEP, AND A FEW FRIENDS AND THEIR UNDIVIDED ATTENTION CAN DO FOR YOU.
WHAT ARE YOU TALKING ABOUT? I DON'T NEED YOU TO LISTEN TO ANYTHING.
THERE'S A LOT OF PEOPLE ON THIS PLANET, SUPERMAN.
IT'S JUST NOT HUMANLY POSSIBLE TO BE RESPONSIBLE FOR THEM ALL, 24/7.
NOW COME ON BEFORE I REALLY TURN ON THE CHARM AND TELL YOU HOW BAD YOU SMELL.

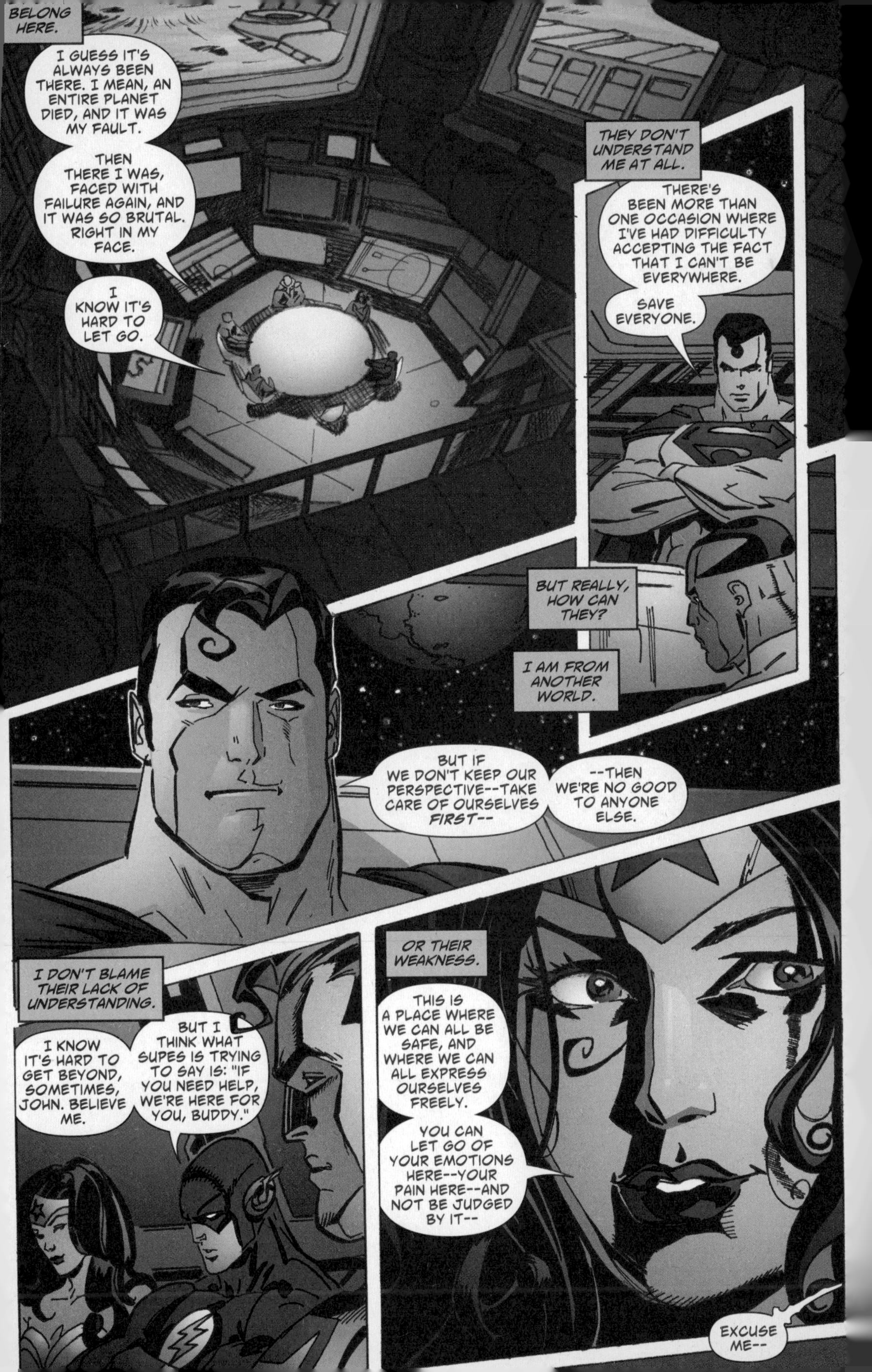
BELONG HERE.
I GUESS IT'S ALWAYS BEEN THERE. I MEAN, AN ENTIRE PLANET DIED, AND IT WAS MY FAULT.
THEN THERE I WAS, FACED WITH FAILURE AGAIN, AND IT WAS SO BRUTAL. RIGHT IN MY FACE.
I KNOW IT'S HARD TO LET GO.
THEY DON'T UNDERSTAND ME AT ALL.
THERE'S BEEN MORE THAN ONE OCCASION WHERE I'VE HAD DIFFICULTY ACCEPTING THE FACT THAT I CAN'T BE EVERYWHERE.
SAVE EVERYONE.
BUT REALLY, HOW CAN THEY?
I AM FROM ANOTHER WORLD.
BUT IF WE DON'T KEEP OUR PERSPECTIVE--TAKE CARE OF OURSELVES FIRST--
--THEN WE'RE NO GOOD TO ANYONE ELSE.
I DON'T BLAME THEIR LACK OF UNDERSTANDING.
I KNOW IT'S HARD TO GET BEYOND, SOMETIMES, JOHN. BELIEVE ME.
BUT I THINK WHAT SUPES IS TRYING TO SAY IS: "IF YOU NEED HELP, WE'RE HERE FOR YOU, BUDDY."
OR THEIR WEAKNESS.
THIS IS A PLACE WHERE WE CAN ALL BE SAFE, AND WHERE WE CAN ALL EXPRESS OURSELVES FREELY.
YOU CAN LET GO OF YOUR EMOTIONS HERE--YOUR PAIN HERE--AND NOT BE JUDGED BY IT--
EXCUSE ME--

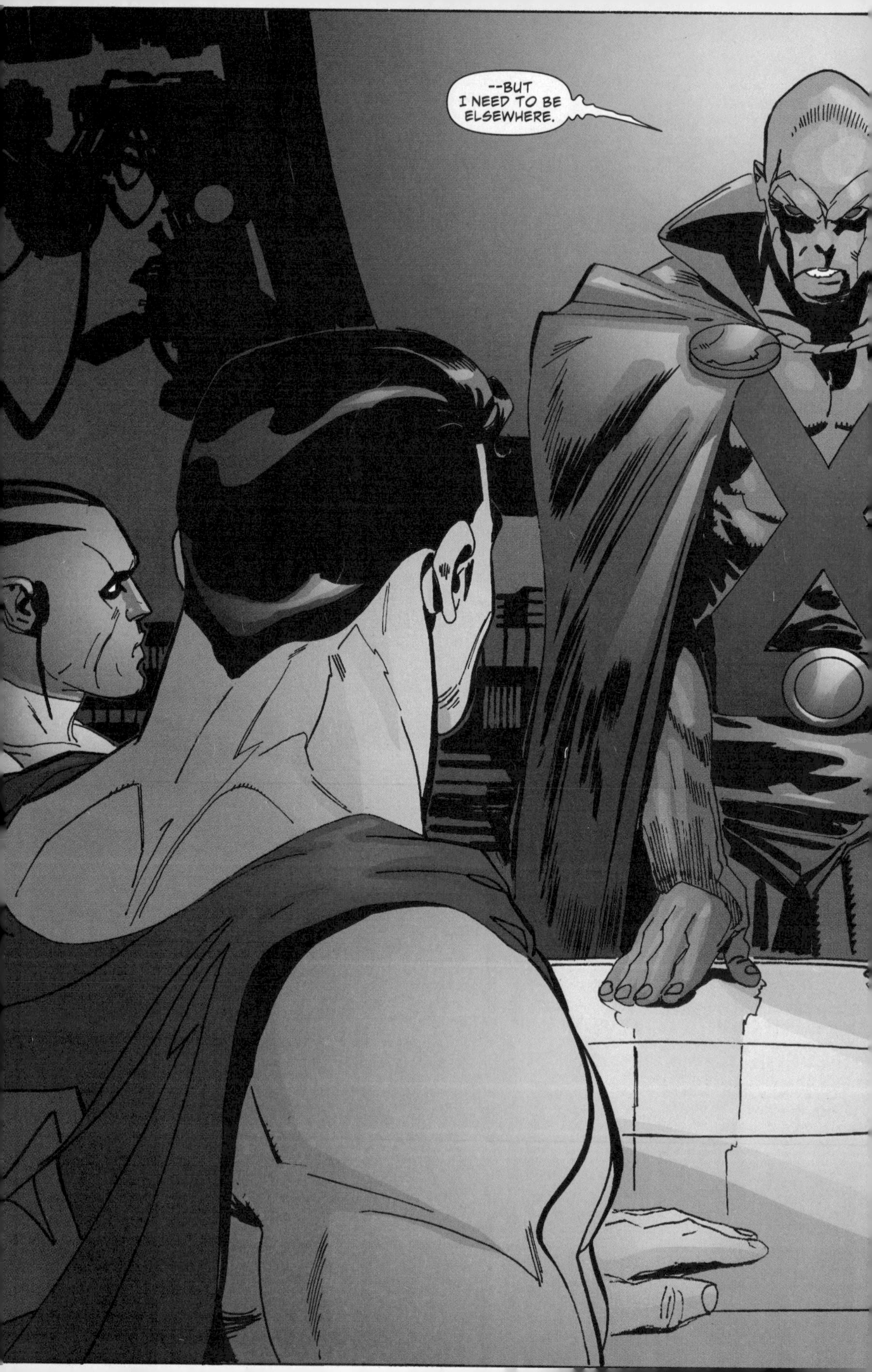
--BUT I NEED TO BE ELSEWHERE.

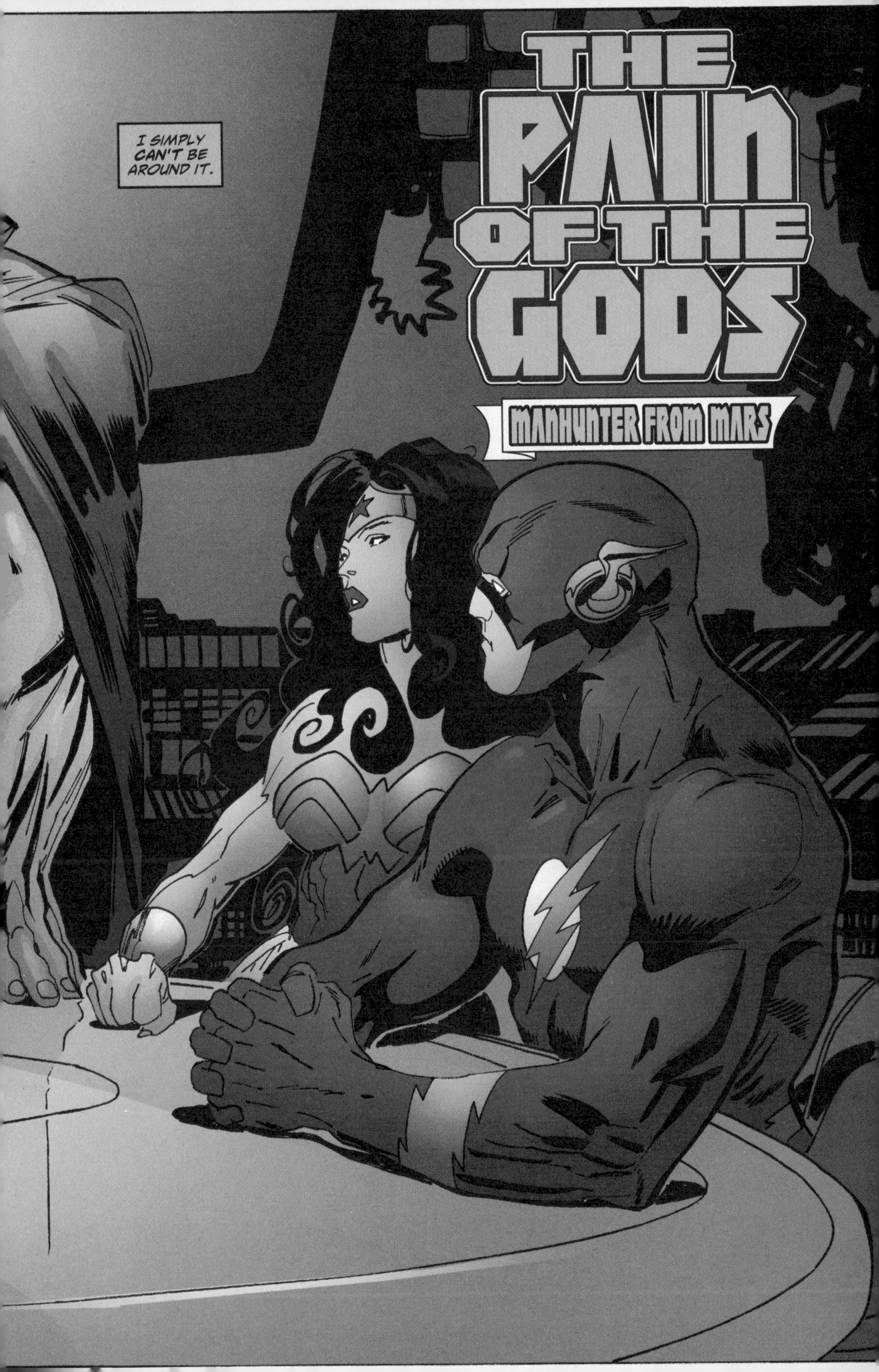
I SIMPLY CAN'T BE AROUND IT.
THE PAIN OF THE GODS
MANHUNTER FROM MARS

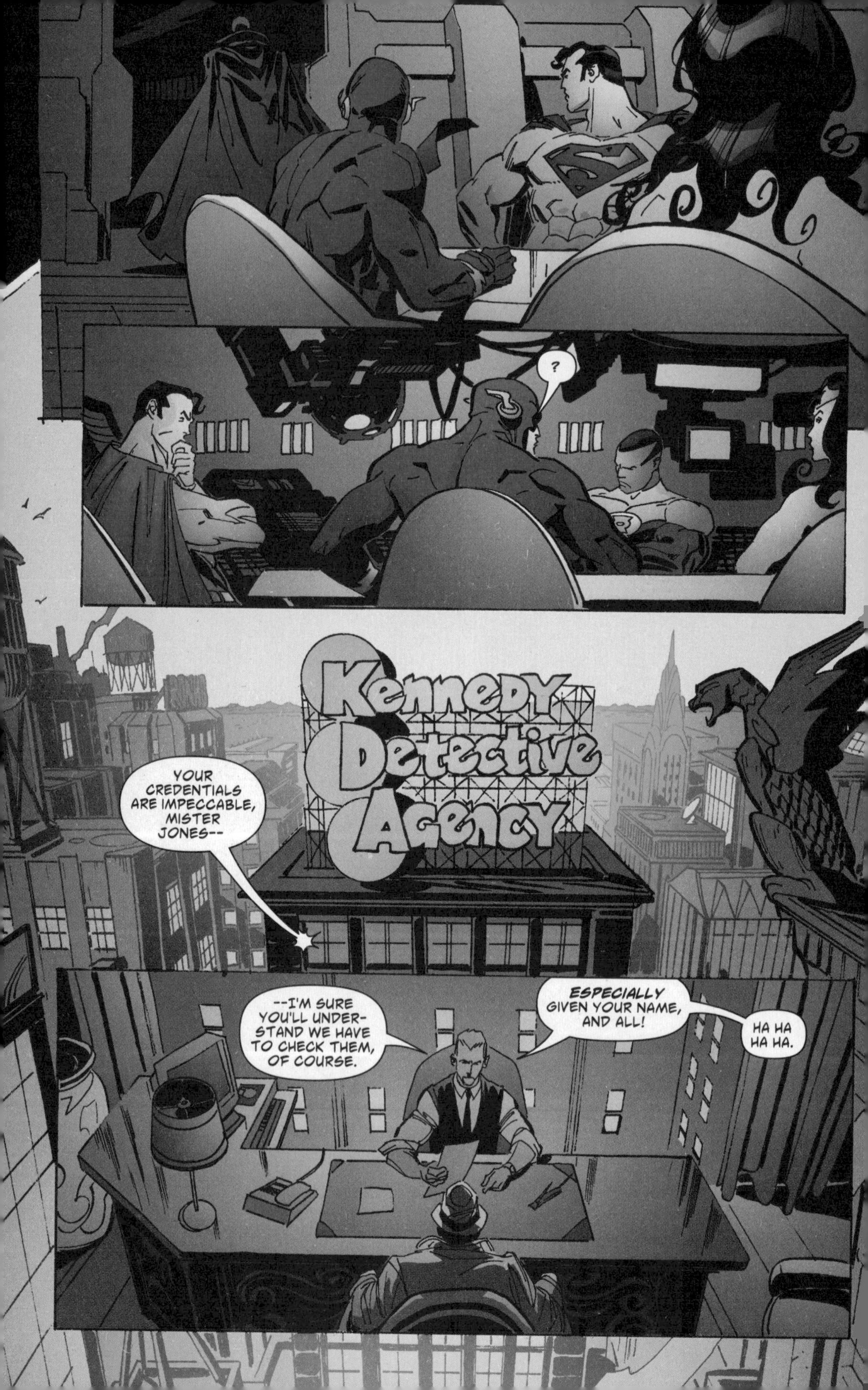
?
Kennedy Detective Agency
YOUR CREDENTIALS ARE IMPECCABLE, MISTER JONES--
--I'M SURE YOU'LL UNDER-STAND WE HAVE TO CHECK THEM, OF COURSE.
ESPECIALLY GIVEN YOUR NAME, AND ALL!
HA HA HA HA.

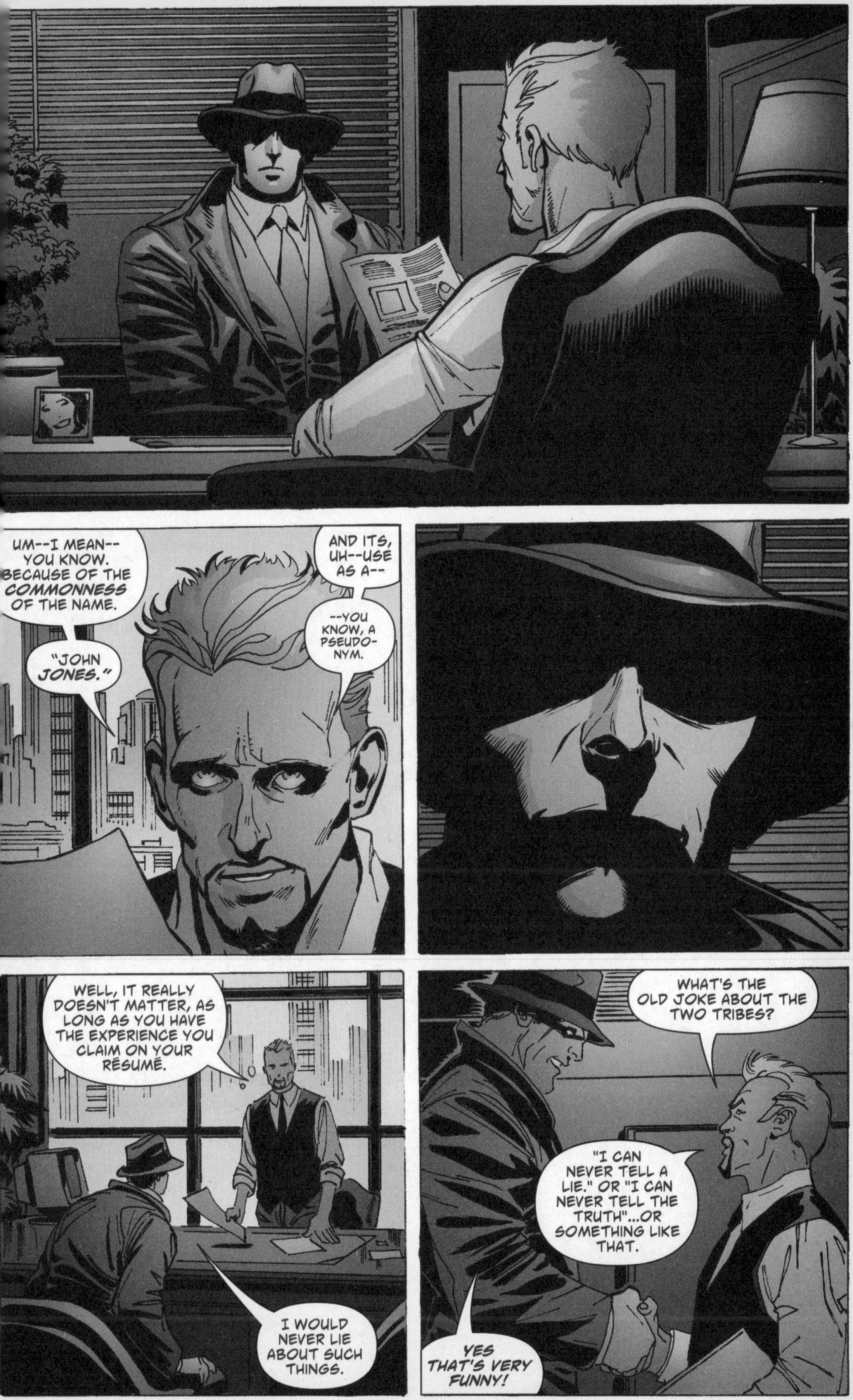
UM--I MEAN-- YOU KNOW. BECAUSE OF THE *COMMONNESS* OF THE NAME.
"JOHN *JONES.*"
AND ITS, UH--USE AS A--
--YOU KNOW, A PSEUDO-NYM.
WELL, IT REALLY DOESN'T MATTER, AS LONG AS YOU HAVE THE EXPERIENCE YOU CLAIM ON YOUR RÉSUMÉ.
I WOULD NEVER LIE ABOUT SUCH THINGS.
WHAT'S THE OLD JOKE ABOUT THE TWO TRIBES?
"I CAN NEVER TELL A LIE." OR "I CAN NEVER TELL THE TRUTH"...OR SOMETHING LIKE THAT.
YES THAT'S VERY FUNNY!

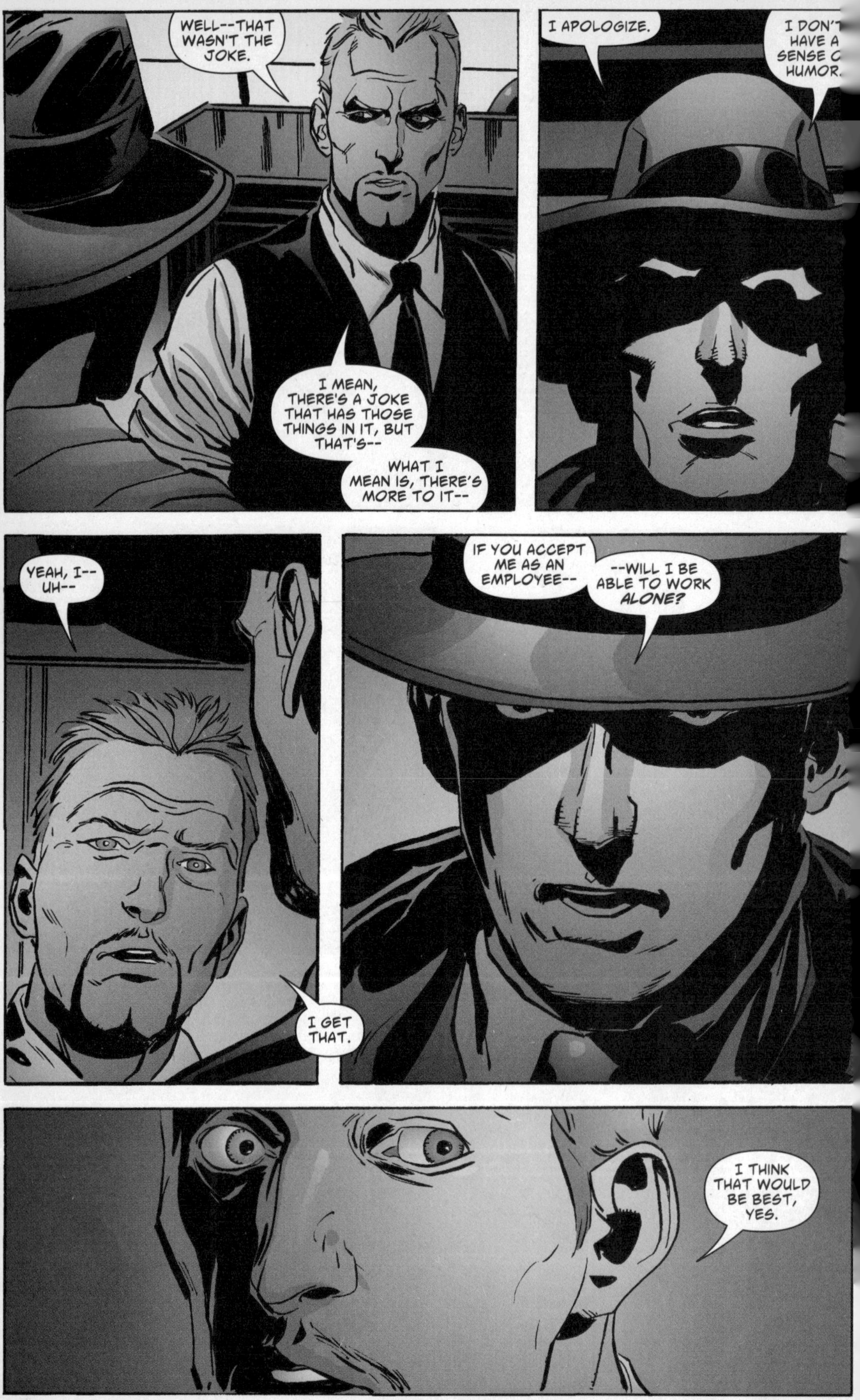
WELL--THAT WASN'T THE JOKE.
I MEAN, THERE'S A JOKE THAT HAS THOSE THINGS IN IT, BUT THAT'S--
WHAT I MEAN IS, THERE'S MORE TO IT--
I APOLOGIZE.
HAVE A
HUMOR.
YEAH, I-- UH--
I GET THAT.
IF YOU ACCEPT ME AS AN EMPLOYEE--
--WILL I BE ABLE TO WORK *ALONE?*
I THINK THAT WOULD BE BEST, YES.

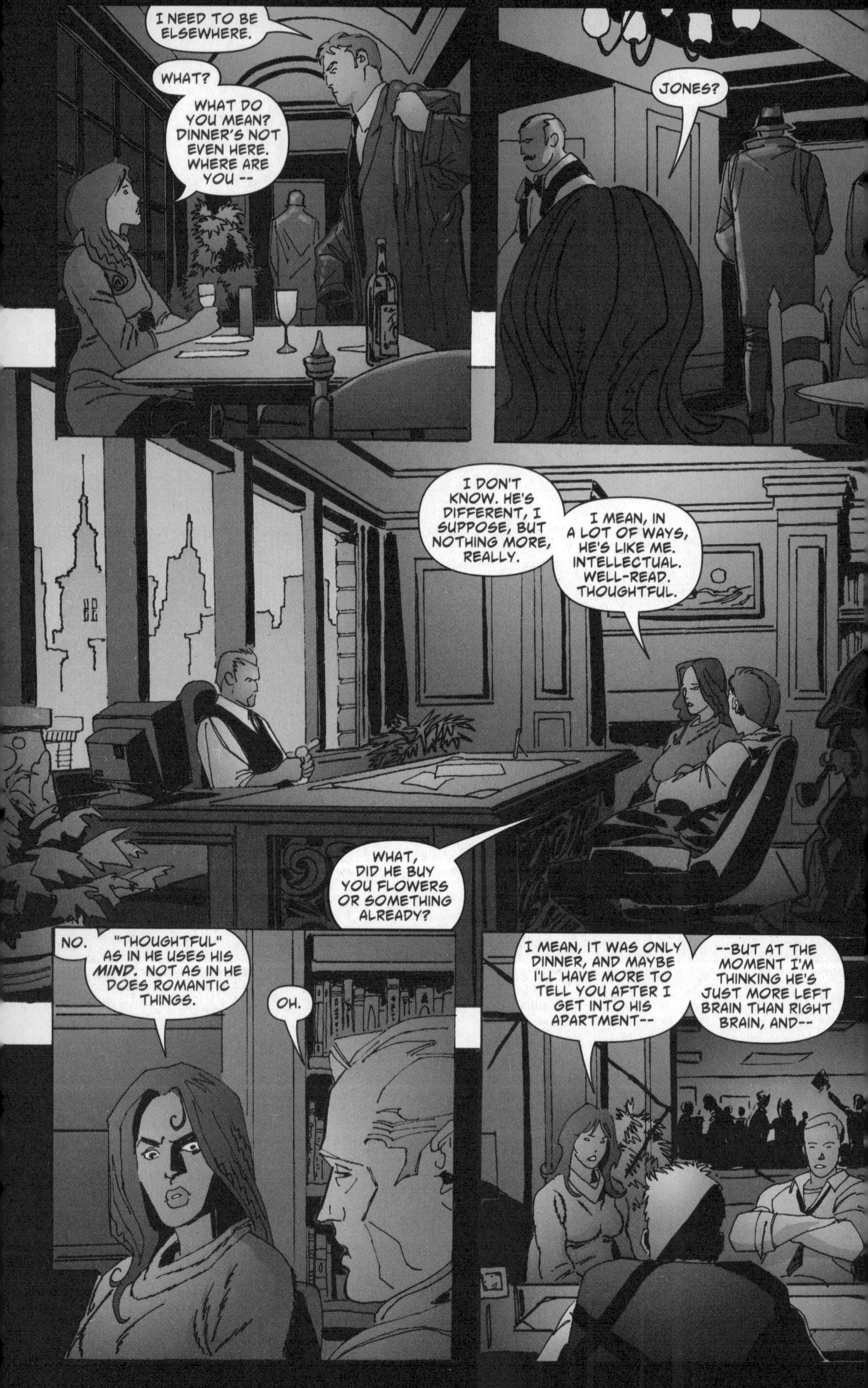
I NEED TO BE ELSEWHERE.
WHAT?
WHAT DO YOU MEAN? DINNER'S NOT EVEN HERE. WHERE ARE YOU --
JONES?
I DON'T KNOW. HE'S DIFFERENT, I SUPPOSE, BUT NOTHING MORE, REALLY.
I MEAN, IN A LOT OF WAYS, HE'S LIKE ME. INTELLECTUAL. WELL-READ. THOUGHTFUL.
WHAT, DID HE BUY YOU FLOWERS OR SOMETHING ALREADY?
NO.
"THOUGHTFUL" AS IN HE USES HIS *MIND*. NOT AS IN HE DOES ROMANTIC THINGS.
OH.
I MEAN, IT WAS ONLY DINNER, AND MAYBE I'LL HAVE MORE TO TELL YOU AFTER I GET INTO HIS APARTMENT--
--BUT AT THE MOMENT I'M THINKING HE'S JUST MORE LEFT BRAIN THAN RIGHT BRAIN, AND--

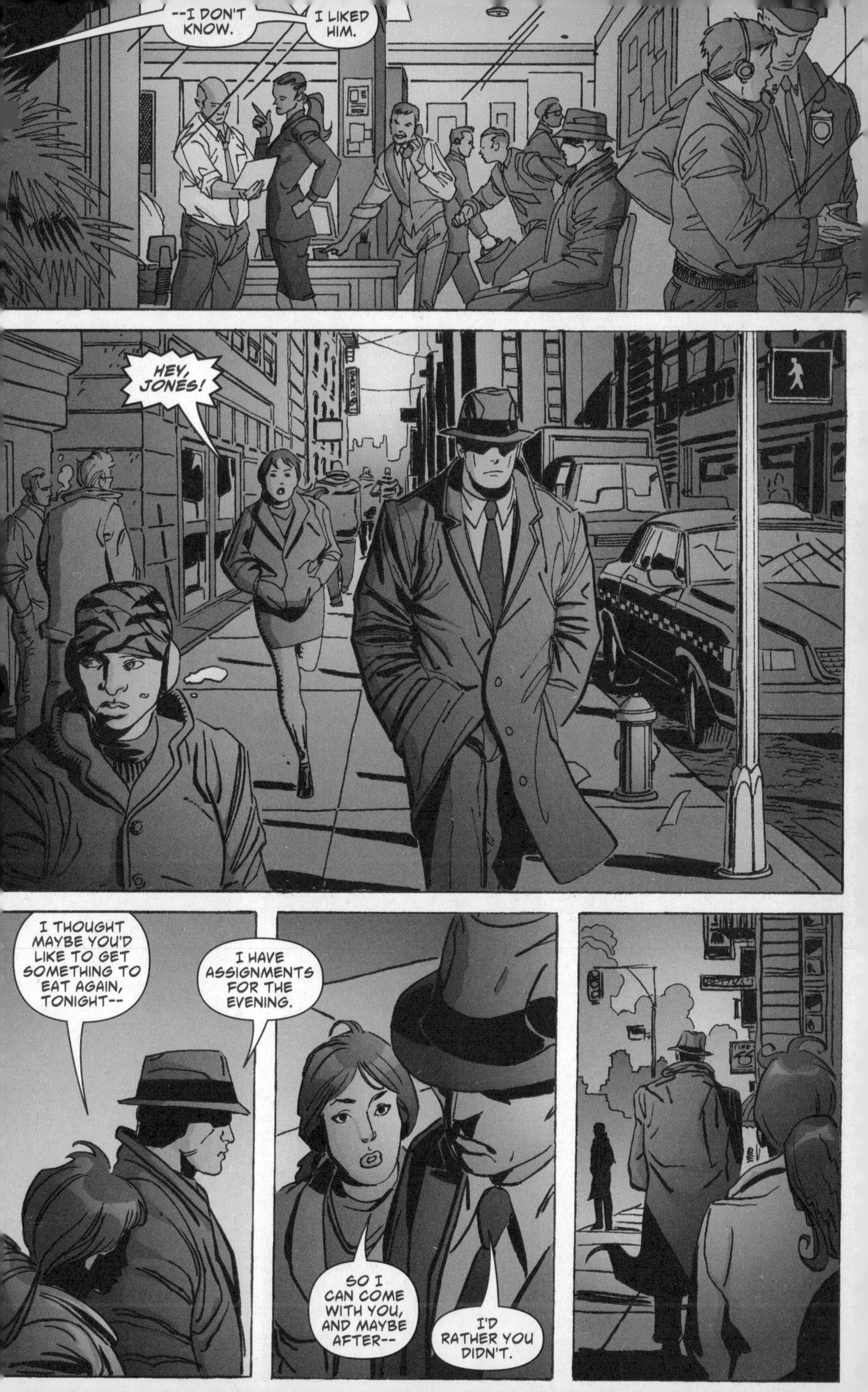
--I DON'T KNOW.
I LIKED HIM.
HEY, JONES!
I THOUGHT MAYBE YOU'D LIKE TO GET SOMETHING TO EAT AGAIN, TONIGHT--
I HAVE ASSIGNMENTS FOR THE EVENING.
SO I CAN COME WITH YOU, AND MAYBE AFTER--
I'D RATHER YOU DIDN'T.

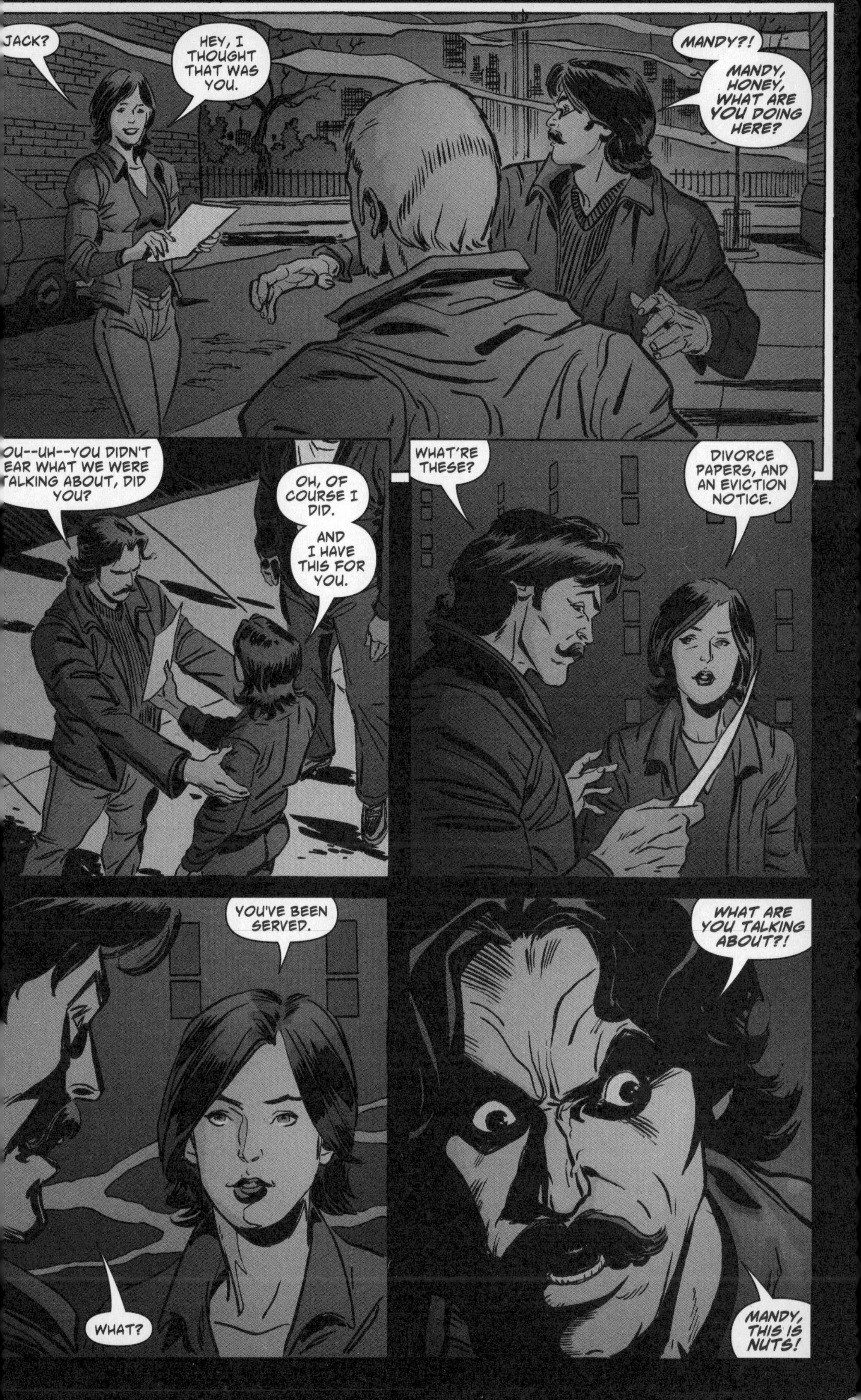
JACK?
HEY, I THOUGHT THAT WAS YOU.
MANDY?!
MANDY, HONEY, WHAT ARE YOU DOING HERE?
OU--UH--YOU DIDN'T EAR WHAT WE WERE TALKING ABOUT, DID YOU?
OH, OF COURSE I DID.
AND I HAVE THIS FOR YOU.
WHAT'RE THESE?
DIVORCE PAPERS, AND AN EVICTION NOTICE.
YOU'VE BEEN SERVED.
WHAT?
WHAT ARE YOU TALKING ABOUT?!
MANDY, THIS IS NUTS!

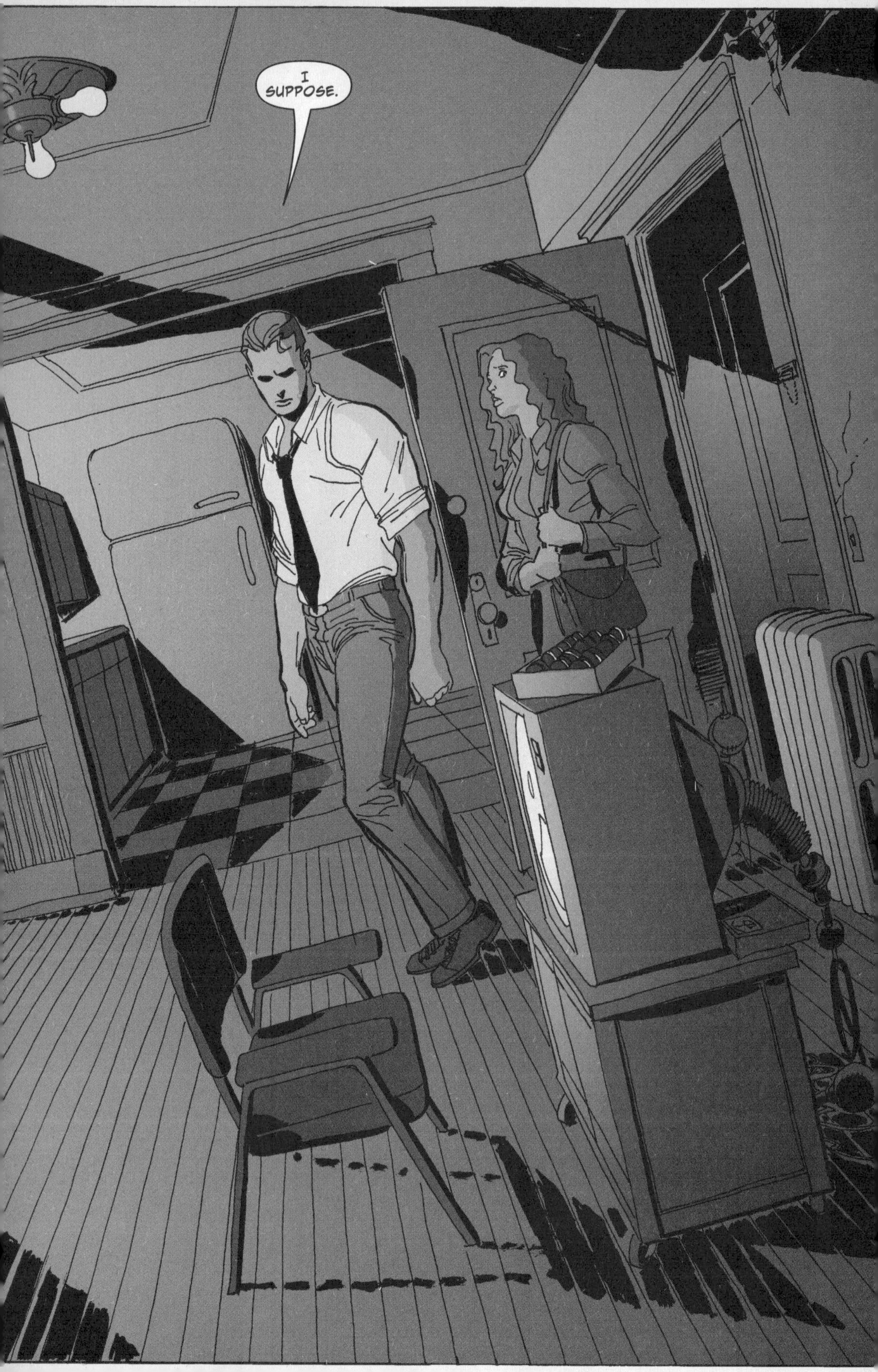
I SUPPOSE.

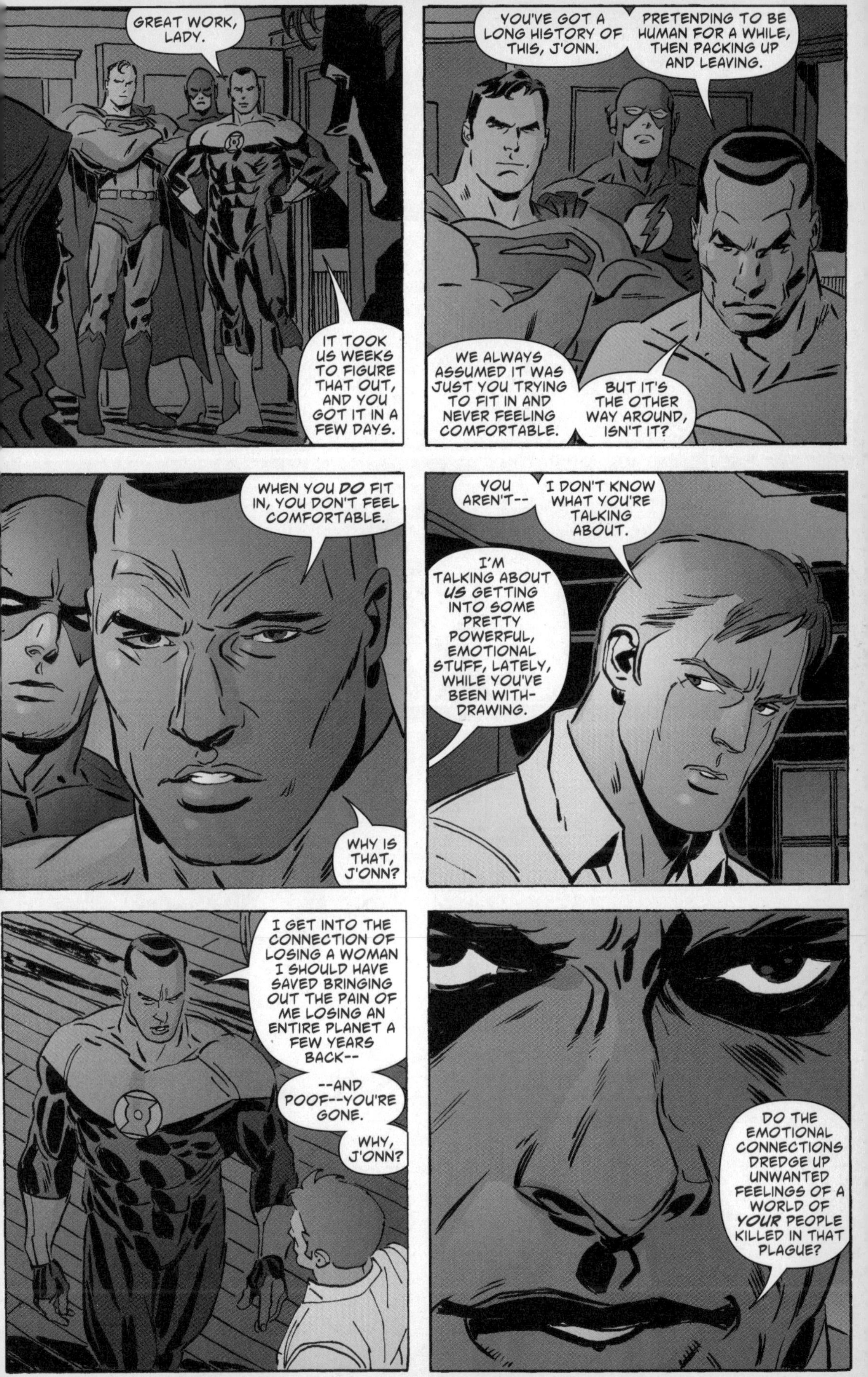
GREAT WORK, LADY.
IT TOOK US WEEKS TO FIGURE THAT OUT, AND YOU GOT IT IN A FEW DAYS.
YOU'VE GOT A LONG HISTORY OF THIS, J'ONN.
PRETENDING TO BE HUMAN FOR A WHILE, THEN PACKING UP AND LEAVING.
WE ALWAYS ASSUMED IT WAS JUST YOU TRYING TO FIT IN AND NEVER FEELING COMFORTABLE.
BUT IT'S THE OTHER WAY AROUND, ISN'T IT?
WHEN YOU *DO* FIT IN, YOU DON'T FEEL COMFORTABLE.
WHY IS THAT, J'ONN?
YOU AREN'T--
I DON'T KNOW WHAT YOU'RE TALKING ABOUT.
I'M TALKING ABOUT *US* GETTING INTO SOME PRETTY POWERFUL, EMOTIONAL STUFF, LATELY, WHILE YOU'VE BEEN WITH-DRAWING.
I GET INTO THE CONNECTION OF LOSING A WOMAN I SHOULD HAVE SAVED BRINGING OUT THE PAIN OF ME LOSING AN ENTIRE PLANET A FEW YEARS BACK--
--AND POOF--YOU'RE GONE.
WHY, J'ONN?
DO THE EMOTIONAL CONNECTIONS DREDGE UP UNWANTED FEELINGS OF A WORLD OF *YOUR* PEOPLE KILLED IN THAT PLAGUE?

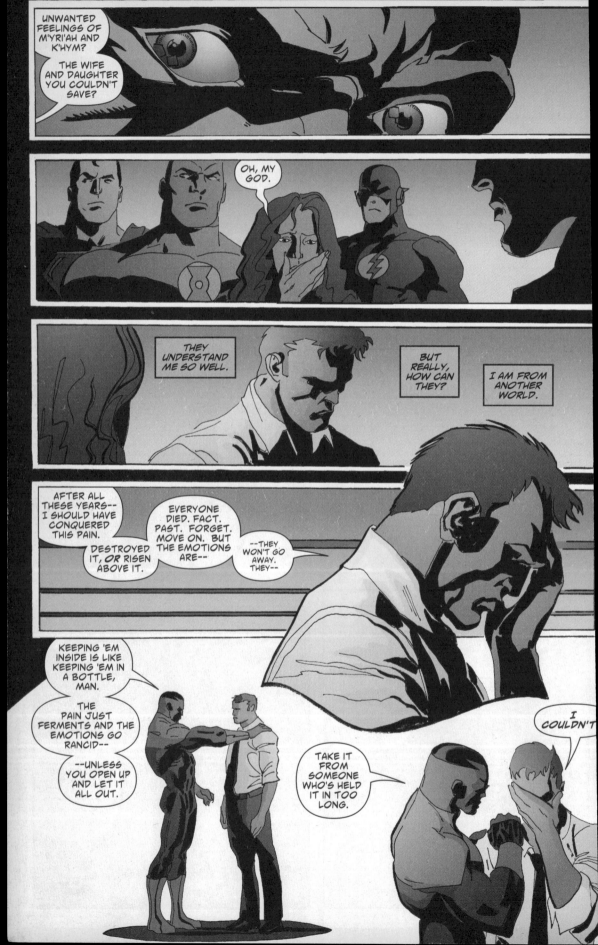

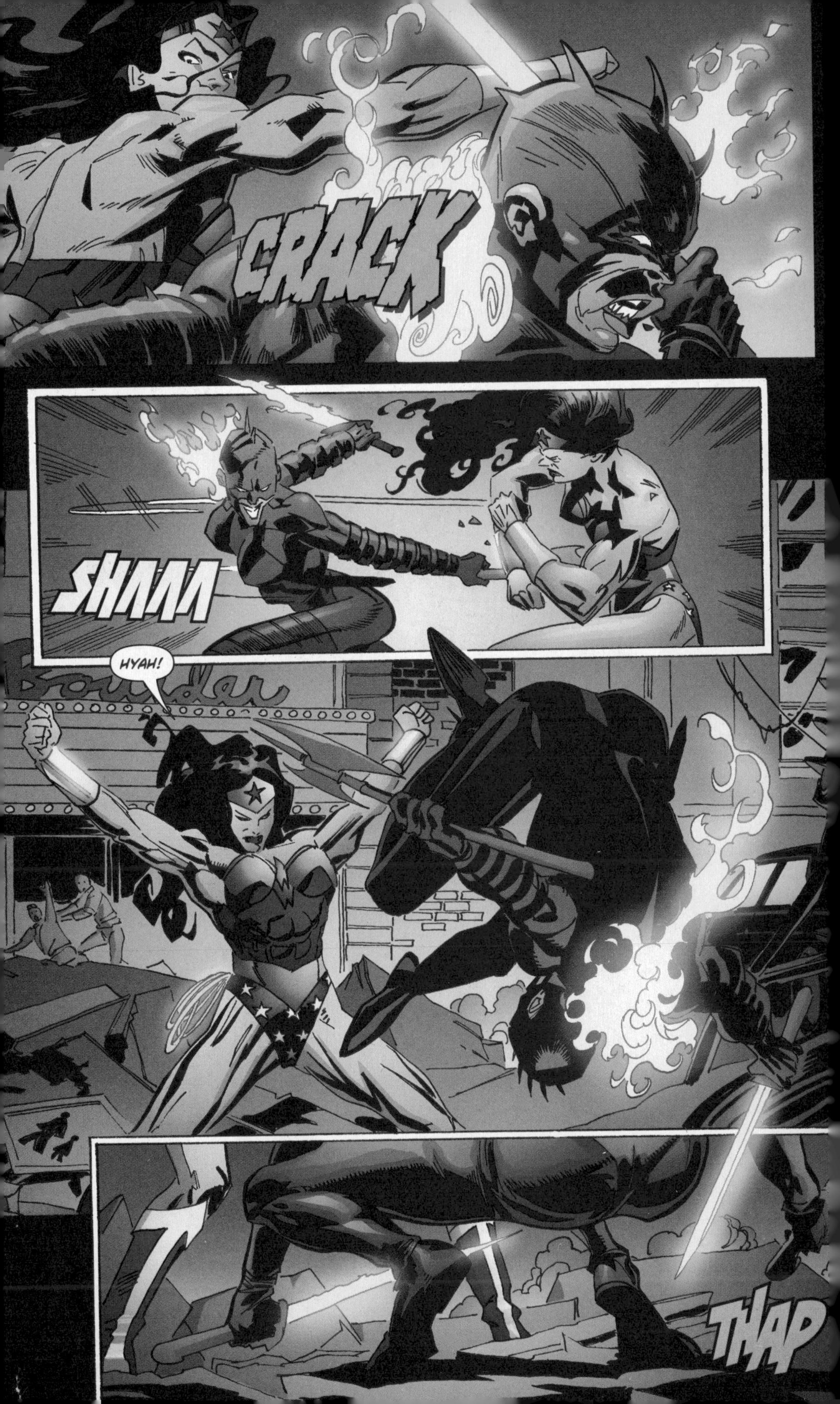

CRACK
SHAAA
HYAH!
THAP

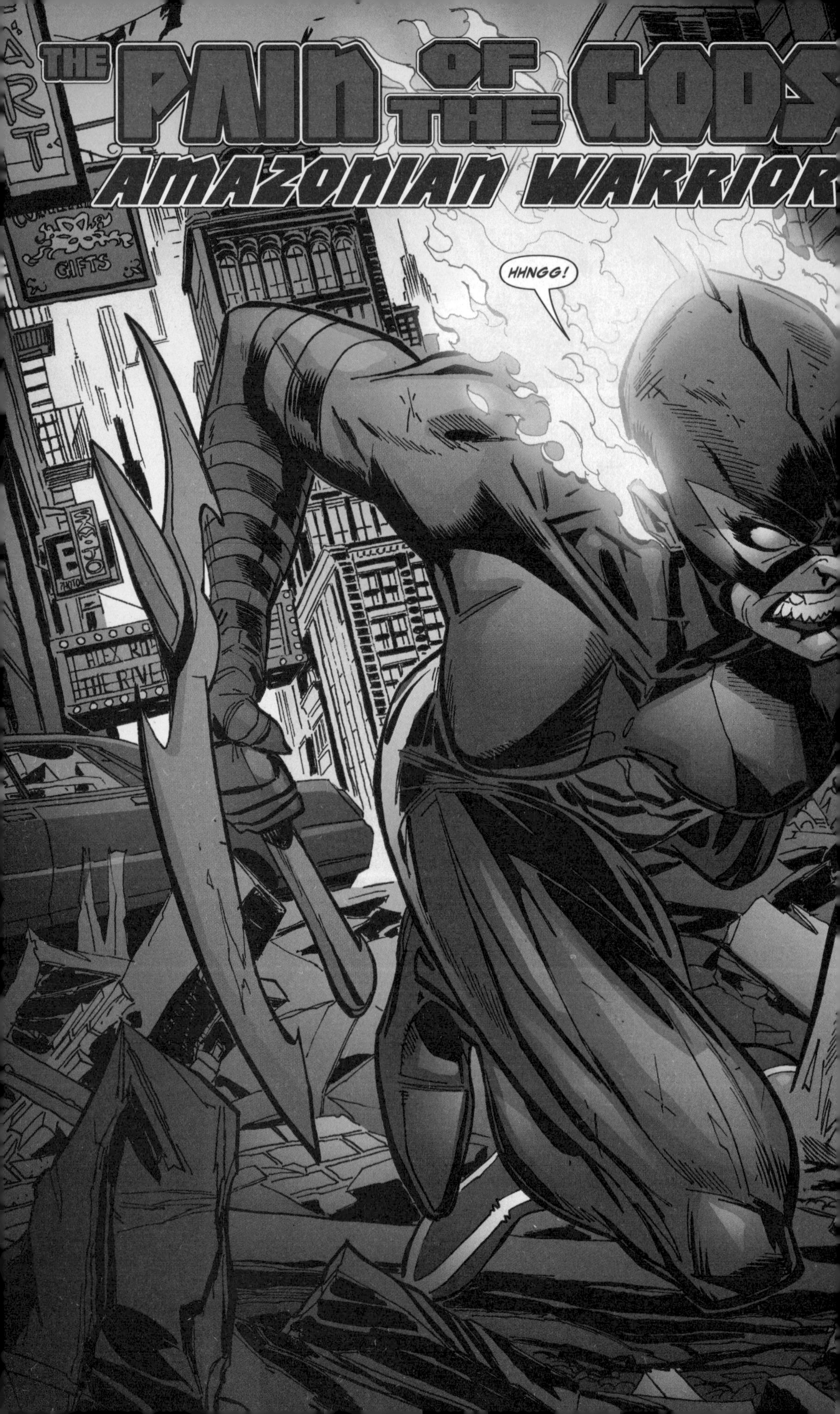
THE PAIN OF THE GODS
AMAZONIAN WARRIOR
HHNGG!

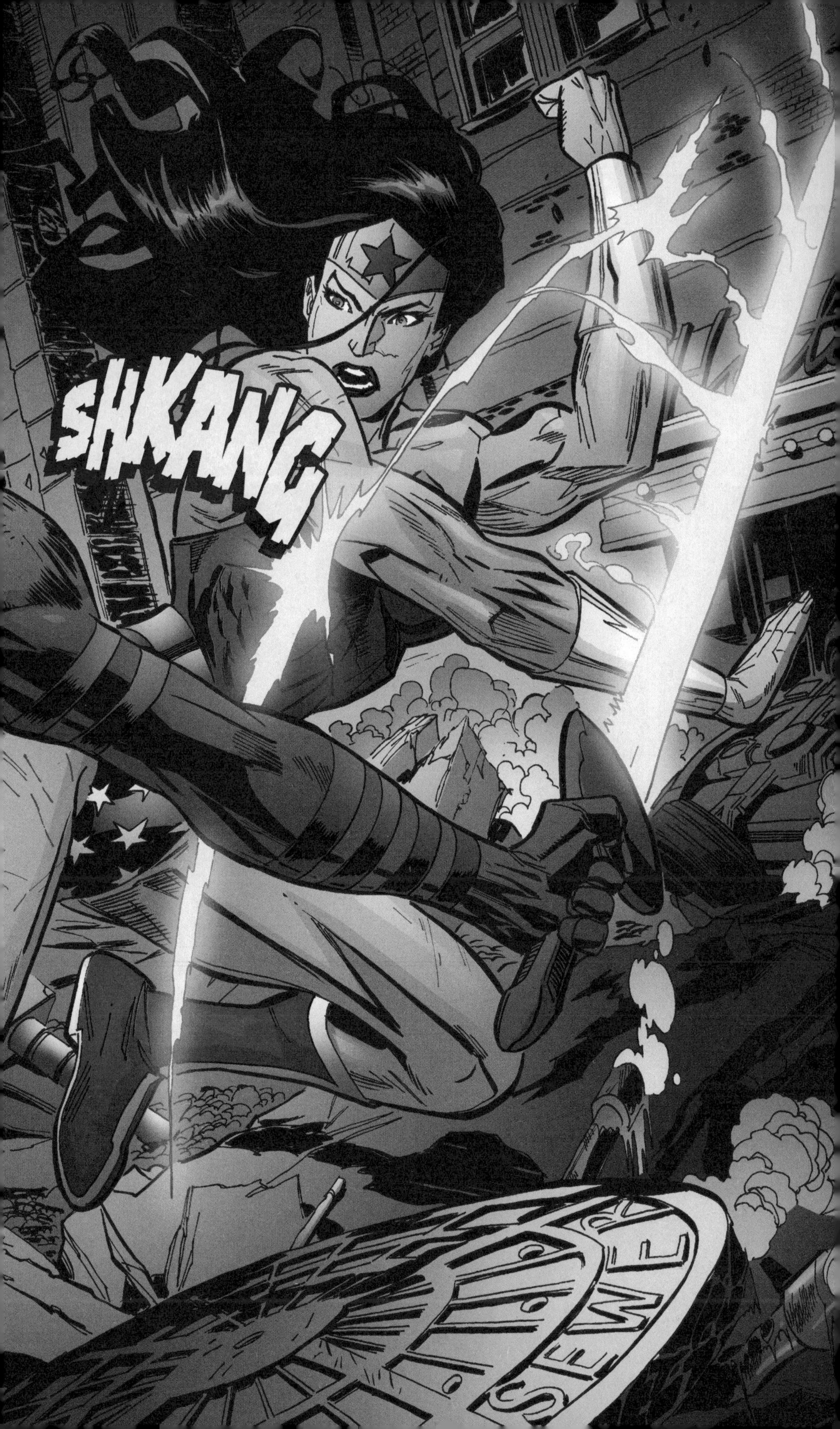
SHKANG

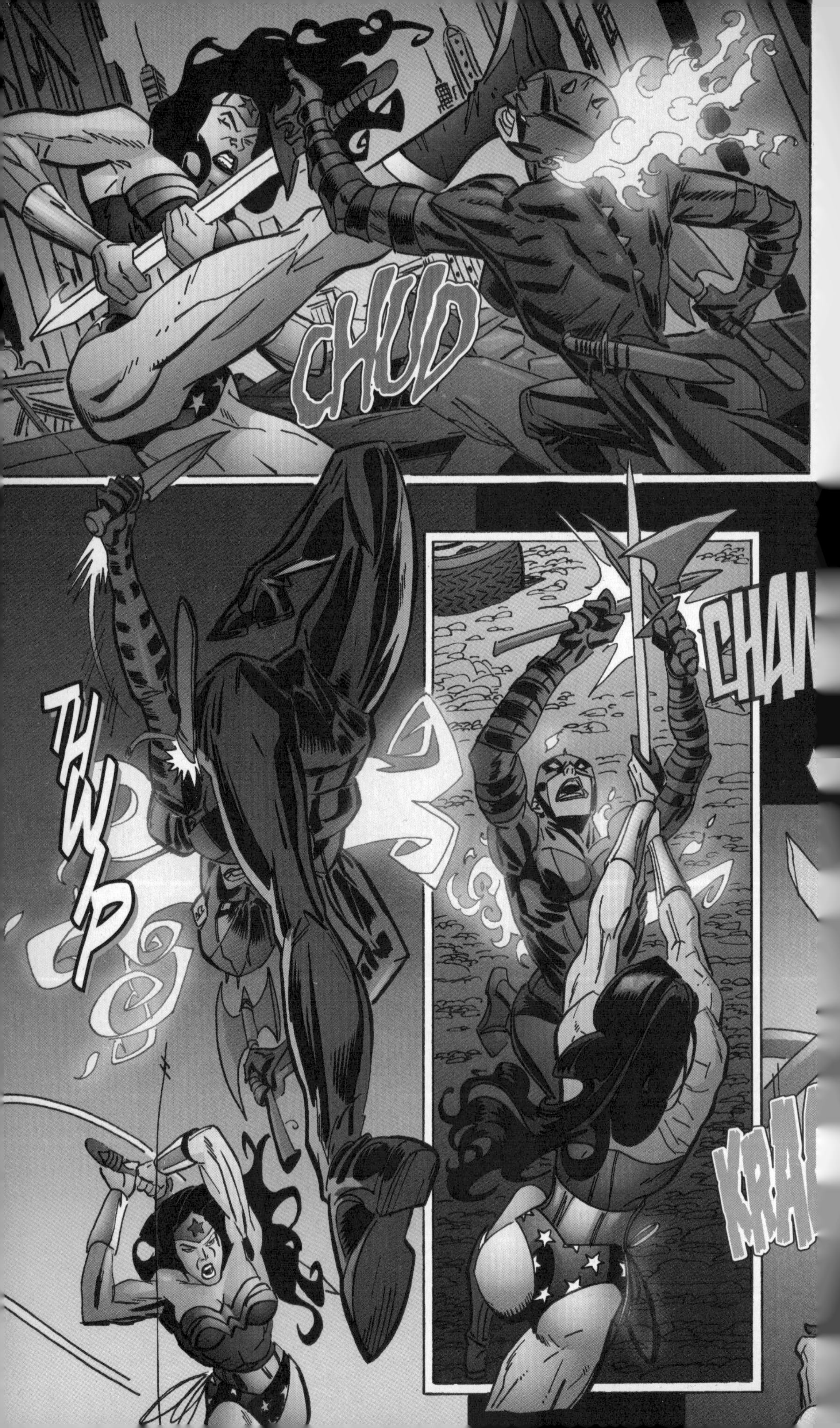
CHUD
THWIP

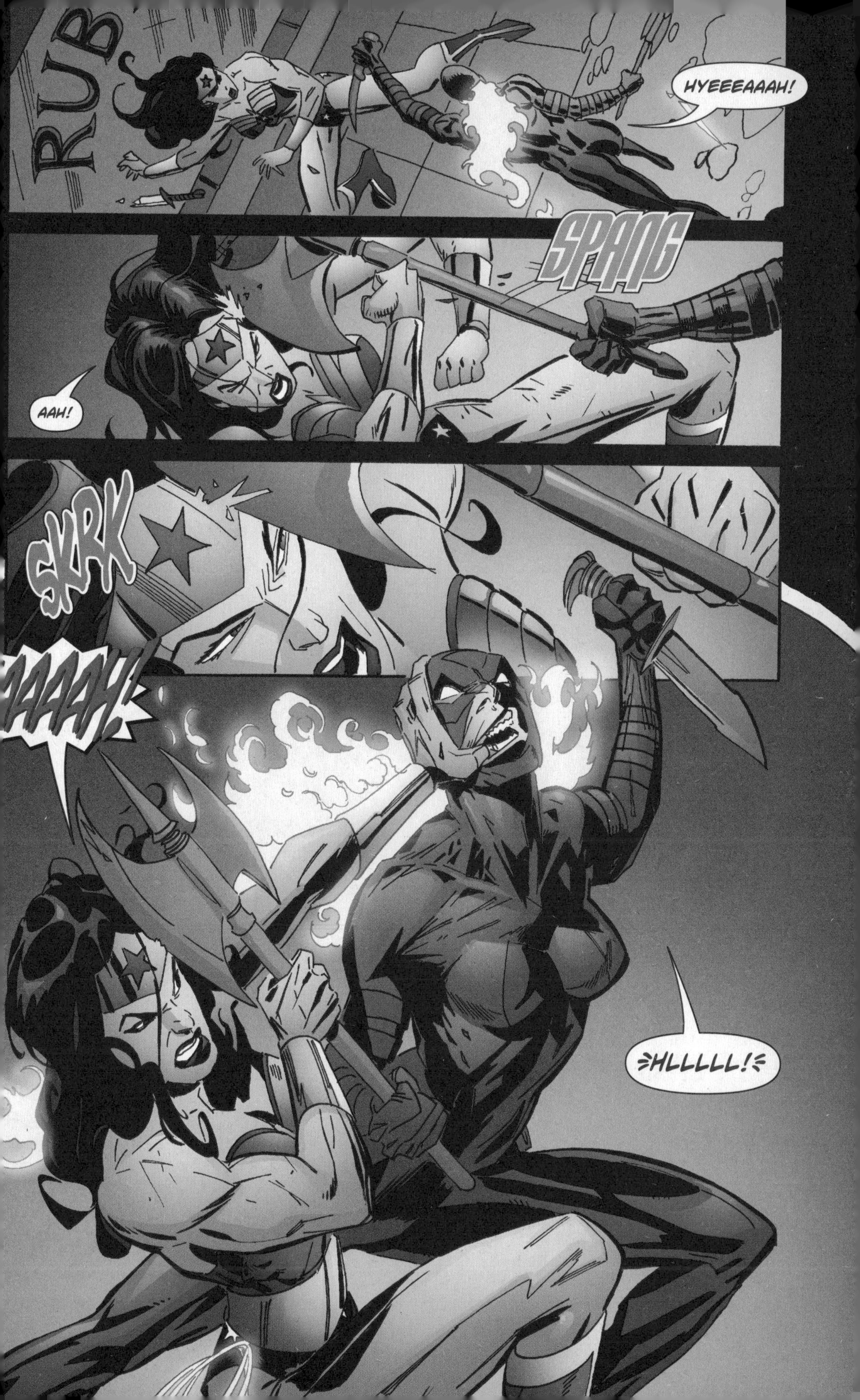
RUB
HYEEEAAAH!
SPANG
AAH!
SKRK
AAAAH!
HLLLLL!

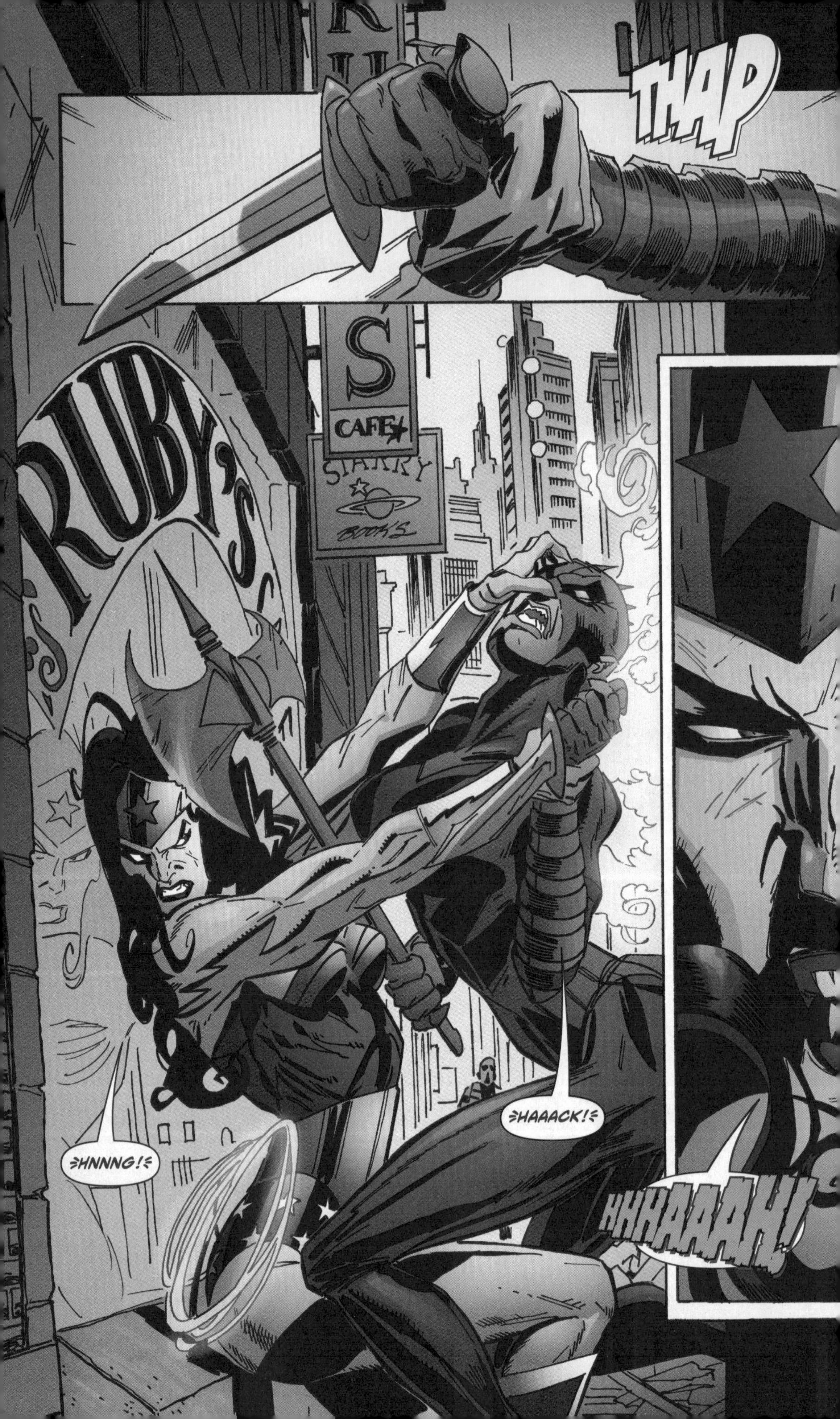
THAP
RUBY'S
S
CAFE
STARRY
BOOKS
HAAACK!
HNNNG!
HHHAAAH!

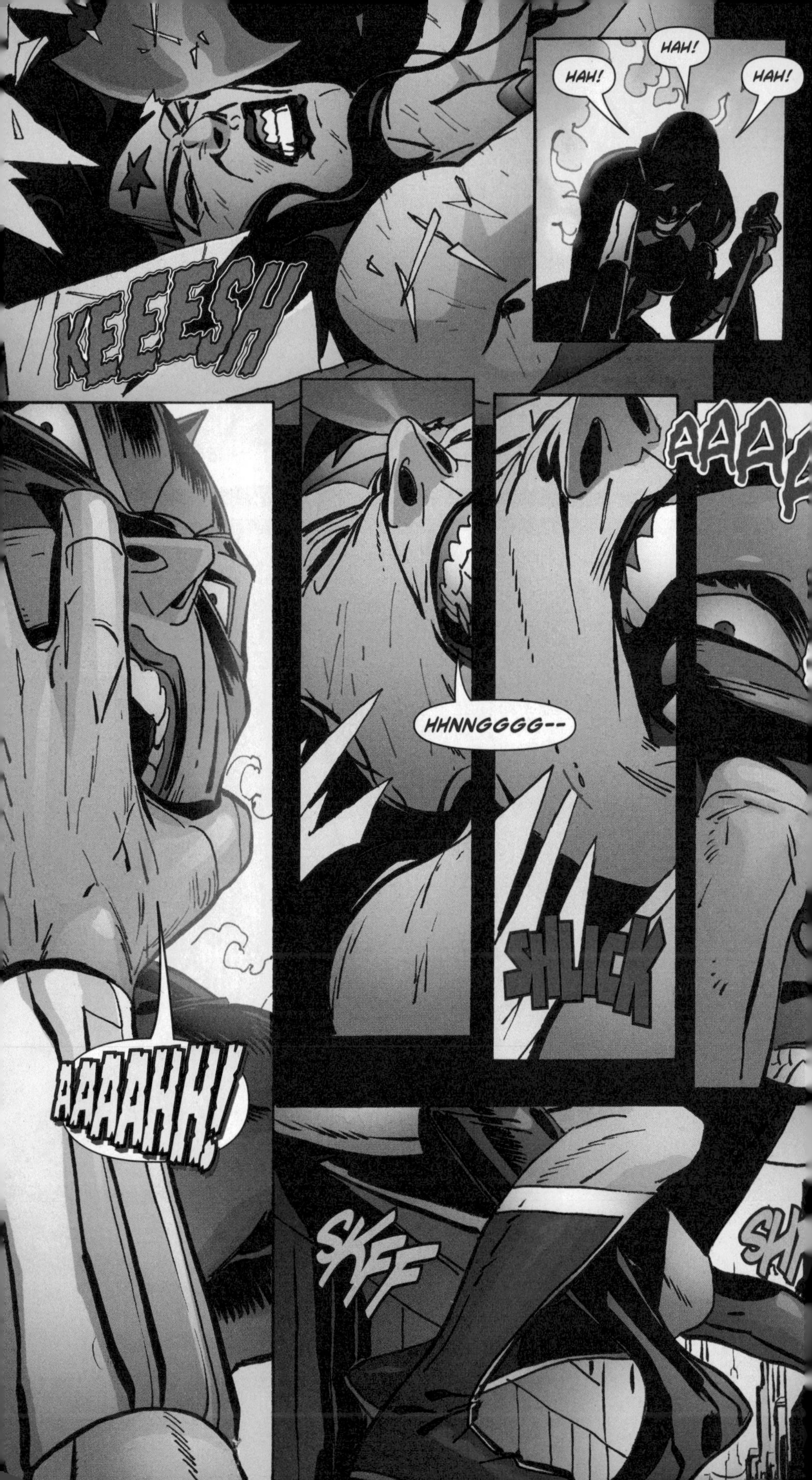

KEEESH
HAH!
HAH!
HAH!
AAAAHH!
HHNNGGGG--
SHLICK
SKFF

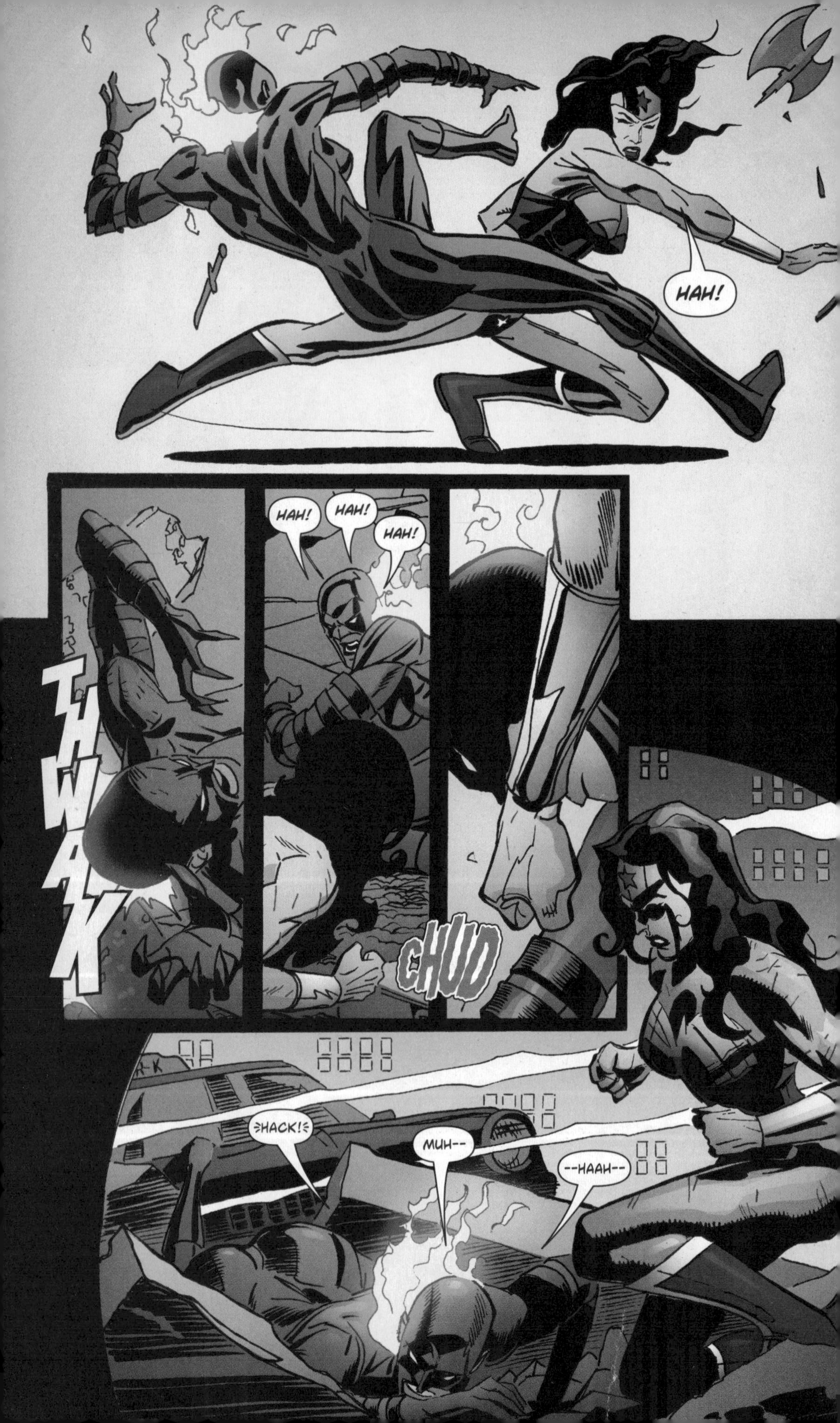
HAH!
THWAK
HAH!
HAH!
HAH!
CHUD
HACK!
MUH--
--HAAH--

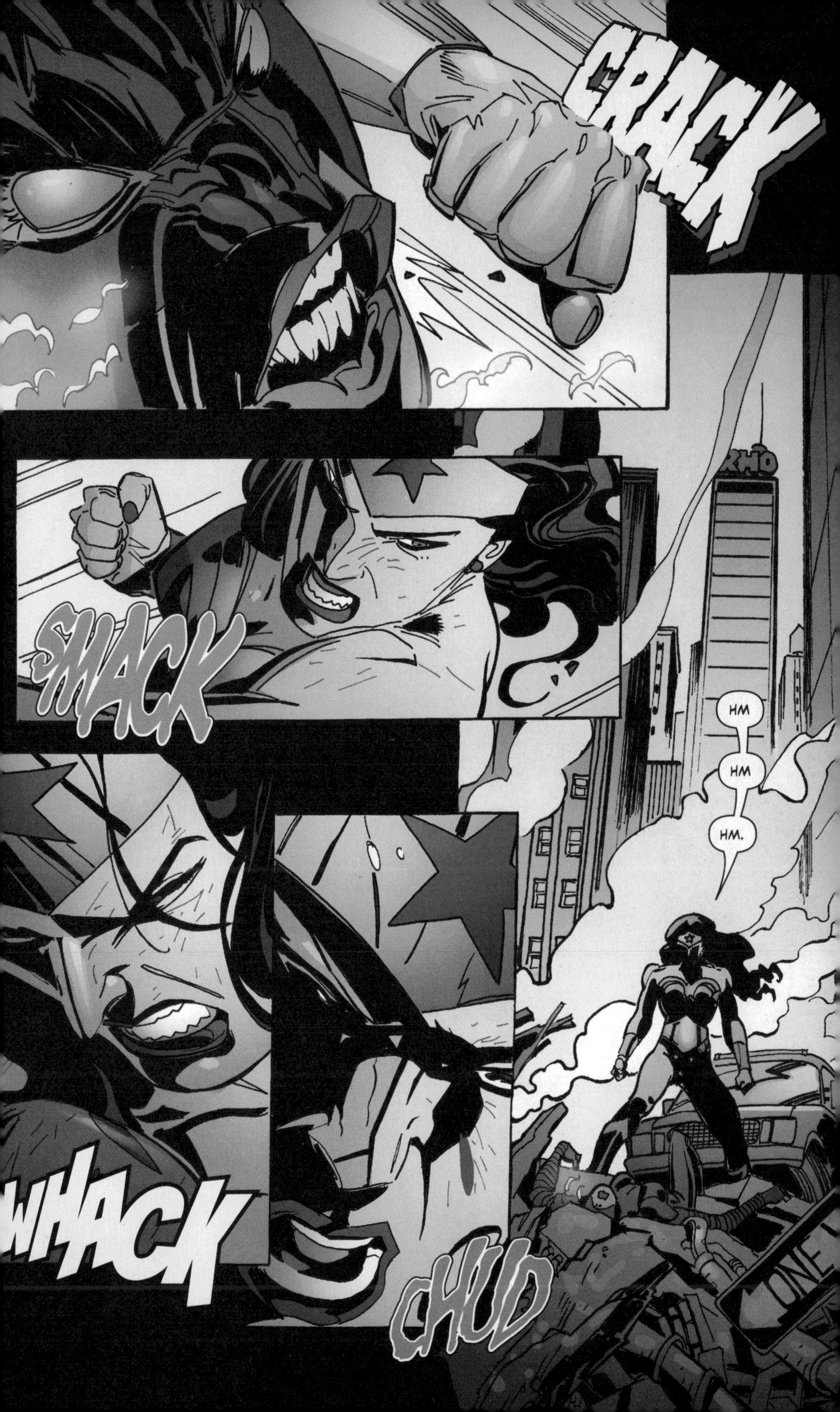
CRACK
SMACK
WHACK
CHUD
HM
HM
HM.

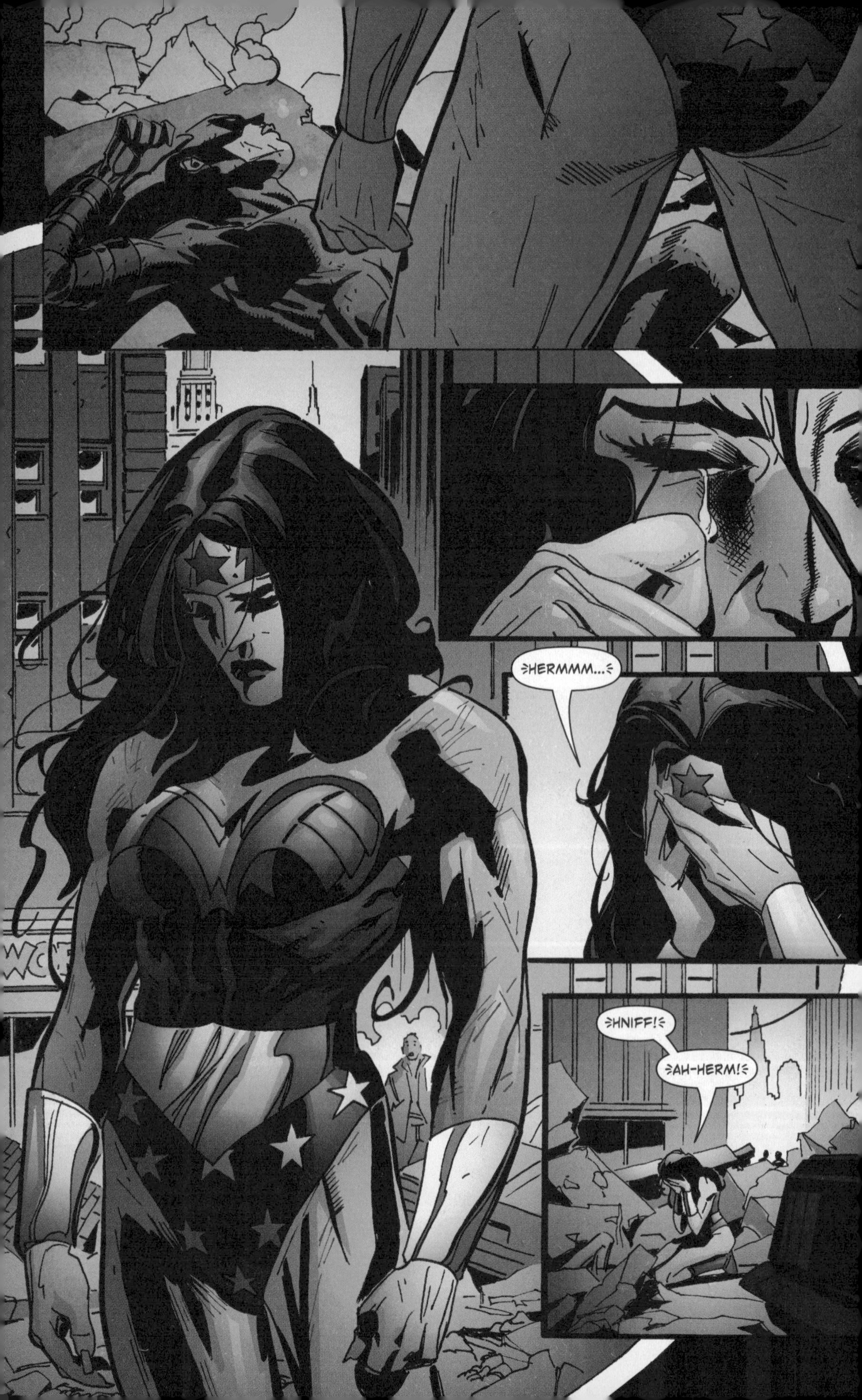
HERMMM...
HNIFF!
AH-HERM!

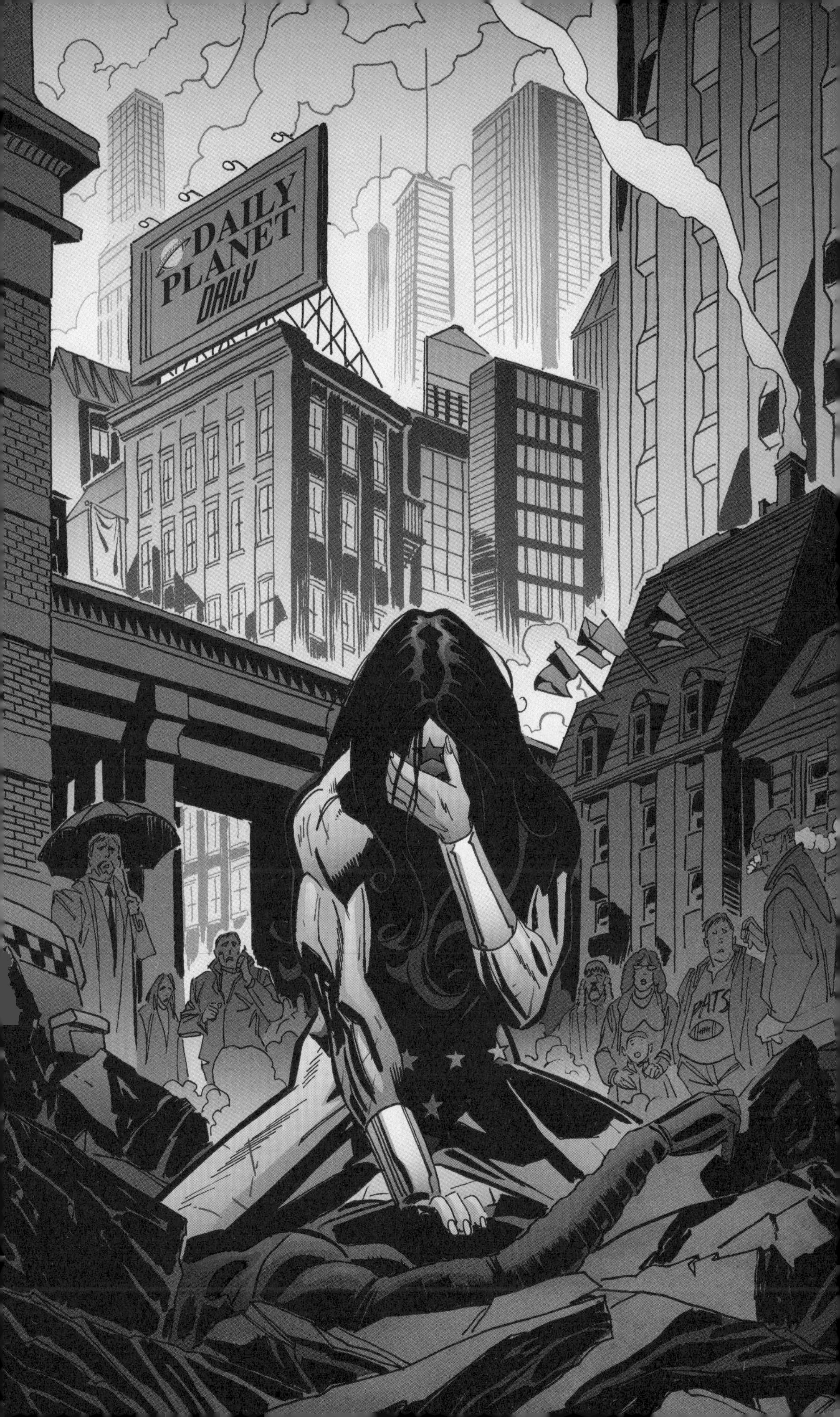
DAILY PLANET
DAILY

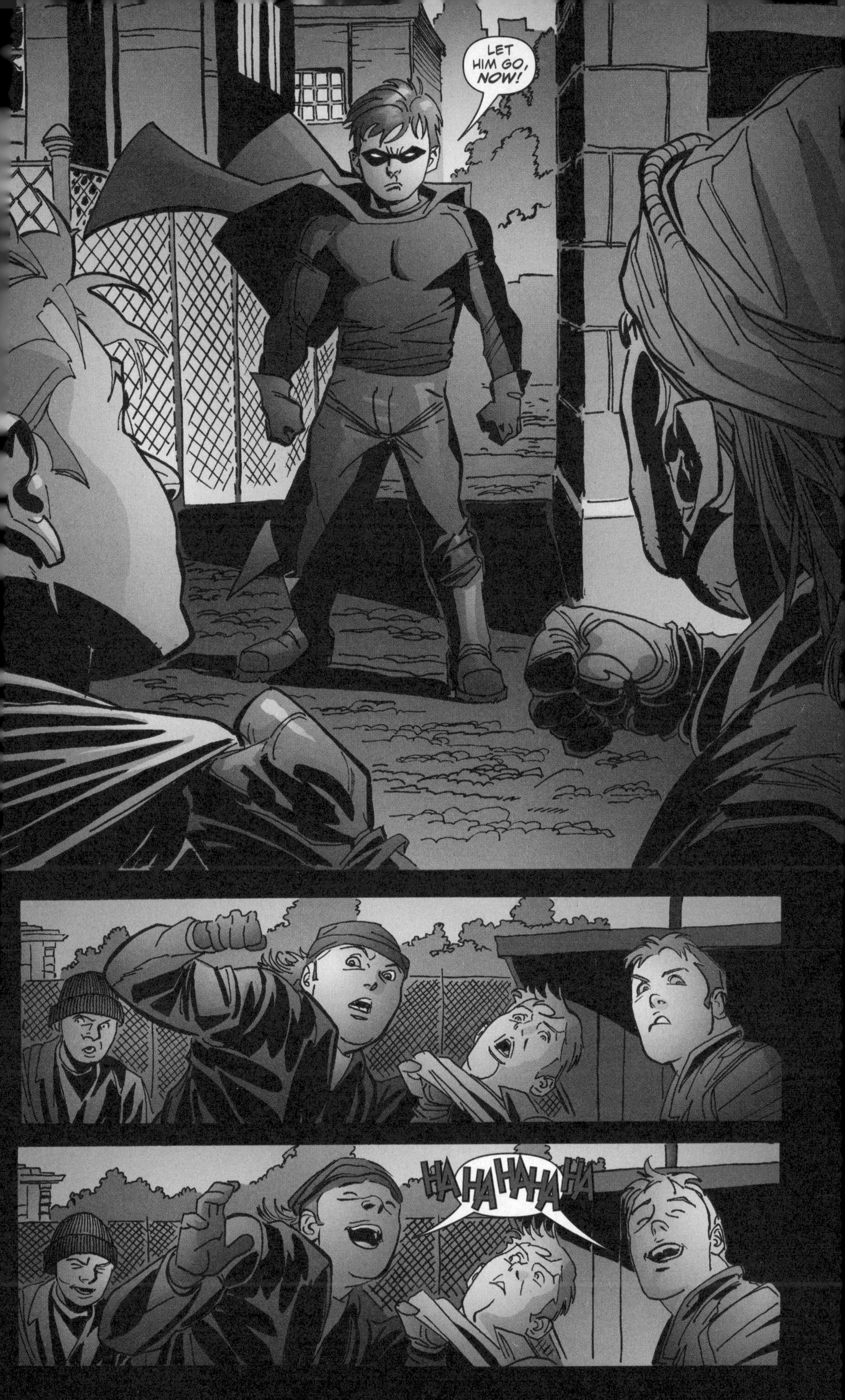
LET HIM GO, NOW!
HA HA HA HA HA HA

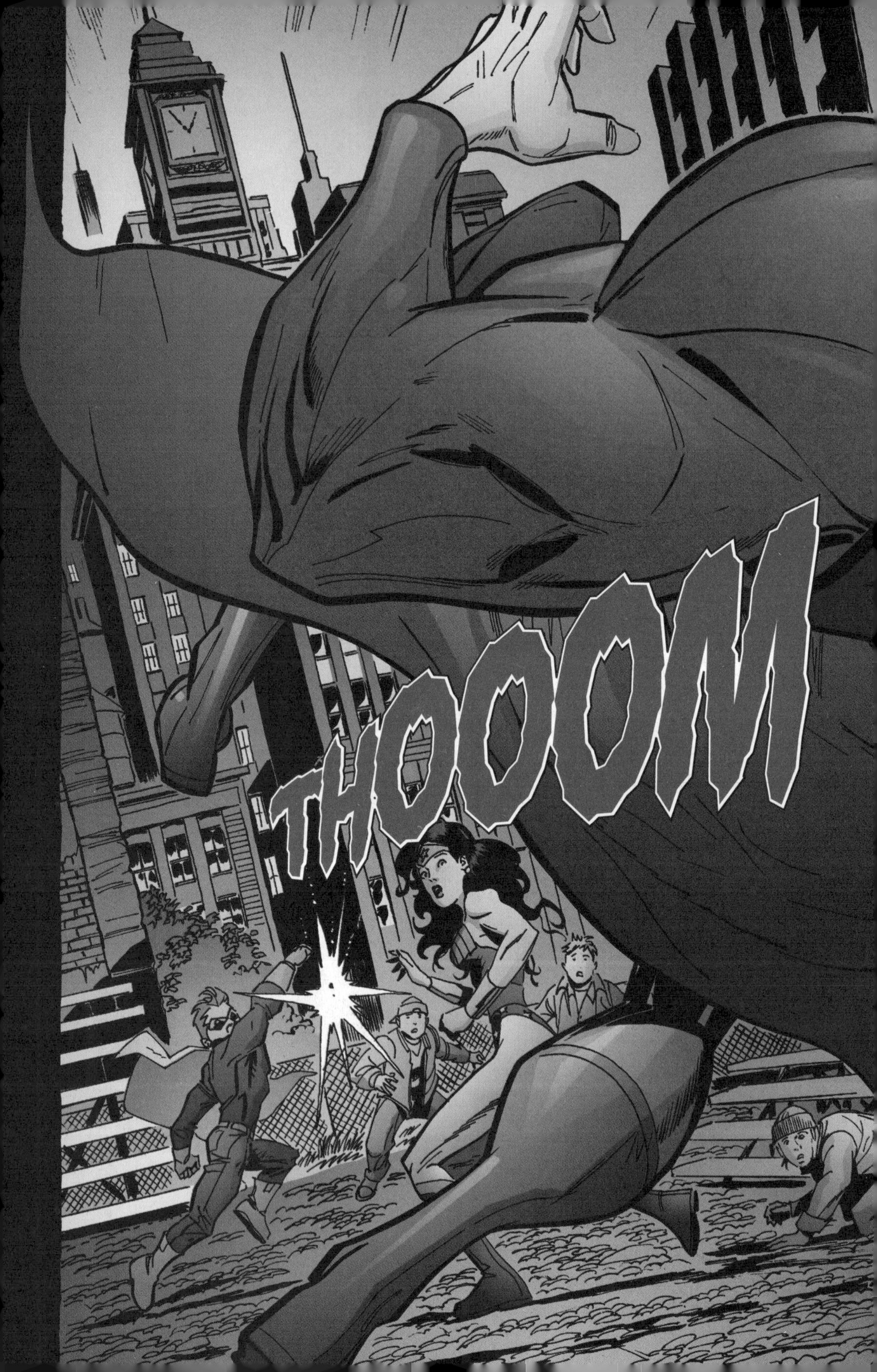
THOOOM

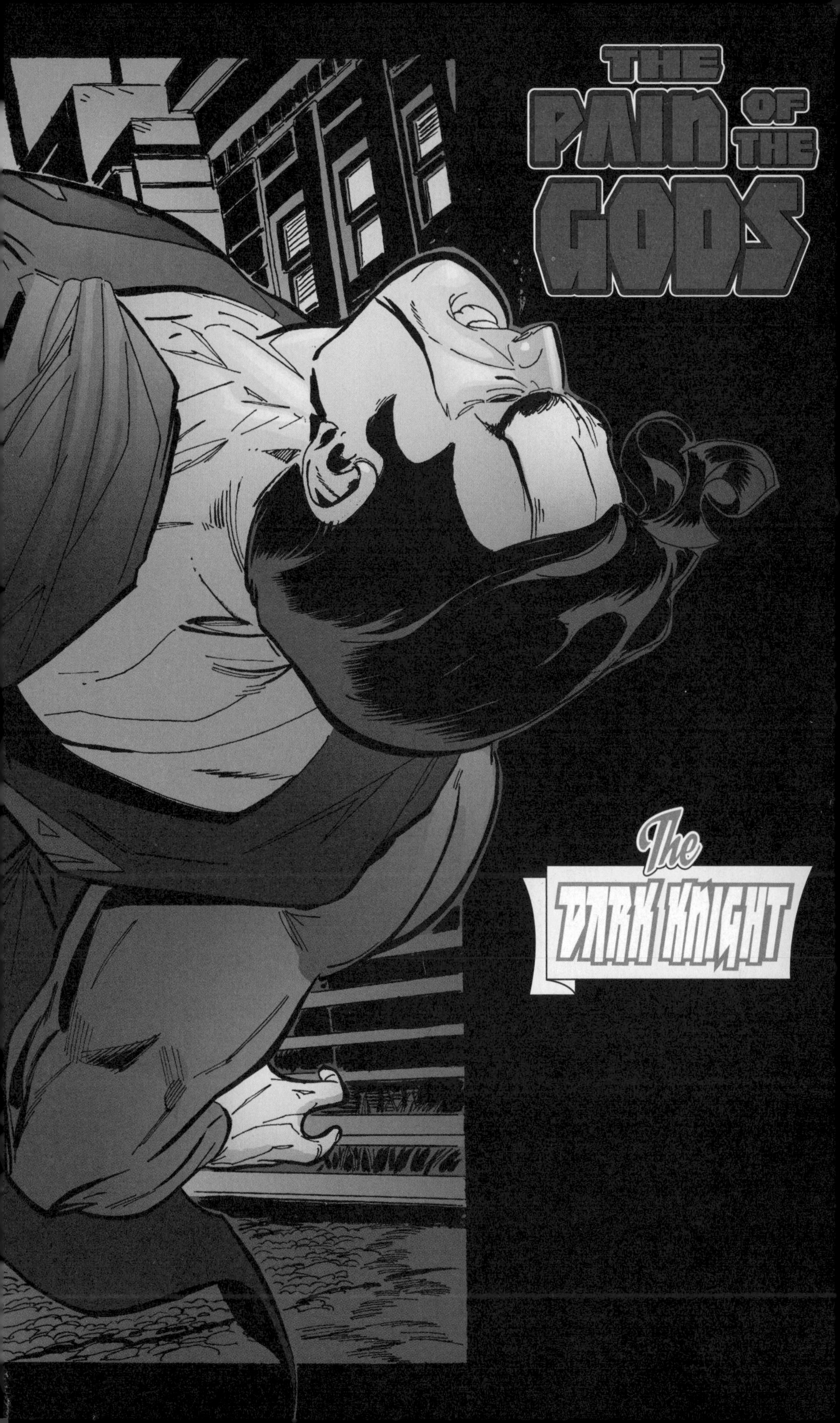
THE PAIN OF THE GODS
The DARK KNIGHT

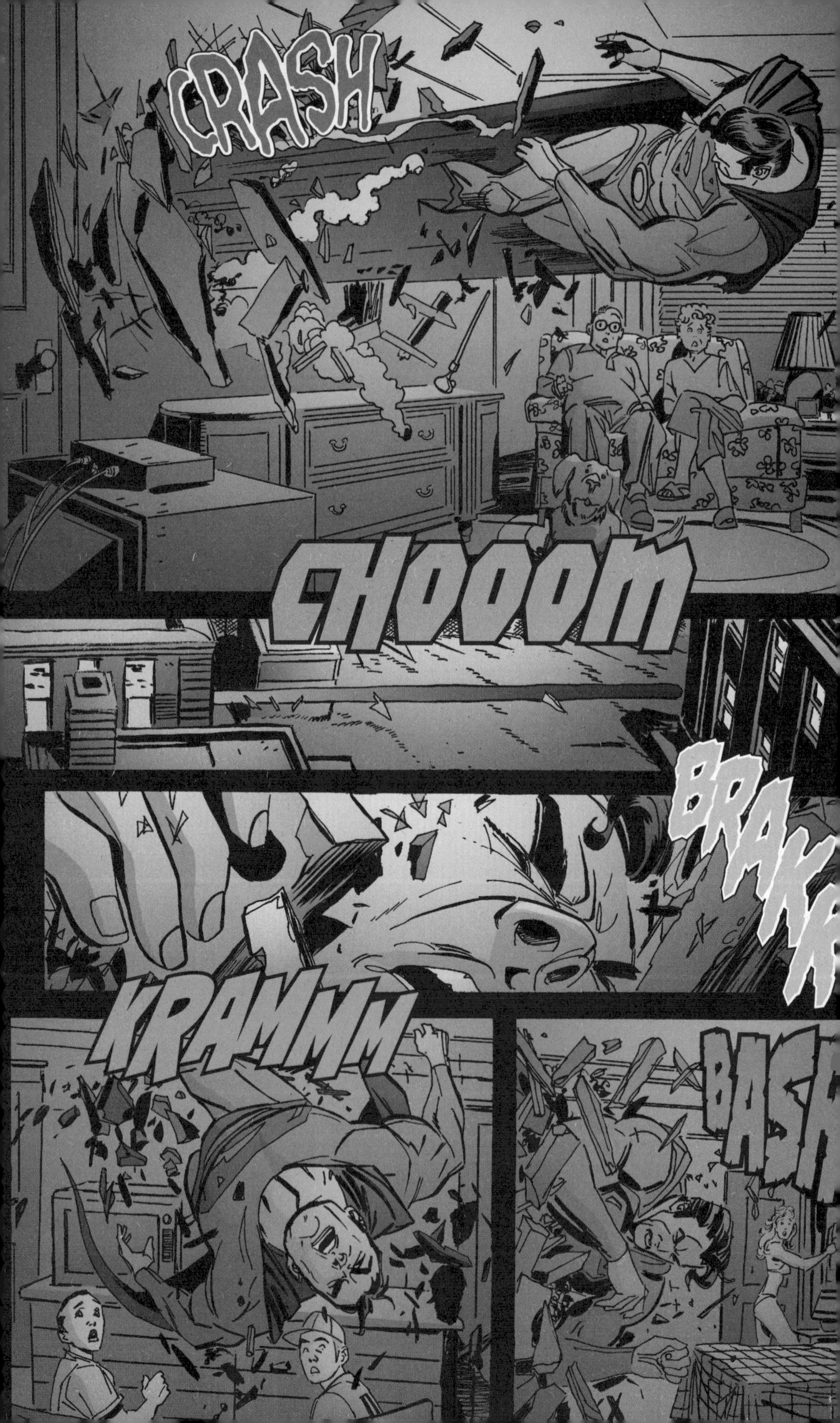
CRASH
CHOOOM
BRAK
KRAMMM
BAS

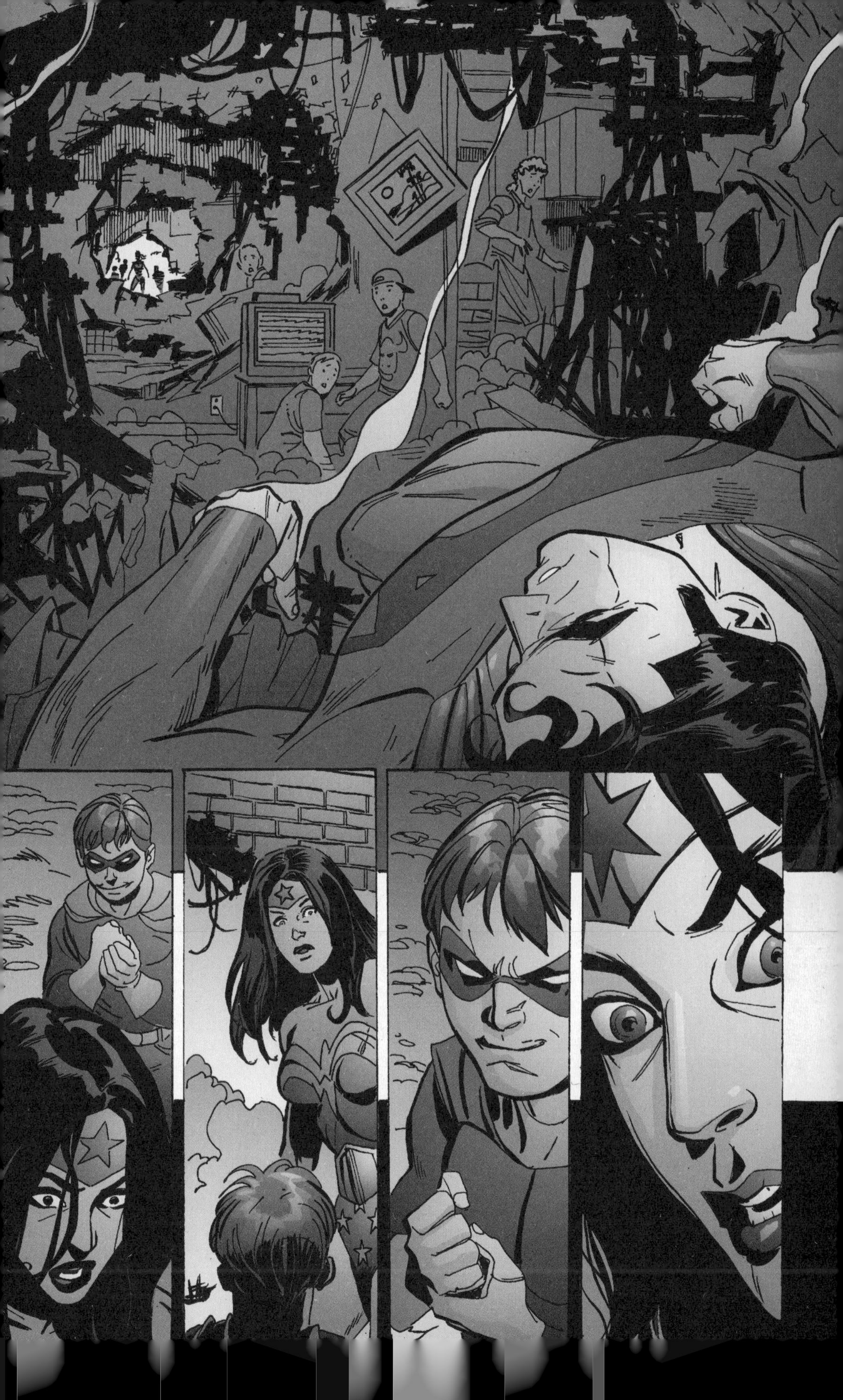

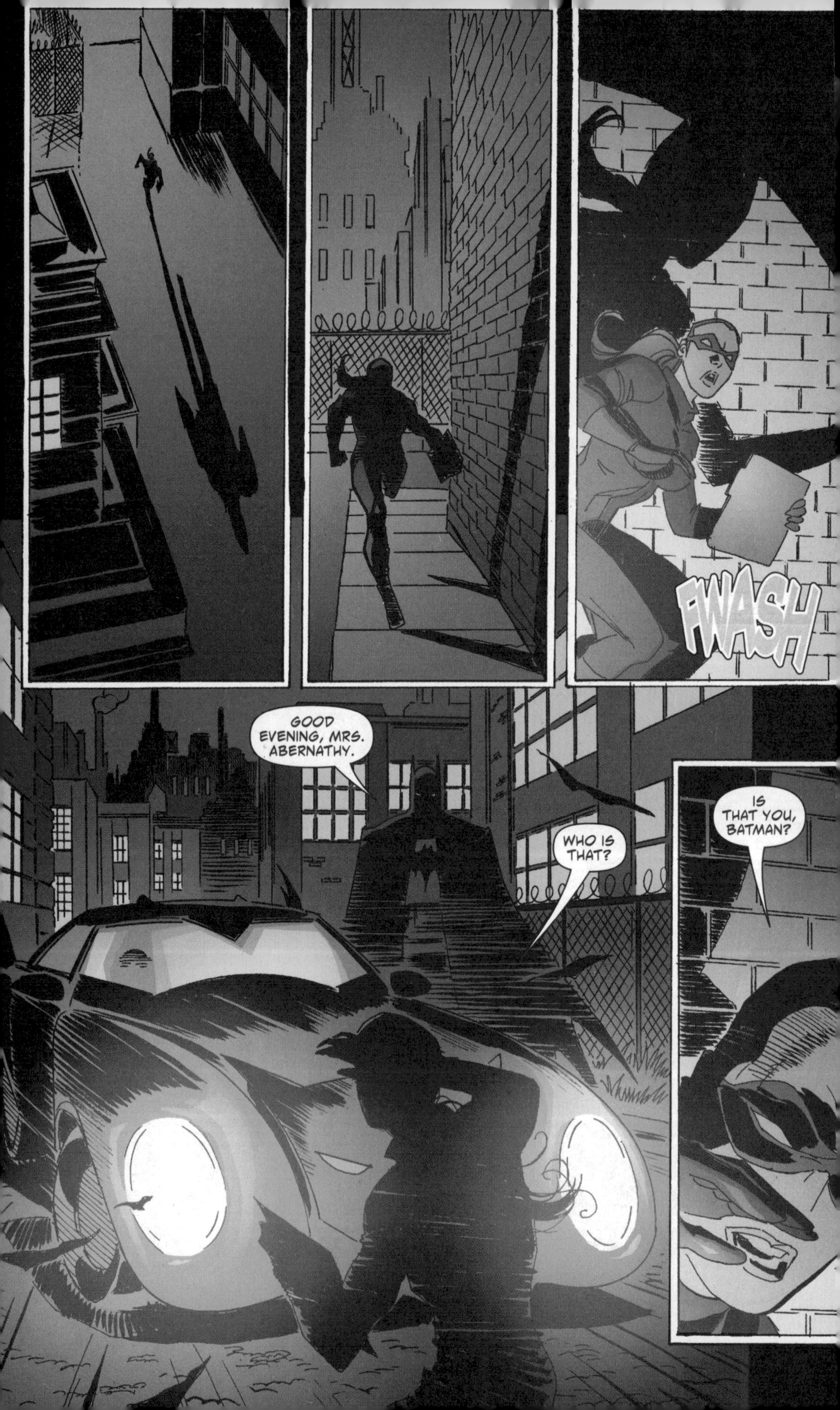
FWASH
GOOD EVENING, MRS. ABERNATHY.
WHO IS THAT?
IS THAT YOU, BATMAN?

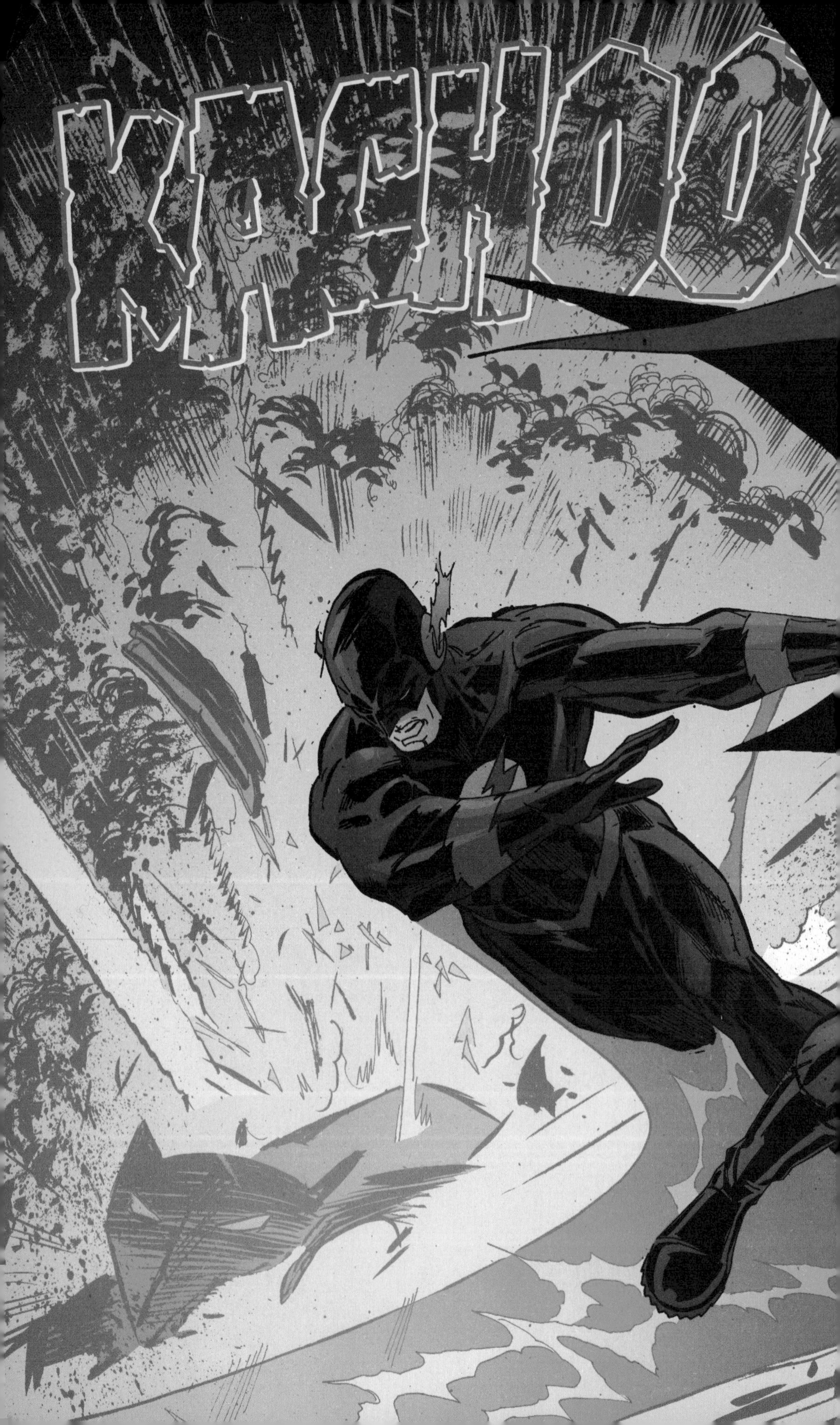
KRASHOO

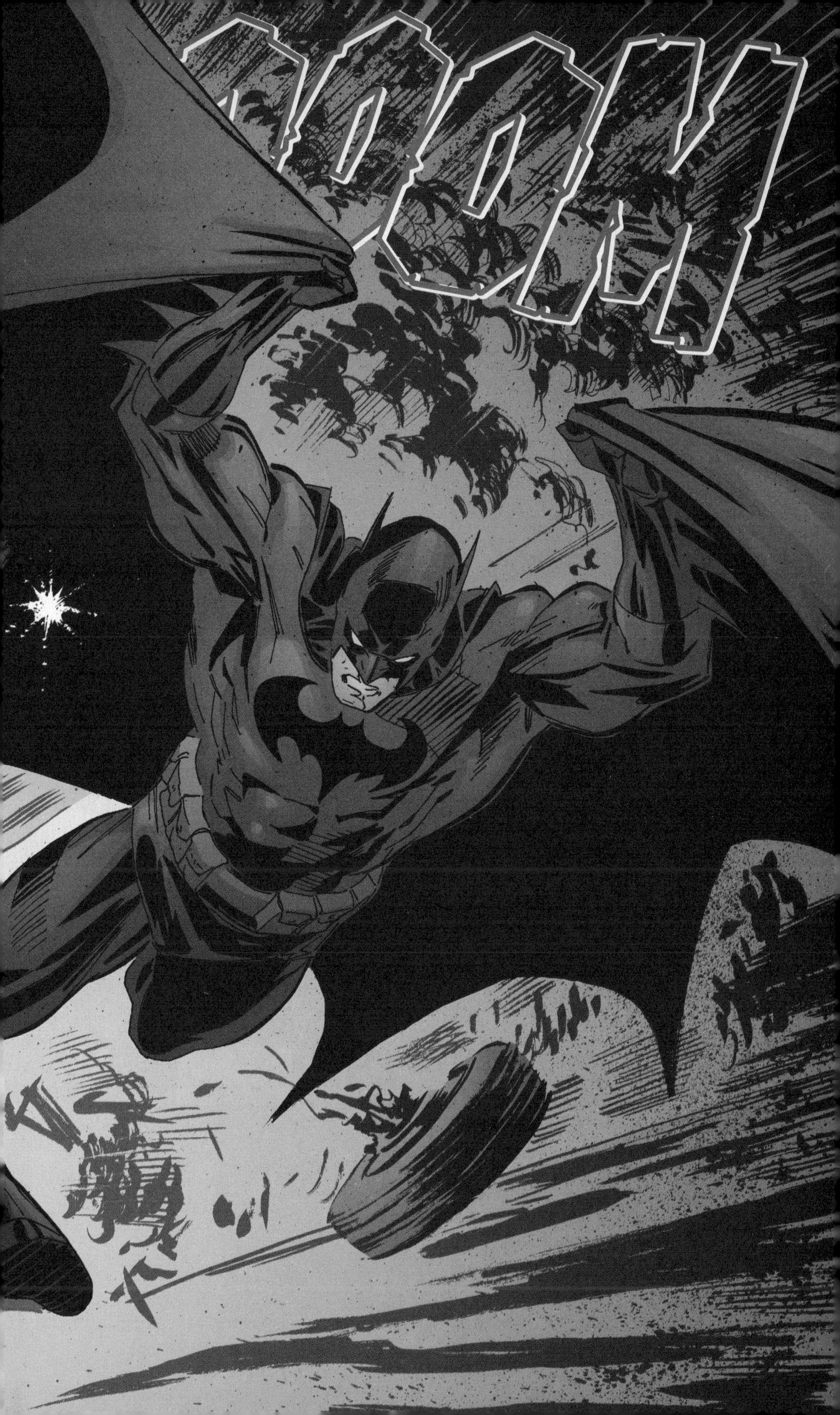
OOOM

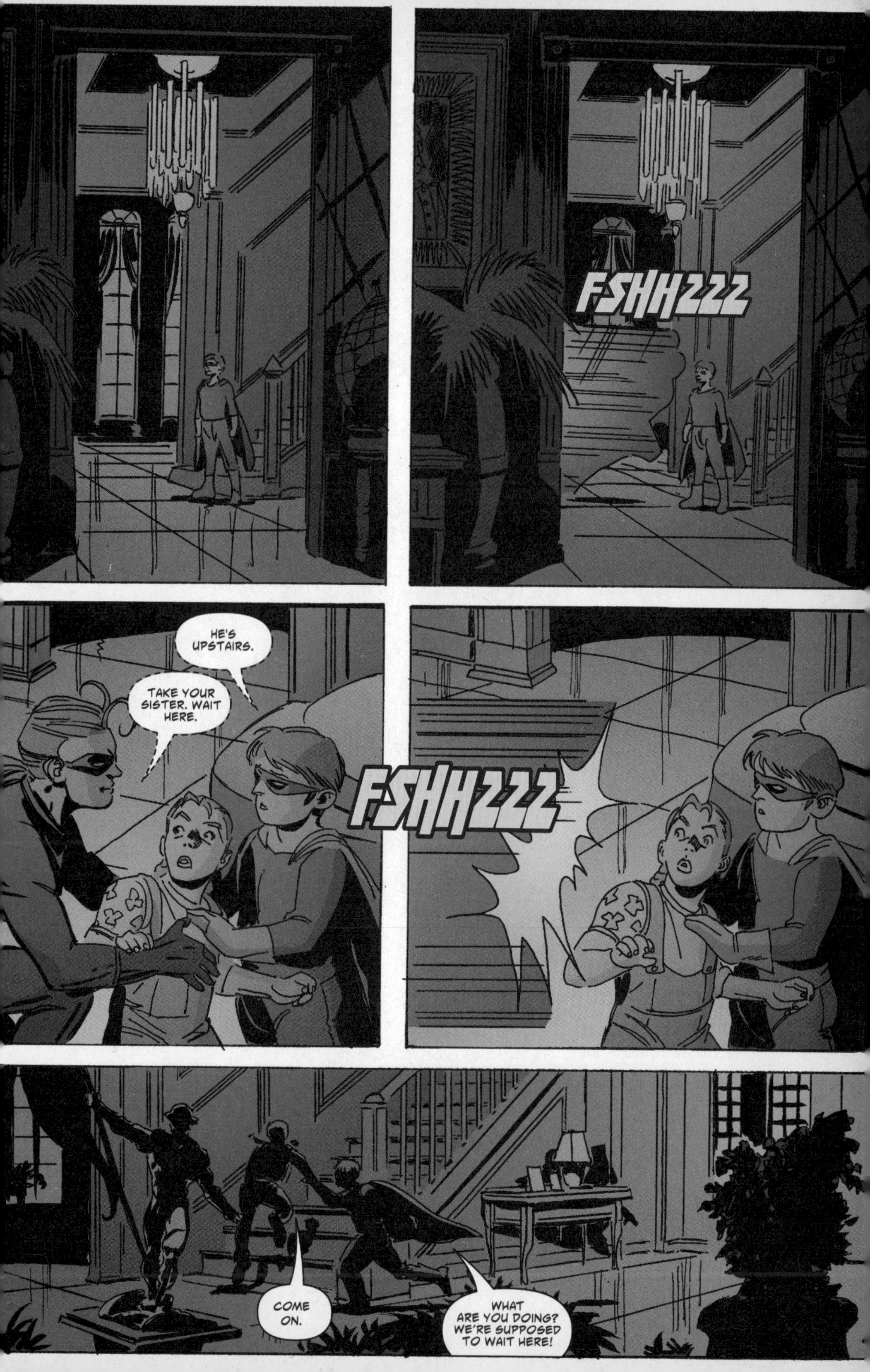
FSHHZZZ
HE'S UPSTAIRS.
TAKE YOUR SISTER. WAIT HERE.
FSHHZZZ
COME ON.
WHAT ARE YOU DOING? WE'RE SUPPOSED TO WAIT HERE!

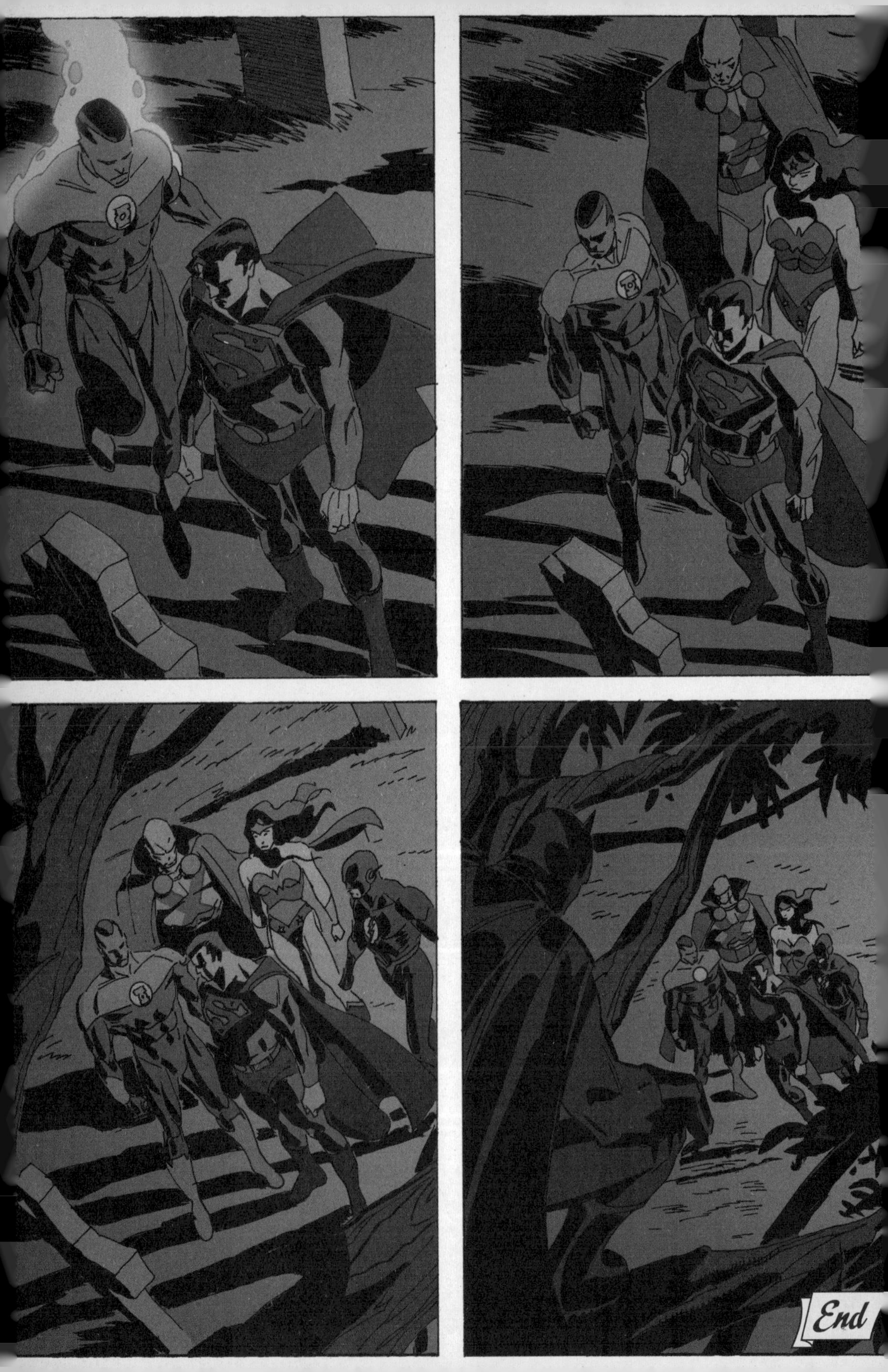
End

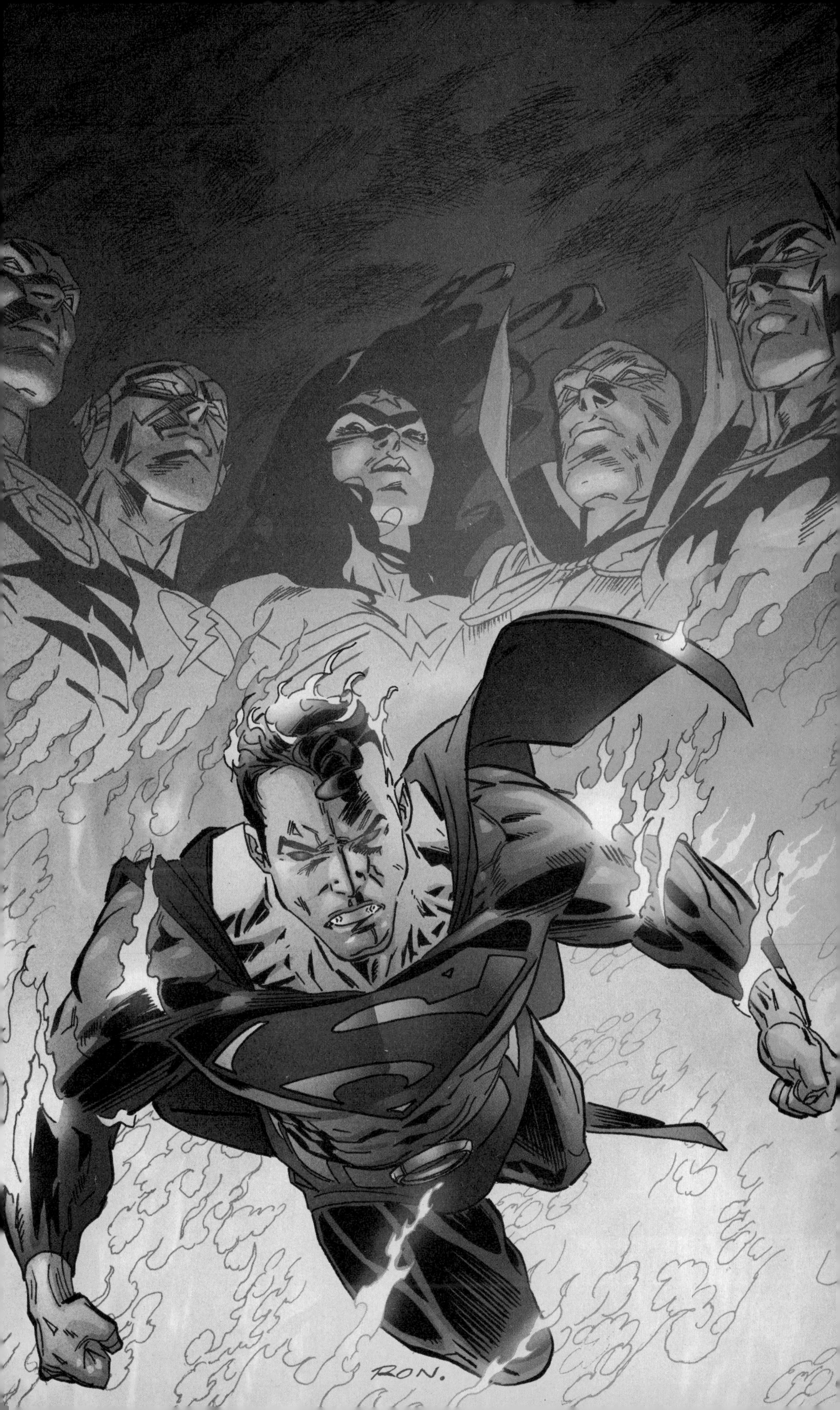
RON.

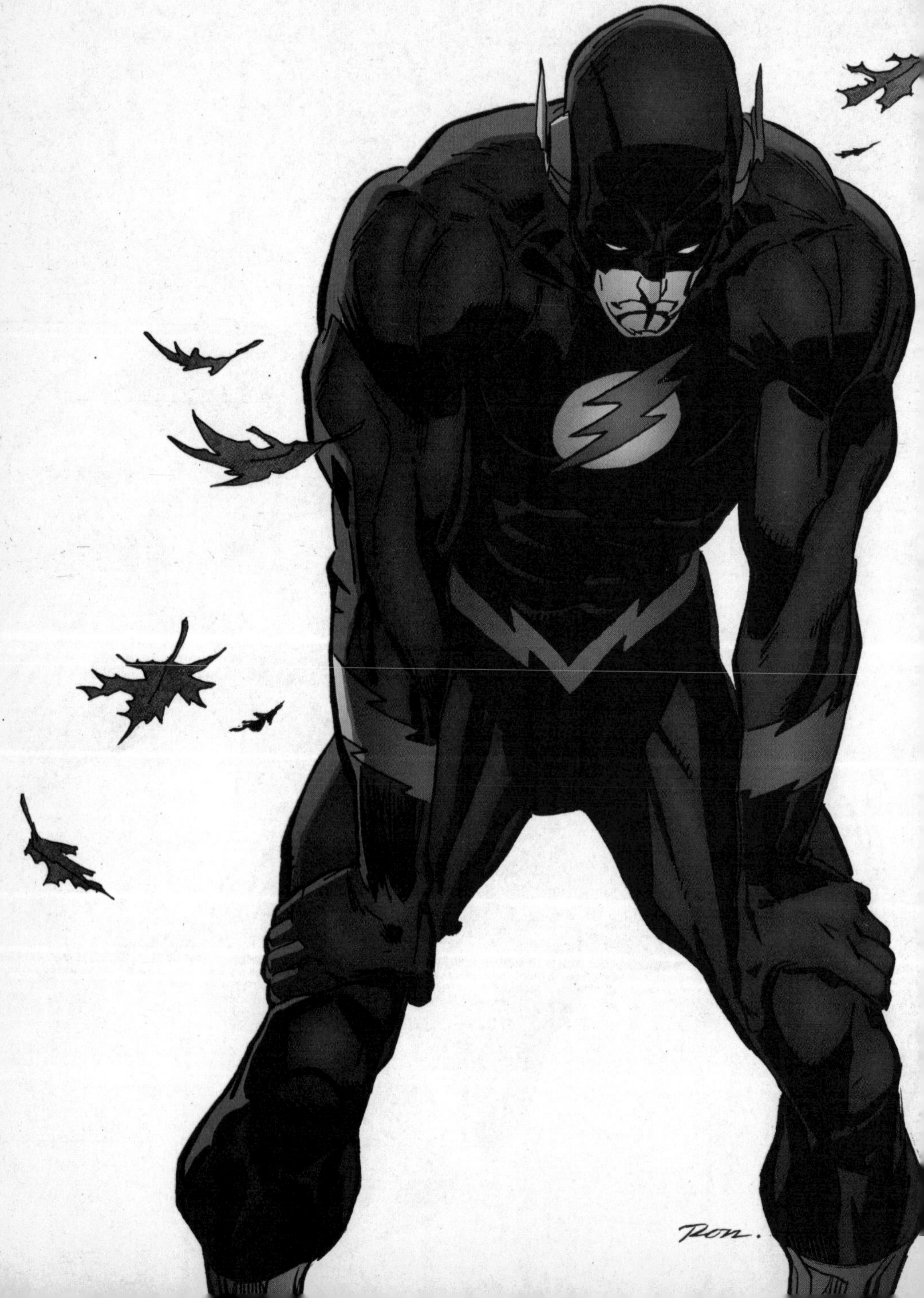

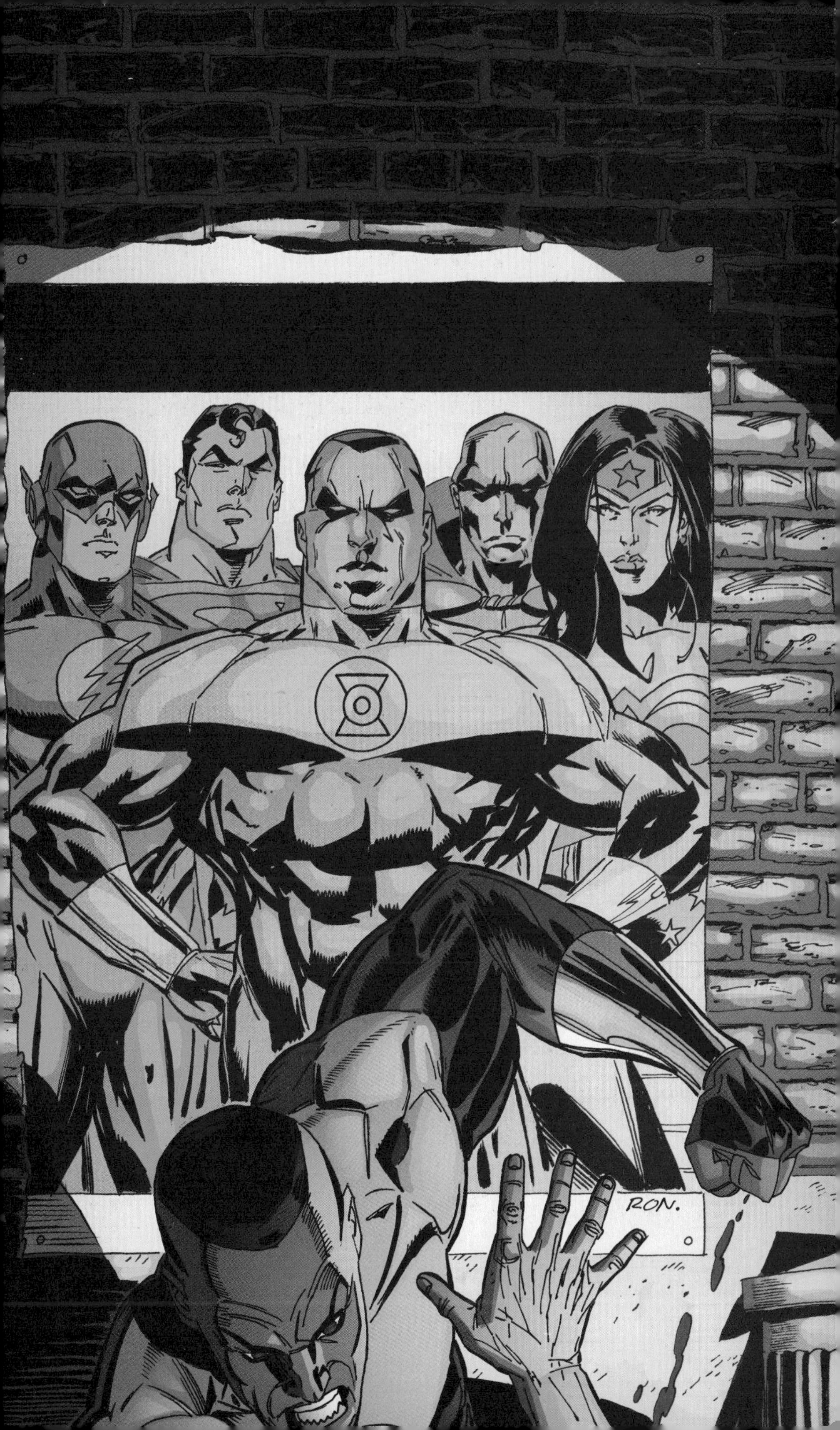
RON.

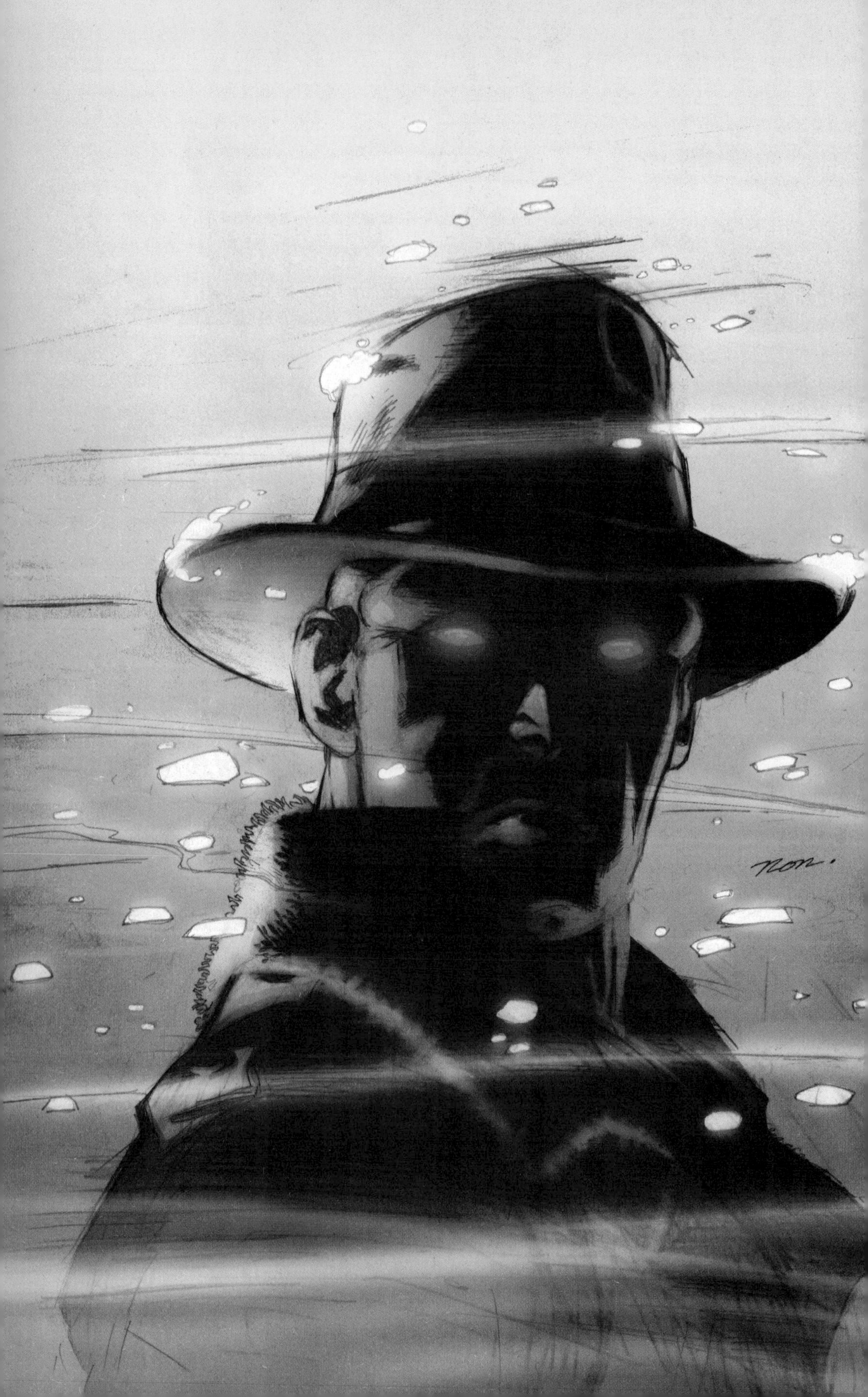

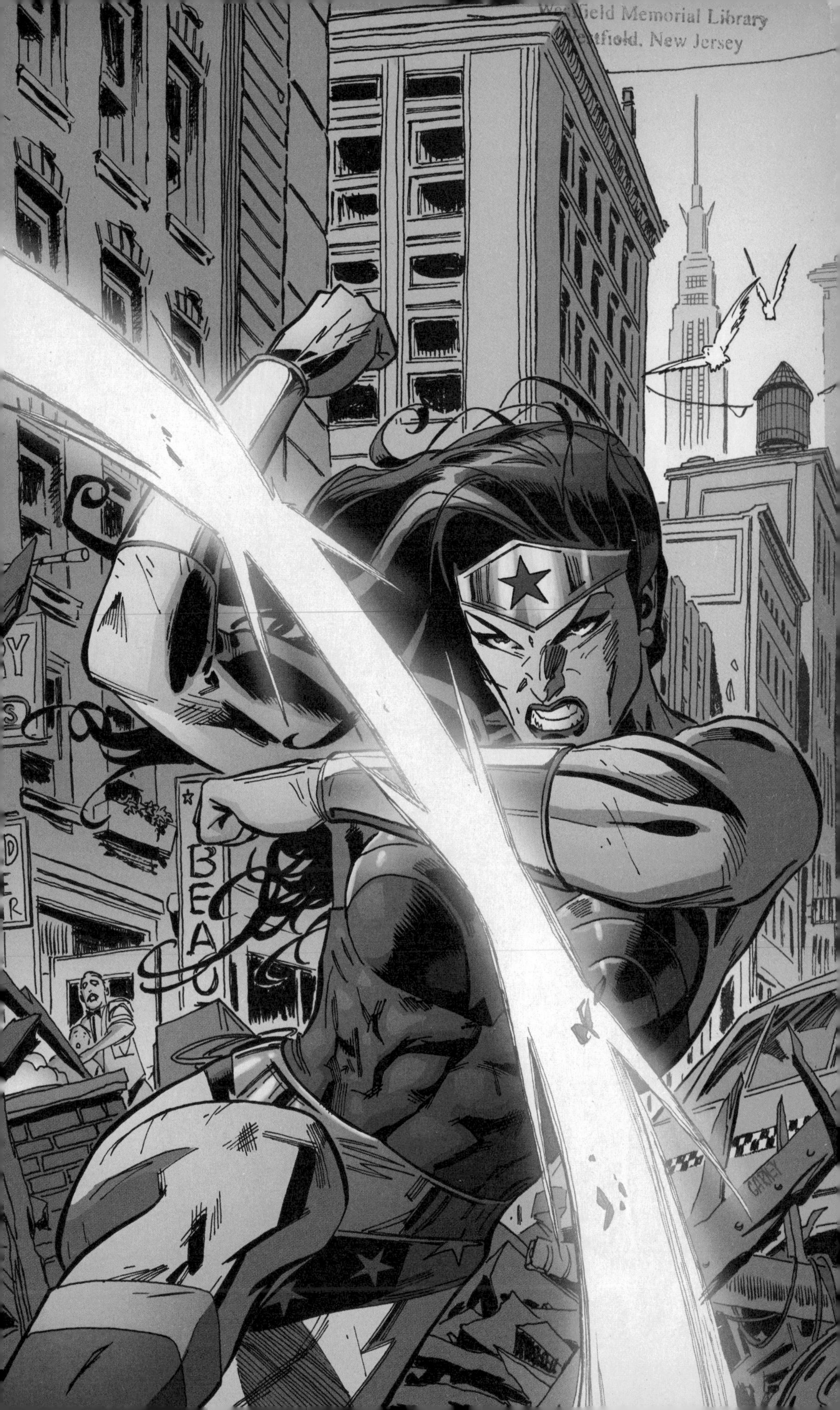
BEAU

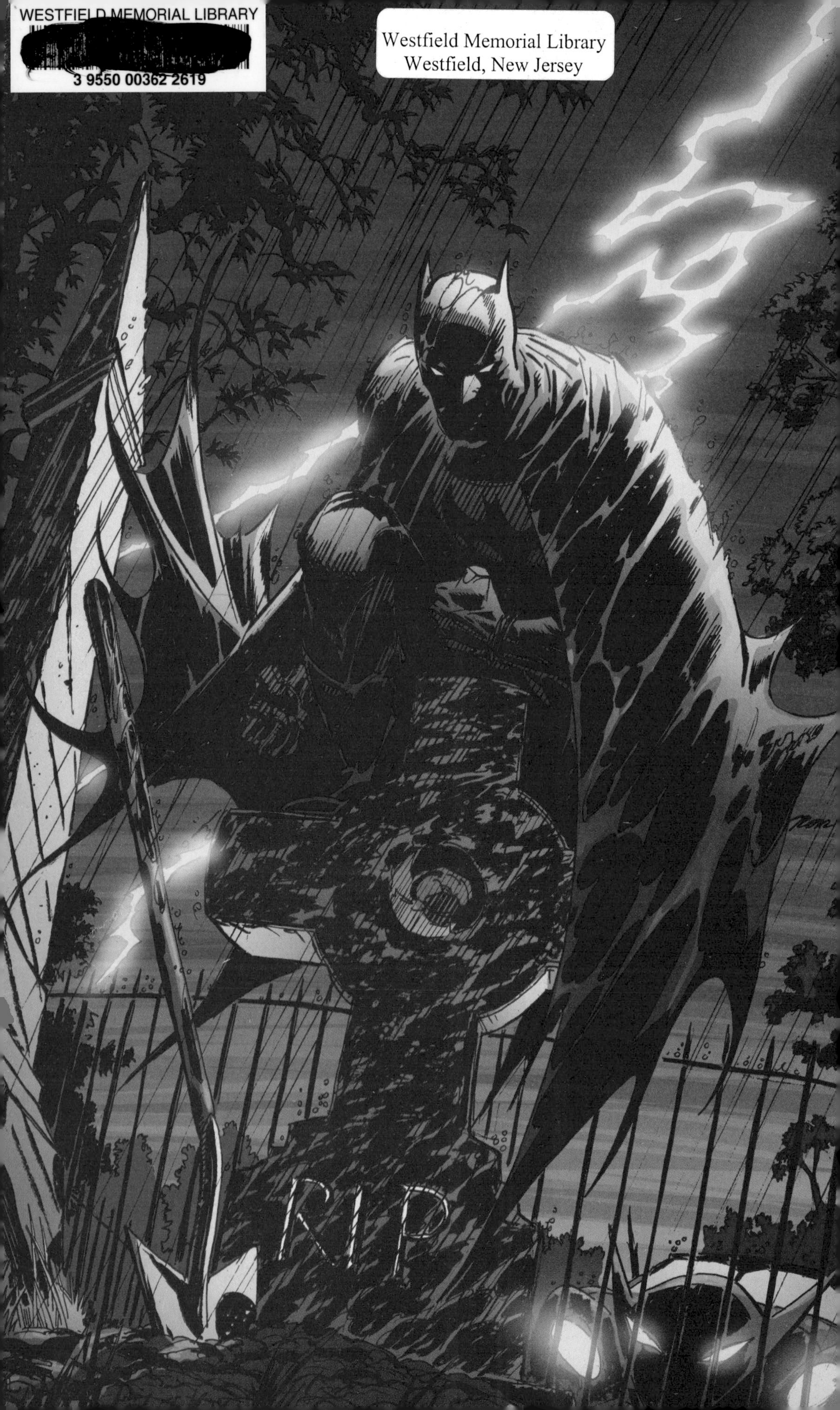
RIP